The Atlas of Cambodia

National Poverty
and Environment Maps

Save Cambodia's Wildlife
with Support from
Danida
Phnom Penh, Cambodia
2006

This document should be cited as
SCW, 2006. Atlas of Cambodia: National Poverty and Environment Maps.
Save Cambodia's Wildlife, Phnom Penh, Cambodia.

ISBN No: 978-99950-814-2-3

Published by
Save Cambodia's Wildlife
#272, St 107, Boeung Prolit,
Khan 7 Makara, Phnom Penh
info@cambodiaswildlife.org
www.cambodiaswildlife.org

Supported By
Danida
Phnom Penh, Cambodia
danida@online.com.kh
www.danida-cambodia.org

The Atlas of Cambodia

National Poverty
and Environment Maps

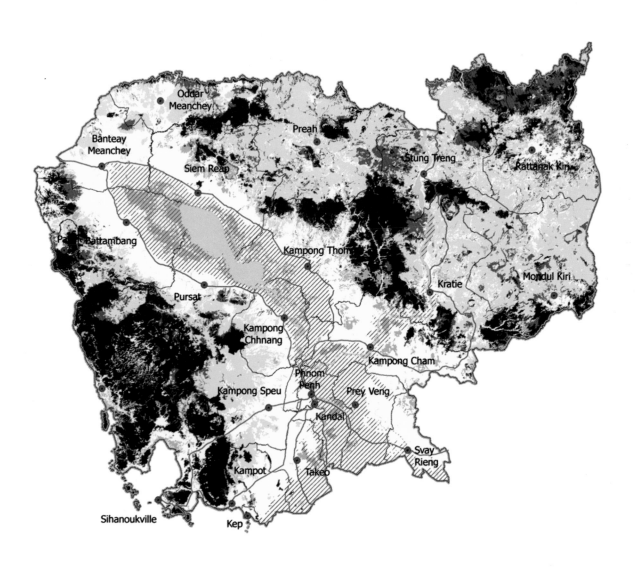

Save Cambodia's Wildlife
2006

CONTENTS

LIST OF MAPS

Foreword

The Atlas of Cambodia: National Poverty and Environment Maps is the first of its kind in Cambodia and has only been possible due to the personal dedication of the people working on the production of the atlas and the strong commitment from the institutions involved. The objective was to ensure the atlas was produced by Cambodians for Cambodians. The work behind the production of this atlas has been immense as compilation of data, its verification and quality assurance at times has required more human resources than first envisioned.

During the process of preparation it also became apparent that public access to data was in some cases restricted and/or not available due to institutional constraints or resistance to provide data for such a publication.

However, it must be fully acknowledged that statistical and GIS data are extremely useful, relevant and could benefit development in Cambodia immensely if appropriate government decisions are put into motion to ensure consistency between data collected in the field and its integration into GIS. A policy and action plan for free inter-ministerial exchange of data within GIS is required. The current project approach in stand alone mode with funding from donors and international NGOs without a requirement for free information sharing neither benefits Cambodia or effectively utilizes donor support. The transaction costs involved in the current state of affairs are enormous.

A large number of institutions and civil servants have contributed to the production of the atlas. Full acknowledgement must be given to the authors, Cambodian experts in their fields working for different ministries, agencies and independent organizations. Gratitude is also given to the many people who contributed data and the independent reviewers who offered advice and support.

The Technical Editorial Committee provided valuable support and direction throughout the development of the atlas to ensure that the most accurate up to date data was utilized. Special thanks are given to Ignas Dümmer and Jan-Peter Mund for their technical expertise in GIS data representation and their commitment to produce an atlas of the highest quality. Credit also goes to Geo-informatics who prepared the maps, Mr Chhut Chheana for design and layout and to Ms Loreen Kerrigan for her role as Editor and Project Coordinator.

H.E San Sy Than
Director General
National Institute of Statistics
Ministry of Planning

Phnom Penh
25 April 2006

Mogens Laumand Christensen
Minister Counsellor
Danida Resident Representative
Royal Danish Embassy - Danida

Preface

The Atlas of Cambodia: National Poverty and Environment Maps is the first atlas devoted entirely to Cambodia providing publicly available cross-sectoral thematic maps, statistics and text giving an overview of environmental and socio-economic aspects of the country. The Atlas of Cambodia project aims to provide a wide array of people such as professionals working for development agencies, government officials, educators and the academia as well as other individuals with high-quality background information which will enable them to better understand the relationship between natural resources and economic and social development in Cambodia. The Atlas could also be used as a frame of reference for planning departments within ministries when developing strategies for utilisation of Cambodia's natural and human resources. It is hoped that the atlas will be particularly useful in effectively disseminating information to those people working in the field at provincial, district and commune levels. It is also intended that the atlas will become an important historical document, whereby comparisons of subsequent editions will clearly outline the improvements made in the capacity to collect, analyze and disseminate data in Cambodia.

Just over a decade ago, Cambodian statistical capacity was virtually non-existent. The wide selection of maps in the Atlas of Cambodia is therefore an indication of the significant improvements made in this area. The collection of data, the establishment of databases and the successful dissemination of such information is an on going process and the atlas of Cambodia provides a good indication of where Cambodia is currently functioning in this process. Every effort has been made to select official sources of data and thanks are given to those ministries who provided valuable support and information to the atlas project. A number of independent data sets were also used in the compilation of many maps and Save Cambodia's Wildlife would like to gratefully acknowledge the important contribution these have made to the atlas. The atlas project team also appreciates the support given by the Department of Geography in supplying accurate base maps, administrative boundaries and codes and the official spelling of place names

Reliable national level statistics are necessary in order to strengthen evidence based planning at all levels. Effective planning is necessary to help Cambodia achieve its objectives of poverty alleviation while maintaining environmental sustainability. With land management approaches moving towards a more community based participatory style, it is hoped that the atlas can further enhance the local community's ability to effectively participate in land management decisions by providing them with access to information.

It is also hoped that the atlas will be of interest to the wider community and visitors to Cambodia as it gives an overview of the environmental and socio-economic issues facing Cambodia today. In addition to this, the atlas provides a glimpse into the unique livelihoods of the largely rural subsistent population of Cambodia.

Finally, Save Cambodia's Wildlife gratefully acknowledges the generous contribution of Danida for their financial support in enabling The Atlas of Cambodia: National Poverty and Environment Maps to become a reality.

Solinn Lim
Director,
Save Cambodia's Wildlife

Introduction

After decades of civil strife, Cambodia is on the road to recovery. The almost total destruction of social and economic institutions and loss of life as a result of Cambodia's dark history left the country to begin from ground zero in 1979. The Paris Peace Agreements in 1991 marked a significant step forward for establishing peace and stability throughout Cambodia and as achievements are progressively made in these areas Cambodia now has an opportunity to focus on long term development. Many achievements have been made in all sectors in recent years such as the introduction of decentralization, a rising GDP, improved access to primary education and declining fertility and mortality rates, all contributing to helping Cambodia meet its Millennium Development Goals. Despite the significant progress made since 1991, Cambodia still faces many challenges including achieving the specific development objectives of poverty alleviation and economic growth while ensuring environmental sustainability.

Cambodia is a developing country with a large proportion of the population living in rural areas. Natural resources such as the abundant fisheries of the Mekong River and Tonle Sap and forests rich in resources have sustained the population for centuries. Traditionally the people have survived on a subsistent balance of growing rice, catching fish and foraging for forest products and a large proportion of the population continue to do so today. While poverty rates have declined in recent years, they still remain relatively high with 36.1 % of the population living below the poverty line, 90 % of which live in rural areas (WB: 2006). Additionally, an increasing population has added greater pressure to the environment by contributing to the encroachment of agriculture and high rates of forest change. This is further enhanced by the inaccessibility of rural hinterlands to services and markets and the relatively low productivity of upland soils.

While many different sectors have reported an increase in yield over the last few years, there are concerns that high value species have declined in favour of low value, labour intensive species. This threatens the livelihood strategies and general well being of the entire population and reduces the possibility of long term poverty reduction. With such dependence on natural resources for survival, the sustainability of the environment is particularly important to the rural poor, especially where alternative livelihood options do not currently exist. As Cambodia moves from subsistence to trade, land management is increasingly significant so that the young generation of Cambodian's have the means and the opportunity to move out of the poverty inflicted on their parents and contribute to the development of their country.

Adequate land management through centralized government led initiatives, local participation and the technical assistance provided by donors has a direct positive impact on the sectors of health and education. With improvements in cash flow, families are more likely to send their children to school for longer periods providing them with the opportunity to move out of the primary sector, given that alternative employment opportunities exist. The provision of adequate health care facilities, wider understanding of reproductive health and a changing perception in health seeking behaviour will help to alleviate some of the problems experienced by large families limiting them to subsistent livelihoods. The cost of healthcare in Cambodia is one of the major contributors to indebtedness experienced by rural families (WB: 2006).

Similarly, health and education statistics provide important poverty indicators helping to identify those areas most likely to experience greatest risk to the sustainability of the environment. The capacity of Cambodia's natural resources to provide such a large proportion of the population with an adequate standard of living is limited. Alternative sources of employment must be found for the majority currently living in subsistent orientated agriculture. Without adequate access to education, the opportunities of progressing from the primary sector are limited for many people. Greater investments in education will help to equip the large young population with the skills necessary for higher wage, greater value added economic activities and help to drive economic transition and long term development so that Cambodia can have a less critical dependence on the environment for survival (WB: 2006).

Natural resource management and environmental stability are key elements in reducing rural poverty. Currently, over 70 % of the population is employed in some form of agriculture including non-paid family workers (NIS: 2005). Over 50% of these workers are women whose opportunities are further limited by gender inequities (UNIFEM: 2003). In 2004, 90 % of the poor lived in rural areas (WB: 2006). These statistics highlight the necessity for rural development, particularly in helping small landholders to increase agricultural productivity that will generate income and decrease their reliance on forest products (ADB: 2000). Another factor underlying rural poverty is the lack of clear land tenure of both private and state land as all cadastral maps and titles were destroyed in the 1970s. Land resource assessments and land suitability studies conducted at local levels will assist the land user and/or land planner to identify possible options for future land use. This is a priority for Cambodia as the relatively low soil fertility produces relatively lower yields thus perpetuating dependence on forest resources in livelihood strategies. Unproductive land holdings also contribute to further encroachment of agriculture as families constantly clear new land to help improve productivity and food security. Thus, without clear land management plans the threat of environmental degradation is ongoing limiting the opportunity for rural poverty reduction.

The Atlas of Cambodia

The Atlas of Cambodia: National Poverty and Environment Maps aims to give an overview of the different sectors in Cambodia and the effect these have on natural resource management. Providing cross-sectoral statistical information, thematic maps and information in the one resource allows for the more efficient dissemination of material that will be useful to a wide variety of people including government departments, national institutions, agencies, educators and the academia. Additionally, the atlas intends to provide easier access to information to those people working in the field at provincial, district and commune levels. The importance of easily accessible reliable data to the development process is widely recognized as it provides a tool for which planners at all levels can identify critical areas and thus facilitates informed decision making. The representation and selection of data in the atlas is also a useful indication of what sectors have effectively collected reliable information, where gaps exist in the availability of reliable statistics and identifies some of the many limitations to data collection in Cambodia today. Hopefully, comparisons of future editions of the atlas will show advancements in the capacity of Cambodia to introduce sector wide approaches to national planning, statistics and poverty monitoring.

The Atlas of Cambodia: National Poverty and Environment Maps includes maps and statistics from the population, health, fisheries, agriculture, energy and forestry sectors. The selection of data intends to give an overview of socio-demographic and environmental information to help identify those areas expected to experience greatest pressure on natural resources in the future. Cambodian statistical capacity was virtually non-existent a decade ago (NIS: 2004). Obvious limitations to collection, such as security, posed significant problems. Additionally, the ability to collect, store and disseminate data was limited. The first full count of the population in 36 years occurred in 1998 with the General Population census. Since that time, with government participation and donor funding, many achievements have been made principally within the National Institute of statistics (NIS) the designated agency commissioned to collect, process and present

data. Additionally, international organizations and NGOs collect data as part of the vast array of projects taking place throughout the country.

Different methodologies such as household surveys, field observation, analysis of satellite images and aerial photographs, GIS and a combination of these are used in data collection and methods selected are largely dependant on who is collecting data and for what purpose. Data collection also occurs at different levels ranging from local, national, regional and global levels. While accurate data exists at disaggregated levels, it is often difficult to make national level comparisons of areas due to the different methodologies used in collection. However, with an understanding of the limitations, comparisons of data either from different years, regions or institutions may be a useful tool in identifying trends affecting the natural environment. In the chapters throughout the atlas additional information about data methodologies and limitations are given in the appropriate sections.

While a wide variety of data exists, access to it is often limited. This is influenced by a variety of factors including poor awareness of what exists due to a lack of clarity of what information is publicly available or confidential. Inappropriate storage techniques may also hinder the identification of data, limit access and dissemination. Consistency in the collection, storage and dissemination of data needs to be encouraged throughout all sectors so that reliable, national level data can increasingly be used to inform policy development and planning. Data sharing also needs to be encouraged between government departments and institutions to ensure that limited financial resources are not strained by the repetitive collection of data. With greater access to reliable quantitative and qualitative data, more time can be given to analysis, implementation, monitoring and evaluation of information thus continually improving the reliability of data sets (Dümmer: 2004).

In the Atlas of Cambodia, every effort has been made to select official data as the basis for map production. Official data sets are those recognized by government departments and often used in policy making. The accuracy of official data sets is varied and often depends on the financial and technical capacity of a department. Also, the nature of information often limits accurate collection in the early stages. For example, the wide variety of fishing gears and the extent to which respondents consider themselves as fishers limits the accurate collection of fish production data, a problem not confined to Cambodia. A lack of consistent terminology may further limit reliability and comparisons of information. A number of independent datasets such as the JICA and Mekong River Commission data sets and the Commune Database established through the Seila Programme are also used throughout the atlas. These data sets have been widely used throughout the development sector in Cambodia and are generally considered to be reliable sources of information.

The compilation of the first Atlas of Cambodia: National Poverty and Environment Maps represents significant developments in data gathering and data sharing in Cambodia in the last ten years. This process is very complicated and ongoing in nature and the reality of any atlas thus represents the state of a nation's technical capacity as it currently exists in relation to gathering and analyzing evidence to effectively inform decision making. Thus this atlas can be seen as the beginning of an ongoing process that will lead to further improvements in the understanding of the interrelationships of different sectors in Cambodia and help the country to achieve its specific objectives of poverty reduction while ensuring environmental sustainability.

Note: references used in the introduction can be found at the end of Chapter One: Territory Overview.

Territory Overview

The Geography of Cambodia

Cambodia is situated in Southeast Asia in the Southern part of Indochina, between 10 to 15 degrees latitude and 102 to 108 degrees East longitude. It covers an area of 181,035 square kilometers with the geographical centre the provincial town of Kampong Thom. The length of Cambodia is approximately 440 kilometers from North to South and the width is approximately 560 kilometers from East to West. Cambodia borders the Lao People's Democratic Republic in the North, the Socialist Republic of Viet Nam in the East/Southeast, the Gulf of Siam in the Southwest and the Kingdom of Thailand in the West. The land border is approximately 2,600 kilometers in length, and the coastline is around 440 kilometers long.

Cambodia has many unique geographical features that may aid development. The complex hydrological system provides one of the most productive fresh water fisheries in the world. The river system also provides valuable transport and trade routes. Although soil productivity is relatively low, the terrain is relatively flat allowing for easier cultivation and the development of infrastructure. Cambodia's forests are rich in biodiversity and an important natural resource that is central to rural livelihood strategies. The forests also provide potential for the development of ecotourism. Finally, the deep water sea port located in Sihanoukville on the Gulf of Siam is a vital link for international trade and the development of industry.

The population of Cambodia has increased from 13.4 million in 2004 to 13.7 million in 2005 with an annual average population growth rate of 1.7% at this time (NIS: 2005). Based on population projections calculated from the 1998 General Census and the Cambodia Inter-Censal Population Survey (CIPS 2004), the projected population in 2005 is 13.7 million. Approximately 85% of the population lives in rural areas. The projection for 2006 calculates an average population density of 82 people per square kilometer with the plains region being the most densely populated at 297 people per square kilometer and the mountain region being the most sparsely populated at 23 people per square kilometer (NIS: 2005).

Ethnicity

Ethnic Khmer's make up 96% of the Cambodian population with the remaining 4% of the population comprised of a variety of ethnic minorities. The largest minority group is the Cham, or Khmer Islam. According to the Cambodian Social Economic Survey (CSES 2004), they constitute 2.2% of the population and generally live in distinct villages in Kompong Cham and neighbouring provinces or in urban neighbourhoods. Although this group demonstrates differences in religion, dress and occupational specialization they otherwise live in much the same way as the Khmer majority (WB: 2006). Following this group are the Chinese (0.2%) and ethnic Vietnamese (0.4%). The smallest ethnic groups are the highlanders also known as Khmer Loeu, Chunchiet or highland tribal groups. These groups mainly live in forested upland areas concentrated in the Northeast provinces of Rattanak kiri, Mondul kiri, Kratie and Stung Treng. The highlanders are comprised of seventeen main groups, each of which numbers between a few hundred and 19,000. Collectively they account for approximately 104, 000 persons, or less than 0.1% of the population (WB: 2006).

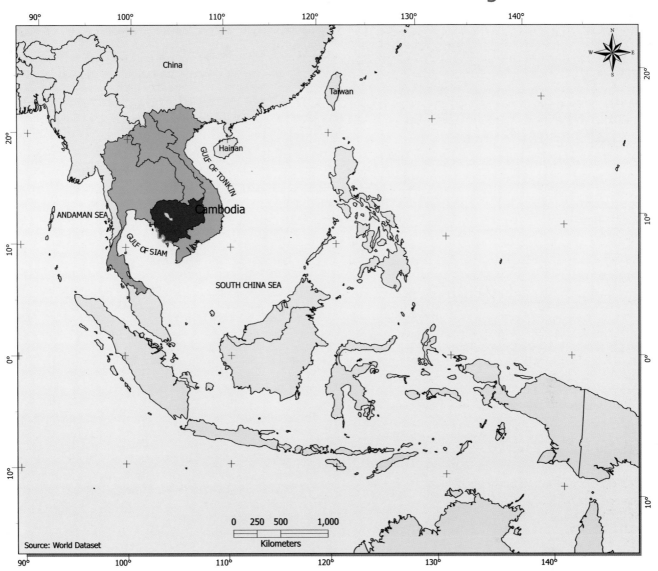

China

Taiwan

Hainan

GULF OF TONKIN

ANDAMAN SEA

GULF OF SIAM

Cambodia

SOUTH CHINA SEA

| 0 | 250 | 500 | 1,000 |

Kilometers

Source: World Dataset

Economy

Cambodia's economic growth rate has been reasonably strong in the last ten years. Annual real gross domestic product (GDP) grew at an average of 6.9% between 1994 and 2004 (at current prices). In 2004 the GDP was 4,888 million US dollars with the per capita GDP at US $357 (NIS: 2005). While per capita GDP has experienced growth in recent years, it still remains the lowest in the ASEAN region. The agriculture fisheries and forestry sectors contributed 30.9% to the GDP, industry 28.9% and services 34.4% in 2004.

The agricultural sector dominated national output in the 1990s accounting for more than 40% of GDP until 1999. However, this trend has declined, mainly as a result of floods and droughts and the depletion of natural resources such as forestry and fisheries. During the last ten years, agriculture, fisheries, and forestry only grew at an annual average of 3.5%. Crops have been the main contributor to the agricultural sector, particularly rice production.

The industrial sector has seen an increasing trend since 1993. It contributed about 13% of GDP in 1993 and almost doubled to 28.9% in 2004 growing at an average annual rate of 21%. This rise can mainly be attributed to the increased export in garments, textiles, and footwear; and the expansion in construction sub-sectors. Garment exports in 2005 were higher than originally projected partly due to the imposition of restrictions on Chinese textile imports in the US and EU markets.

Administrative Boundaries

Cambodia is divided into twenty provinces each of which is headed by a governor, and four municipalities. These are the provinces of Banteay Meanchey, Battambang, Kampong Cham, Kampong Chhnang, Kampong Speu, Kampong Thom, Kampot, Kandal, Kratie, Mondul Kiri, Preah Vihear, Pursat, Rattanak Kiri, Siem Reap, Stung Treng, Svay Rieng, Takeo, Prey Veng, Koh Kong and Oddar Meanchey. The municipialities of Phnom Penh, Sihanoukville, Kep and Pailin have provincial government status.

Each province is divided into districts (srok) with a total of 185 districts in Cambodia. Each district is further divided into communes (khum), totaling 1621. The communes are then divided into villages (phum) with approximately 13,694 villages occurring in the country. However, according to the constitution, the villages are not in the administrative order.

Decentralized government bodies where first elected in Cambodia in 2002. These are in the form of commune councils with 11,261 elected members. The principle underlying the establishment of commune councils is that the elected members of the council serve the interests of the local people and are responsible to them. Commune Councils may also be seen as an agent of the central government. Commune councils provide an important function in terms of natural resource management as land use planning becomes more participatory and community based. The commune councils can provide a key role in helping to identify the needs of the local people while incorporating their knowledge in establishing land suitability and resource assessments in order to formulate effective land management plans.

In terms of data collection, the administrative boundaries should provide clear demarcations for statistical evidence at the commune level. However, the commune boundaries are often not official, with various discrepancies in data. At present, many commune boundaries consist of sketched drawings. There is a need for these boundaries to be redone and this process is intended to begin in 2006.

Cambodia at a Glance

People		Economy		Land Distribution million hectares	
Population (millions)	13.7	GDP (US$)	$357	Forest	11.1
Population Growth Rate	1.7 %	GDP Growth rate	6.9%	• Forest Concessions	3.3 *
Average Population Density	75 pp/km²	GDP Composition by Sector		• Protected Areas	3.3 *
Ethnicity: Khmer	96%	Agriculture	20%	• Protected Forests	1.3 *
Religion: Theravada Buddhism	95%	Fisheries	9%	• Other Forests	3.3
Languages: Khmer	95%	Forestry	2%	Cultivated Areas	2.7
Infant Mortality Rate	95/1000	Industry	29%	Scrub Land	1.4
Maternal Mortality	4/1000	Services	34%	Fishing Concessions	1.0 *
General Fertility Rate	129/1000	Per capita HFCE (in '000 Riels)	1,091	Towns	1.0
Life Expectancy	54.4 years	Unemployment rate	0.8	Agricultural Concessions	0.8 *
Net Enrollment Ratio for Primary School	91.9	Labour force participation Rate	74.6%	Land mine/UXO area	0.1 *
Literacy Rate (15-44)	79%	Poverty rate	36.1%	Total	18.1

Source : NIS Statistical Year Book 2005, CDHS 2000, State of the Environment Report 2004
Note : * denotes a boundary. HFCE - House hold final consumption expenditure

Administrative Boundaries

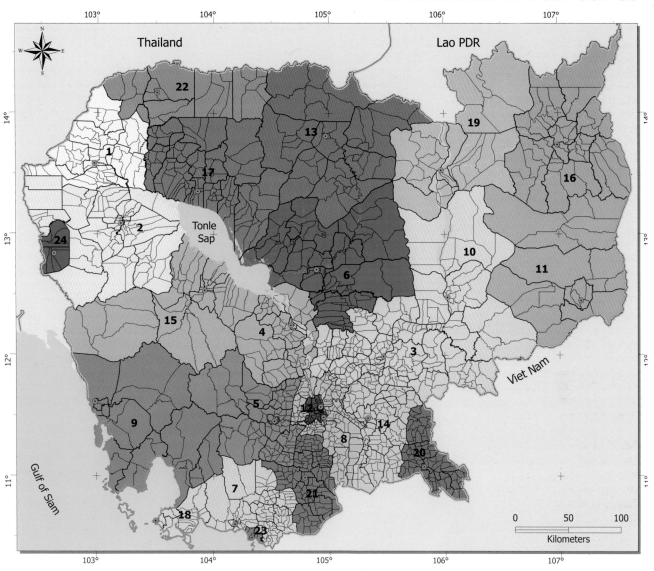

Legend

- Provincial Center
- Water Body
- —— Commune Boundary
- —— District Boundary
- —— Provincial Boundary
- —— International Boundary

Data Sources:
Administrative Boundaries and Provincial
Center: Department of Geography 2005
Water Body: JICA Dataset 2002

Code	Province	Provincial Center	No. Districts	No. Communes	Area Km²
1	Banteay Meanchey	Serei Saophoan	8	64	6,679
2	Battambang	Battambang	13	96	11,702
3	Kampong Cham	Kampong Cham	16	173	9,799
4	Kampong Chhnang	Kampong Chhnang	8	69	5,521
5	Kampong Speu	Chbar Mon	8	87	7,017
6	Kampong Thom	Stueng Saen	8	81	13,814
7	Kampot	Kampong Bay	8	92	7,873
8	Kandal	Ta Khmau	11	147	3,568
9	Koh Kong	Smach Mean Chey	8	33	11,160
10	Kratie	Kratie	5	46	11,094
11	Mondul Kiri	Saen Monourom	5	21	14,288
12	Phnom Penh	Toul Kouk	7	76	290
13	Preah Vihear	Tbaeng Mean Chey	7	49	13,788
14	Prey Veng	Kampong Leav	12	116	4,883
15	Pursat	Kandieng	6	49	12,692
16	Rattanak Kiri	Ban Lung	9	49	10,782
17	Siem Reap	Siem Reap	12	100	10,299
18	Sihanoukville	Mittapheap	3	22	868
19	Stung Treng	Thala Barivat	5	34	11,092
20	Svay Rieng	Svay Rieng	7	80	2,966
21	Takeo	Doun Kaev	10	100	3,563
22	Oddar Meanchey	Samraong	5	24	6,158
23	Kep	Damnak Chang Aeur	2	5	336
24	Pailin	Pailin	2	8	803
	Total		**185**	**1,621**	**181,035**

Source: NIS 2005, DoG 2005

Geographical Relief

The central geographical feature of Cambodia is the Tonle Sap Lake and the Bassac and Mekong River systems. The Tonle Sap Lake and the lower basin of the Bassac and Mekong rivers form the basis of the lowlands region with elevations generally less than 100m. This region is considered the food basket of Cambodia because it is rich in fertile farms and the rivers, streams and lakes supply water all year around. This region is also the most densely populated area of the country with a projected average population density of 82 people per square kilometer in 2006 (NIS: 2005).

To the South of the central lowlands the elevation increases to form the Cardamom Mountains which are originated generally in a Northwest - Southeast direction. Mount Aoral, Cambodia's highest peak, is located in the Northeastern region of the Cardamom Mountains and rises to 1,813 meters above sea level.

The Elephant Range extends Southeast of the Cardamom Mountains to the coastal province of Kampot. The Elephant Range rises in elevation from 500 to over 1000 metres above sea level.

Located on the Southwest of the Cardamom Mountains and the Elephant Range is a fairly narrow coastal plain extending from Koh Kong, through Sihanoukville and Kampot to Kep.

North of the central lowlands, the elevation averages 50 to 100 metres above sea level with some small areas rising to 500 metres above sea level. The Dangrek Mountains on the Northern rim of the Tonle Sap Basin adjoins the Korat Plateau of Thailand marking the boundary between the two countries.

The Highland region occupies the Northeastern part of the country with the Rattanak Kirri Plateau and the Chlong Highlands in the East merging with the Central Highlands of Viet Nam. This area is mostly covered with fertile volcanic soil.

The water network in Cambodia is divided into three systems: The Mekong River system, The Tonle Sap Lake system and the Coastal zone. The hydrological systems are central to life in Cambodia and Phnom Penh itself is located on the confluence of three important rivers; the Mekong, the Tonle Sap and the Bassac.

The Mekong River system includes the Mekong River, the Tonle Touch (small river), and the Tonle Bassac and their tributaries. With a length of 500km crossing Cambodia's territory from the Northern to the Southern border. The Mekong is Cambodia's most important river, and some would argue resource, as the people depend on the river for silt to provide rich agricultural land and fish constitutes a major proportion of protein in the diet. The Mekong River has two distinct seasons; the season of flooding from June to October and the season of subsidence from November to May.

The Tonle Sap system includes the Tonle Sap Lake, the Tonle Sap River and their tributaries. The Tonle Sap Lake is the greatest source of fish in Cambodia and as a result experiences the greatest population density as many people rely on the lake as a form of income. This region floods annually with the lake covering approximately 10,000 square kilometers in the wet season and only 3, 000 square kilometers in the dry season. The flooded forest of the Tonle Sap Lake with its floating villages is an easily recognizable part of Cambodian culture. The Tonle Sap River is well known for its rare ability to change its direction of flow. During the rainy season, as the pressure of water flow of the Mekong River traveling from its source is greatest, water flows Northwest along the Tonle Sap River into the Tonle Sap Lake. During the dry season as the Mekong water flow subsides, the water flow of the Tonle Sap River reverses direction and flows Southeast back towards the Mekong. The change in direction is marked by the Water Festival in Phnom Penh where brightly coloured long boats are raced along the Tonle Sap River.

Geographical Relief

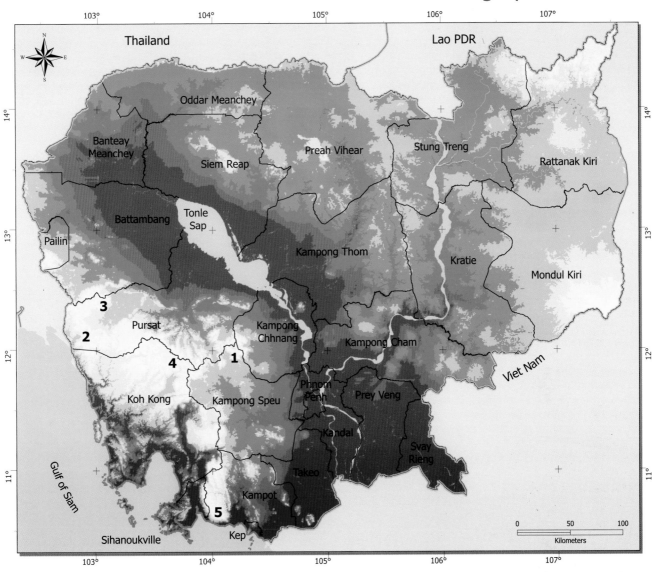

Legend

- ■ 0 - 15 m
- ■ 16 - 25 m
- ■ 26 - 50 m
- ■ 51 - 100 m
- 101 - 250 m
- 251 - 500 m
- 501 - 750 m
- 751 - 1,000 m
- 1,001 - 1,500 m
- 1,501 - 1,756 m
- Water Body
- — Provincial Boundary
- — International Boundary

Data Sources:
DEM: MRC
International and Provincial Boundary:
Department of Geography 2005
Water Body: JICA Dataset 2002
Note: elevation calculated using grid
system may cause variation in total area
size. Offical Area = 181,035 Km².

No.	Mountain Name	Height (m)
1	Phnom Aoral	1,813
2	Phnom Samkoh	1,717
3	Phnom Krapang	1,711
4	Phnom Knang Trapeng	1,213
5	Phnom Bokor	1,080

Elevation	Area (Km²)
0 - 15 m	41,181
16 - 25 m	13,556
26 - 50 m	22,854
51 - 100 m	47,041
101 - 250 m	35,102
251 - 500 m	12,231
501 - 750 m	5,924
751 - 1,000 m	2,704
1,001 - 1,500 m	999
1,501 - 1,813 m	15
Total:	**181,607**

Climate

Cambodia's climate is governed by monsoons and is characterized by two distinct seasons: from mid-May to early October, strong prevailing winds from the Southwest bring heavy rains and high humidity and from early November to mid-March, winds and humidity are low. Between these two seasons is a transitional period. The rainfall patterns change with elevation. It is heaviest in the mountains along the coast which receive from 2,500 mm to more than 5,000 mm of precipitation annually as the Southwest monsoon reaches the coast. The average annual rainfall is 1,400 mm in the central lowland regions and may reach 5,000 mm in certain coastal zones or in highland areas. The relative humidity is high at night throughout the year usually exceeding 90%. During the daytime in the dry season humidity averages about 50% or slightly lower, but it may remain at about 60% in the rainy period. Temperatures can approach 40 degrees celsius in April, while the coldest temperatures can be as low as 17 degrees celsius in January. The annual average temperature is 28 degrees celsius.

The coastal zone of Cambodia experiences high relative humidity with mean annual relative humidity values ranging around 85%. Minimum average humidity is recorded in December and January, while maximum relative humidity occurs in August through October. Wind speed in the coastal areas ranges from 2 to 4 m/s. Strong offshore winds of 16 m/s have been recorded and almost every year Cambodia's coastal zone is affected by tropical cyclones from the Pacific Ocean. However, the country is rarely exposed to the full force of a typhoon because it is surrounded by mountain chains which dissipate the full force. Storms occur more frequently during the period from August to November, with the highest frequency in October (MoE: 2001).

Prior to 1970 there were extensive rainfall stations in Cambodia. At present the number of operating stations has decreased dramatically. Similarly, air temperature is only recorded in six stations. There is only one station that records other climatic variables such as evaporation, radiation and wind.

Climate Change and its Impact on Cambodia

As an agrarian country, Cambodia is highly vulnerable to the impacts of climate change. Agriculture, a major sector of the national economy, is dependent on the natural rainfall and the annual flooding and recession of the Mekong River and the Tonle Sap Lake. Cambodian agriculture is therefore particularly sensitive to potential changes in local climate and monsoon regimes. Data from the past five years indicate that more than 70% of rice production loss in Cambodia was primarily due to flooding while drought was responsible for about 20% of the losses (MoE: 2001).

A study conducted by the Ministry of Environment suggested that by 2100 rainfall in Cambodia would increase by 3% to 35%, while temperature increase would be in the range of 1.3 degrees celsius to 2.5 degrees celsius.

Climate change may increase wet season rainfall and decrease dry season rainfall. Based on studies in Stung Metoek, Russei Chrum, Stung Sala Munthun and Stung Chhay Areng, the dry season river flow may decrease by 4 m³/s, while the wet season flow might increase by up to 10 m³/s (EVS: 1996). These findings would suggest that under climate change, the risk of drought and flood in Cambodia might increase.

Over the last decade Cambodia has experienced social, economic and environmental impacts caused by irregular, severe and more frequent floods, droughts and windstorms, which are believed to be related to changes in local and global climate. In the Social and Economic Development Plan II (SEDP II), these climate hazards are recognized as the main contributors of poverty. Severe floods that occurred from 2000 to 2002 resulted in 438 casualties and caused damages amounting to US $205 million (NCDM: 2002).

Sea level rise will severely affect the 435km long coastline, large parts of the Mekong River flood plain and the Tonle Sap ecosystem, which is the heart of Cambodia's economy, culture and environment. A study conducted by the Cambodian Climate Change Office indicates that a sea level increase of one meter would inundate many coastal areas of Cambodia, specifically the province of Koh Kong.

The country is also vulnerable to the health impacts of climate change due to its geographical location, the poor healthcare system, poverty predomination among the majority of people, and low awareness of people about healthcare measures. Cambodia already has the highest malaria fatality rate within Southeast Asia with some 500 deaths per year (MoH: 2004).

Cambodia is vulnerable to climate change with flood and drought the two major climate hazards commonly experienced. Their impacts include the yearly destruction of infrastructures, properties, crops, livestock and losses of lives. The adaptive capacity to flood and drought is relatively low in Cambodia. However, a number of projects addressing the need to reduce and mitigate the impacts of floods and droughts have been implemented, with over ten projects started in the last ten years.

The Royal Government of Cambodia has formulated long-term strategic sectoral plans and programs through the support of international donors to address the climate change problems. However, there is a need for policy makers to improve their understanding of climate change as well as capacity to mobilise resources to implement identified projects to address climate change. National policies and regulation should take into consideration climate change aspects, and it is urgent to assist local communities in increasing their adaptive capacity to climate variability.

Rainfall and Temperature Patterns

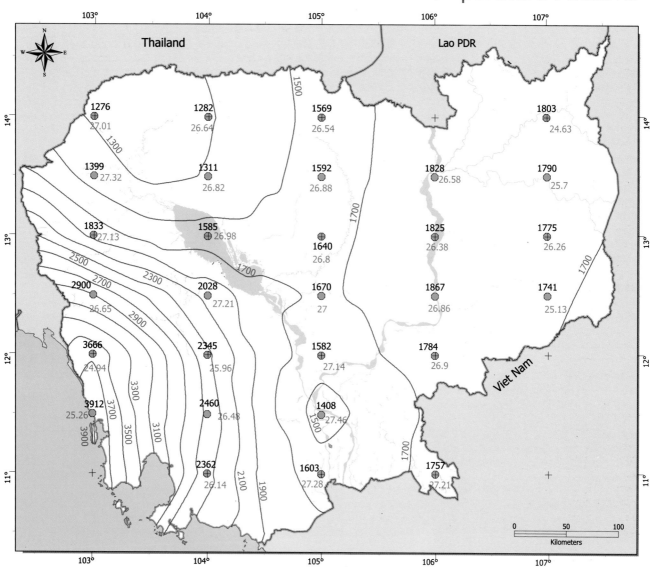

Legend

- ⬤ Introperlated Data Points
- — Introperlated Isohyets
- 1224 Rainfall (mm)
- 26.9 Temperature (°C)
- (shade) < 4 months dry
- (shade) > 4 months dry
- (shade) Water Body
- — Provincial Boundary
- — International Boundary

Note:
Remote sensing data - Secondary calculations.
1 month dry < 40 mm rainfall

Data Sources:
Precipitation and Temperature: FAO
Dry Periods: Gene-Ecological Zonation
of Cambodia (Tree Seed Project FA/
Danida /DED) 2003
International and Provincial Boundary:
Department of Geography 2005
Water Body: JICA Dataset 2002

Dry Periods

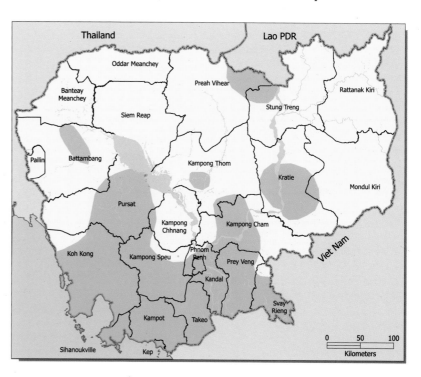

Atlas of Cambodia National Poverty and Environment Maps **9**

Land Use

Well defined land management techniques are critical to the socio economic development of Cambodia, as 85% of the population rely on a fragile balance of agriculture, fisheries and forest products for survival. Cambodia's total land area of 181, 035 km² is comprised of 54.1% forests, 23.4% agriculture, 6.8% wetlands, 15.6% wood and grasslands and 0.1% settlements (JICA dataset 2002). Cambodian agriculture is predominantly organized on the basis of small farmer communities. The plight of these communities in relation to access to natural resources and land ownership is possibly one of the most significant factors facing land use issues in Cambodia today.

Over the last decade, the main form of land use management has been the establishment of industrial concessions in the forestry, fisheries and more recently, in the agricultural sectors. The unsustainable use of many of these concessions, combined with their inability to increase economic activity at the local level, has led the RGC to seek alternative management practices that will support its goal of poverty alleviation combined with increased environmental sustainability.

Agriculture

Rice production dominates the agricultural sector, occupying 90% of cultivated area. While Cambodian soils generally exhibit low to medium soil fertility, the vast floodplains of the Mekong and Tonle Sap provide suitable conditions for extensive areas of rain-fed lowland rice. Multi cropping also exists along the banks of the Mekong. A combination of traditional systems, such as swidden agriculture and a diversification into cashew plantations, occur in the Northern highlands. The coastal zone, while becoming increasingly reliant on tourism and the industrial sector, includes a composition of land use types such as paddy fields, aquaculture, salt pans and plantations.

An increasing trend towards large scale economic concessions has emerged as a contentious issue in Cambodia (SOER: 2004). Currently there are 32 economic concessions recognized by MAFF covering a total of 773,749 ha. There are a further 17 economic concessions covering 115,590 ha which have not yet signed a contract. With clear resource assessments and management plans, economic concessions have the potential to stimulate the economy at a local level by providing employment and production. However, only 5% of the concession land granted has been active in growing crops. The rest have faced dispute over boundaries and have not been implemented (map pg 93).

Forestry

Comparison of forest cover data is invariably inconsistent, largely as a result of incomparable datasets. However, many government and independent analysis indicate that the extent of agricultural land has increased at the expense of the forests, not always productively (MRC: 2003). While 60% of Cambodia's forests remain, most have been disturbed with the Independent Forest Sector Review (2004) categorizing only 27% as less disturbed. The unsustainable use of the forestry concessions has left large tracts of land clear-felled and much of the remainder has been reduced in quality. Currently, the status of many of the forest concessions is uncertain.

While some have been cancelled, the rest have either no viable resources left or their legal status is in question. None are operating legally as the moratorium on logging established in 2001 is still in place.

An increasing population, low soil fertility and outdated farming practices has increased forest land encroachment. While this occurred mainly on the fringes of agricultural land during the 1990s, a variety of issues have led to the forests being more deeply penetrated in recent years (Dümmer: 2004).

The Forestry Administration broadly lists Cambodia's forest cover into four main categories; Evergreen forests, Semi Evergreen forersts, Deciduous forests and other forests (including bamboo, shrub and woodland, plantations, inundated forests, mangrove and forest regrowth). For more detail, refer to *Forest Resources*.

The late 90s and early 2000s saw an increase in the number of protected areas ranging from multiple use areas, wildlife sanctuaries, protected forests and globally recognized conservation areas. The jurisdiction of these fall under a variety of government departments. With inconsistent policies and management techniques, many of these areas remain under threat.

Fisheries

Cambodia has one of the largest inland fresh water fisheries in the world with thirteen provinces considered fishing provinces and six of these bordering the Tonle Sap. Fish remains the greatest source of protein in the Cambodian diet with annual consumption of fish and other aquatic animals estimated at over 30kg per person per year (Baran: 2005). Statistical data often underestimates the importance of fisheries as difficulties arise in determining the importance of the subsistent nature of fishing to many communities. For more detail refer to *Fisheries*.

Land Issues

Following many years of civil strife and displaced persons the problem of land tenure remains one of the most pressing issues facing the RGC today as many land title documents were destroyed. The lack of secure land tenure has resulted in an increasing trend of illegal ownership of large areas and incidents of land grabbing. Additionally, without the clear demarcation of state and privately owned land there are many land disputes surrounding economic land concessions. Generally, land registration occurs through two processes. The first is the systematic registration of land where people are currently living or operating and this occurs on a village by village basis. This process is heavily funded by the World Bank and has registered some 20,000 land titles per month. The second process is the sporadic registration of land controlled by the RGC where requests are made based on individual cases. Recently the RGC has also focused on the implementation of local land concessions through the Land Allocation for Social and Economic Development (LASED). The aim of LASED is to reduce poverty through facilitating approximately 10,000 landless and poor families to gain access to land, supporting infrastructure and livelihood services. It is expected that LASED will become operational by late 2006 and run for a duration of five years.

Landuse

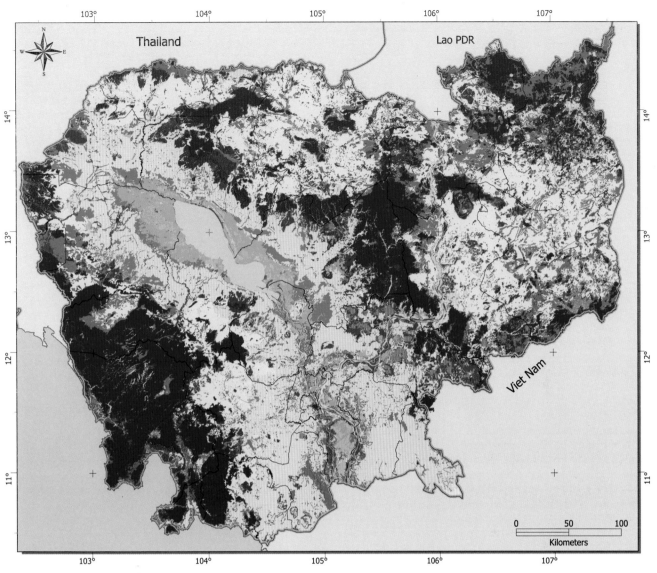

Thailand

Lao PDR

Viet Nam

Territory Overview

0   50   100
Kilometers

Legend

Landuse Type	Ha
Rice Field	3,163,000
Field Crops	372,600
Swidden Agriculture	349,700
Village Garden Crops	198,300
Receding Rice and Floating Rice Fields	194,000
Rubber Plantation	88,300
Urban, and Built-up Areas	18,100
Orchards	8,800
Salt Evaporator	6,100

Note: Vegetation types are broadly defined. For greater detail refer to Terrestial Vegetation and Landuse Patterns map.

	Ha
Evergreen broad leafed forest	3,922,638
Deciduous forest	3,549,993
Mixed forest from evergreen and deciduous species	1,429,007
Woodland and Scattered trees	1,266,100
Shrubland	1,094,000
Grassland	861,600
Flooded Shrub	533,200
Flooded Grassland	173,500
Barren Land	27,200
Sand Terrain	7,500
Rock Outcrops	1,800

	Ha
Perennial Water Body	91,100
Mangrove	64,900
Marsh or Swamp	44,600
Flooded Forest	20,600
Water Body	
—— Provincial Boundary	
—— International Boundary	

Data Sources:
Landuse: JICA Dataset 2002
International and Provincial Boundary :
Department of Geography 2005
Water Body: JICA Dataset 2002

Poverty Mapping

The Ministry of Planning in close collaboration with the United Nations World Food Programme (WFP) has created a set of maps showing poverty at provincial, district and commune levels in Cambodia. The maps have served as a basis for formulating plans for various social interventions carried out by the WFP. They have also been used as a valuable tool to establish programmes and strategies to combat poverty by the RGC, donors and other organizations.

Existing data from the Cambodian Socio-economic Surveys (CSES) allow for the estimation of poverty indicators but this is only accurate over large geographical areas. Thus, pockets of poverty or poor areas surrounded by non-poor areas cannot be identified from the socio-economic surveys alone. The surveys do not provide for a reliable estimation of poverty at the provincial, district or commune levels.

It is often the case that what policy makers really need is information at geographically disaggregated levels. Therefore, poverty maps have been created by combining data from the socio-economic surveys, the 1998 Cambodian Population Census, and other geographic data compiled with a GIS. Using a recently developed statistical technique "Small Area Estimation", the strengths of these various datasets were combined to generate poverty estimates at geographically disaggregated levels thus providing more useful information. In the present Atlas of Cambodia, maps are shown with poverty rates at the commune level.

Overview of Poverty Mapping Methodology

The mapping exercise uses consumption (the monetary value of the goods and services consumed by a person) as the measure of poverty. Data is taken on household consumption from the socio-economic survey, which is combined with data on household and village-level characteristics from the population census and GIS data. Statistical analysis is applied to these data to estimate a relationship between consumption and household and village-level characteristics. This relationship is known as the consumption model and is used to generate estimates of consumption for large numbers of households across the country.

Next, a given level of consumption is chosen as a poverty line. Households whose consumption is below this level are considered poor, and those with consumption above it are considered non-poor. From here, standard poverty indicators, such as poverty incidence, poverty severity, and poverty gap can be calculated. The calculations also produce measures of error for the estimates, which can be used to assess their validity. Finally, maps are generated to show the geographical distribution of these indicators across communes, districts and provinces.

Consumption as the Measure of Poverty

Household consumption expenditure is used to measure the welfare of people. Consumption is not the only possible measure and can capture only certain aspects of poverty. For example, consumption measures cannot capture health and nutrition poverty or education poverty. However, because consumption is expressed in monetary terms its meaning is easily understood.

Income is also a useful monetary measure but when a large informal sector exists, or a large fraction of production is for self-consumption, it is unlikely to accurately reflect welfare. Consumption may be thought of as a good proxy indicator for measuring true welfare, although it is by no means the perfect measure.

Choice of the Poverty Line

To ensure comparability with the national poverty rate of 36.1%, the poverty lines were chosen so that the same poverty rate would be replicated for the three strata of the CSES surveys. Calculations were conducted so that the poverty line for each stratum would be set at a rate that would have 36.1% of the population of the strata below it. As a result, the poverty lines, in terms of per capita per day consumption, are 1,629 Riel for Phnom Penh, 1,214 Riel for other urban areas and 1,036 Riel for Rural areas[1]. This means that people in each of the three strata whose daily consumption has a value of less than these rates are considered poor. The differences in the rates reflect differences in the cost of living in Phnom Penh, other urban areas and rural areas.

Poverty Rate

The poverty rate (also know as poverty incidence or the headcount index) is the most commonly used measure of poverty. It refers to the proportion of the population living below the poverty line. As such, the measure is easy to understand. However, it has an important weakness in that it fails to take the intensity of poverty into account. The poverty rate only shows the proportion of people below the poverty line and contains no information about how far they fall below it. A population that has many people just below the poverty line will have the same rate as one that has many people far below the line.

Essentially, the poverty rate implies that there is a jump in quality of life at the poverty line, suggesting that the lives of those just below the line are very different from the lives of those just above the line. This difference is not found in reality.

A recently published report by the World Bank establishes that the poverty rate fell by 1-1.5% per annum between 1993/4 (45-50%) and 2004 (35%) (WB: 2006). However, while there has been a decrease in overall poverty, the report found the distribution of wealth uneven with the gap between rich and poor increasing. Overall the findings are encouraging, although international evidence indicates that a decline in poverty after the establishment of a stable government and the corresponding improvements in infrastructure and economic growth, are to be expected. The challenge ahead for Cambodia lies in the continuing decline in poverty, particularly for those people in rural areas (Conway: 2005).

---

[1] The average official exchange rate in 1998 was USD 1=3807.8 Riels

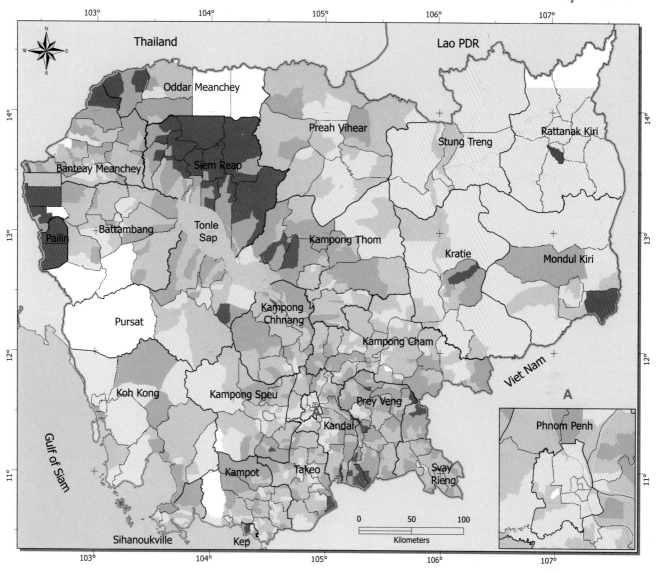

Legend

Poverty Rate
(CSES 97 + Census 98)

- ■ > 75% poor
- ■ 50 - 75% poor
- ■ 25 - 50% poor
- ▨ < 25% poor
- □ No Data
- ■ Water Body
- ┄┄ District Boundary
- ── Provincial Boundary
- ── International Boundary

Note: This map reflects the poverty situation in 1998. An updated version will be available following the 2008 census.

Data Sources:
Poverty Rate: WFP 2002
International, Provincial and District Boundary:
Department of Geography 2005
Water Body: JICA Dataset 2002

Poverty Rate

Province	Poverty Rate %	Est No. of poor people (000's)
Banteay Meanchey	40.9	228.8
Battambang	26.4	198.7
Kampong Cham	12.1	190.1
Kampong Chhnang	44.6	179.9
Kampong Speu	18.2	105.3
Kampong Thom	29.1	158.9
Kampot	18.7	97.3
Kandal	18.4	192.3
Koh Kong	8.2	8.7
Kratie	38.6	97.8
Mondul Kiri	19.9	6.2
Phnom Penh	11.9	109.4
Preah Vihear	29.1	32.9
Prey Veng	53.1	493.6
Pursat	40.7	140.2
Rattanak Kiri	8.8	8.1
Siem Reap	53.7	356.8
Sihanoukville	34.1	50.4
Stung Treng	16.4	12.6
Svay Rieng	43.5	205.5
Takeo	15.2	117.9
Oddar Meanchey	39.1	24.5
Kep	49.0	9.6
Pailin	97.2	6.0

Landmine and UXO Distribution

The Cambodian problem of landmines and unexploded ordinance (UXOs) is the direct result of decades of war and conflict which have devastated the country in every sense. Today, the people of Cambodia have to deal with one of the worst impacts of landmines and UXO contamination on the surface of the globe. In the course of these conflicts, each warring faction has polluted indiscriminately and scattered without record or regard to later consequence their killing tools of landmines and UXOs. It has been estimated that between 4 and 6 million landmines have been laid - the frightening statistic of one landmine for every two Cambodians. In addition, there are the UXOs - the remains of a massive air bombing campaign, and the ordinance that litters the many battlefronts, which are part of the two to three million tons of ammunition expended from 1970 to 1997.

The National Level One Survey reveals the following results: 6,422 Cambodian villages identified as contaminated, or 46.2% of the total villages in Cambodia; 4,466 km² of land is contaminated leaving over 5 million Cambodian people at risk; and over 11,000 EOD tasks have been identified. It should be noted that the mine problem in Cambodia is mainly concentrated in the Northwestern part of the country bordering Thailand while the UXO problem is heavily concentrated in the Southeastern part of the country bordering Viet Nam. This is due to the different nature of conflicts in two distinct regions.

Based on the outcome of the survey, every Cambodian province and city is to some degree affected by landmines and/or UXO. Today, this heavy and abundant contamination is one of the most important factors hindering the socio-economic reconstruction and development of Cambodia. It threatens personal safety, access to economic sources and activities. The presence of landmines and UXOs, or even the suspicion of their presence, impinges on almost every aspect of post conflict recovery that faces Cambodia. With the cessation of fighting, the battlefields are now once again available to be returned to their former use. As social and economic activities start to take root and grow on old battlefields, people are constantly faced with the dangers of stepping on a landmine or exploding a UXO causing expensive social and economic loss to the individual, family and society.

Today, landmines and UXOs continue to kill and injure close to 1,000 people every year. This number of casualties still remains one of the highest casualty rates in the world, and probably the highest among peaceful countries. Despite the landmine/UXO risk, education and clearance efforts by all demining organizations, including informal deminers, landmines and UXOs still pose formidable risks to personal security, economic recovery and national development. Landmine and UXO accidents occur as people have no choice but to carry out livelihood activities on the contaminated land. Children are especially vulnerable to landmines as they help their parents in livelihood activities such as collecting firewood and herding animals. They are also exposed to the dangers of UXOs as they tamper with them out of curiosity and for economic reasons. Poverty, the recent rise in metal price and the uncontrolled development of cheap detecting technology have worsened UXO incidences. Recently, the number of casualties caused by

UXOs throughout Cambodia is on the increase, a trend due to the attractive price of scrap metal. Despite constant and persuasive UXO awareness campaigns, villagers and ex-soldiers have entered into the dangerous venture of turning UXO into income by selling the shells of UXOs after removing the explosives and detonators. Unfortunately, these ventures are not always successful and are often costly, not only to the victim and their families, but also to their communities. One way or another, all accidents cause injury or death and this has a severe negative impact on the social and economic well being of the community.

Roads, agricultural land, community areas such as schools, pagodas, ponds and wells are often considered as part of the suspected areas. This makes access dangerous, prevents adequate development in the long term and puts the population at high risk. Local populations are frequently under economic pressure to resettle on contaminated land resulting in an increase in the number of victims.

Landmines and UXO clearance effort is essential to support humanitarian, poverty reduction and development causes. Clearance helps to reduce risk and poverty, re-establish social integrity, develop infrastructure, provide assistance to environmental preservation activities, and return the basic right of personal security to the people. It should be noted that Cambodia is probably the only country in the world which has targeted mine clearance in the Millennium Development Goals.

Landmine and UXO Contamination

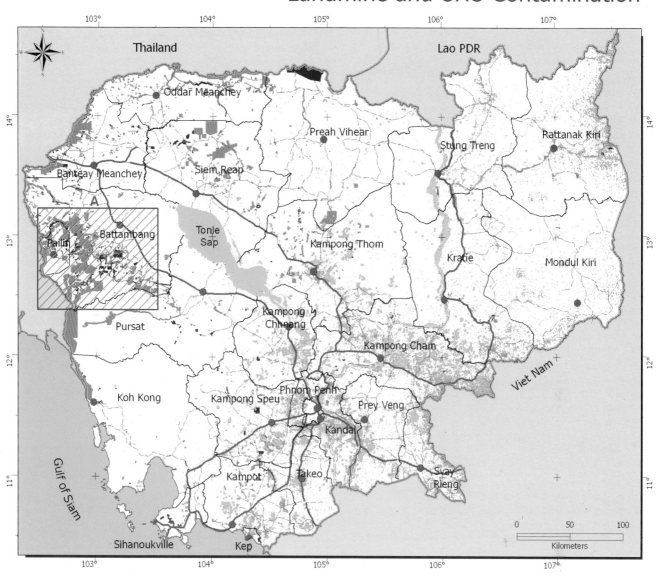

Legend

- Air Attack Targets
- Provincial Center
- Mine Location (Level one survey)
- Mine Location (Confirmed, Suspected, Residual)
- B52 Bombing Targets
- Water Body
- Main Roads
- Secondary Roads
- Provincial Boundary
- International Boundary

Data Sources:
Mine Location: Level One Survey, CMAA 2001
Mine Location: Confirmed, Suspected, Residual, CMAC 2005
Air Attack Targets and B52 Bombing Targets: US-DSCA
(US-Defense Security Cooperation Agency) 1970-1975
International and Provincial Boundary and Provincial Center:
Department of Geography 2005
Main Roads, Secondary Roads and Water Body:
JICA Dataset 2002

A

References

ADB. 2000. Priority Sectors for ADB's Future Operations. Priority Sector One: Rural Economic Development. In, Cambodia: Enabling a Socio-economic Rennaissance. Accessed at:
www.adb.org/Documents/CSSs/CAM/ cam405.asp

Baran, E. 2005. Cambodian Inland Fisheries: Facts, Figures and Context. WorldFish Center. Penang, Malaysia

CM. 2004. Significant Achievements of Royal Government of Cambodia in 1998-2003. Office of Council Ministers. Phnom Penh, Cambodia

Conway, T. 2005. How the Poverty Line and Poverty Rate are Calculated. The World Bank Newsletter, Volume 3, Number 12. December 2005. Phnom Penh, Cambodia

Dümmer, I. 2004. Information and Knowledge Based System for Land Suitability Analysis in Cambodia. A Paper Prepared for the Land Resource Assessment Forum (14-17 September 2004).
Accessed at: www.danida-cambodia.org

EVS Environment Consultants. 1996. Coastal and Marine Environmental Management for Cambodia: Final Report. Phnom Penh, Cambodia

FAO, Guidelines for Land-use Planning: FAO Development Series 1. United Nations Food and Agriculture Organization.

MoEYS. 2001. Social study 7 (Geography and History). Department of Pedagogy Research, Ministry of Education, Youth and Sport. Phnom Penh, Cambodia

MoE. 2001. Vulnerability and Adaptation Assessment to Climate. Ministry of Environment. Phnom Penh, Cambodia

MoE. 2005a. Analysis of Policies to Address Climate Change Impacts in Cambodia. Phnom Penh: Climate Change Office: Ministry of Environment. Phnom Penh, Cambodia

MoE. 2005b. Clean Development Mechanism in Cambodia. Phnom Penh. Climate Change Office. Ministry of Environment. Phnom Penh, Cambodia

MoH. 2004. Health Statistic Report for 2002. Ministry of Health. Phnom Penh, Cambodia

MoH. 2004. Achievements of the Ministry of Health in 2003 and Direction for 2004. Ministry of Health. Phnom Penh, Cambodia

MOWRAM. 2003. Report on Activities and Outputs of the Ministry of Water Resources and Meteorology 2003. Ministry of Water Resources and Meteorology. Phnom Penh, Cambodia

MRC. 2003. State of The Basin Report: 2003. Mekong River Commission. Phnom Penh. ISSN: 1728:3248

NCDM. 2002. Summary of Micro Projects Completed in Phase 3. National Committee on Disaster Management. Phnom Penh, Cambodia

NIS. 1999. General Population Census of Cambodia 1998. National Institute of Statistics, Ministry of Planning. Phnom Penh, Cambodia

NIS. 2000. Cambodia Demographic Health Survey. National Institute of Statistics, Ministry of Planning. Phnom Penh, Cambodia

NIS. 2002. Country Paper - Cambodia, for the Subcommittee on Statistics, first session Bangkok 18-24 February 2004. National Institute of Statistics, Ministry of Planning. Phnom Penh, Cambodia

NIS. 2004. Cambodia Inter-censal Population Survey 2004: General Report. National Institute of Statistics, Ministry of Planning. Phnom Penh, Cambodia

NIS. 2005. Statistical Yearbook 2005. National Institute of Statistics, Ministry of Planning. Phnom Penh, Cambodia

SOER. 2004. State of Environment Report 2004. Ministry of Environment, Phnom Penh, Cambodia

UNIFEM, WB. ADB, UNDP and DFID/UK. 2004. A Fair Share for Women: Cambodia Gender Assessment. UNIFEM, WB. ADB, UNDP and DFID/UK. Phnom Penh, Cambodia. ISBN: 1-93287-00-5

WFP, MoP. 2002. Estimation of Poverty Rates at Commune Level in Cambodia. Using the Small Area Estimation Technique to Obtain Reliable Estimates. United Nations World Food Programme and Ministry of Planning. Phnom Penh, Cambodia

World Bank. 2006. Cambodia Halving Poverty by 2015? Poverty Assessment 2006. The World Bank, Phnom Penh, Cambodia

Population and Settlement

Population

Reliable demographic data is necessary in order to monitor the real needs of the population in relation to factors such as health, education, employment and infrastructure. It is also important to identify demographic trends and the resultant effect these will have on natural resources. This is particularly true for Cambodia where a high proportion of the population still rely heavily on natural resources to meet their daily needs. Reliable quantitative and qualitative demographic data is needed to increase understanding of population issues such as increasing youth and elderly populations and migration in order to inform effective policy, strategies and planning to aid development. In the last five years, significant improvements have been made in Cambodia in the capacity to collect and analyse data with the introduction of several household surveys. However, there are still some problems remaining with limited resources available to undertake research on emerging population issues (UNFPA: 2005). This is particularly so at provincial, district and commune level where local planners often don't have access to data or the capacity to analyse this data as part of the participatory planning process.

The main source of demographic data is the General Population Census of Cambodia (GPCC) conducted in 1998. The GPCC was the last full count of the population in 36 years since the GPCC in 1962. The next GPCC is scheduled to take place in 2008. In the interim, to help support and update the information collected from the GPCC 1998, the National Institute of Statistics (NIS), in the Ministry of Planning has conducted a number of household surveys. These include the Cambodian Inter-censal Population Survey (CIPS 2004), Cambodian Social Economic Survey (CSES 2004) and the Cambodian

Demographic Health Survey (CDHS 2000). An updated CDHS is scheduled for publication in 2006. As the various titles imply, the household surveys are used to support different sectors. The CIPS 2004 contains updated information on population characteristics, household facilities and amenities. It was conducted in a nationwide representative sample of 21,000 households within a selected 700 villages. The demographic data included in the Population and Settlement chapter of the atlas has been sourced from the NIS Statistical Yearbook 2005, CIPS 2004 and the Commune Data Base. The Commune Data Base has been included as a source as it provides useful information at commune level.

Population Overview

Cambodia's total population in 2004 was 13.4 million. Based on population projections from the GPCC 1998 and CIPS 2004, the projected population in 2005 is 13.7 million indicating an increase of 1.7% (NIS: 2005). In 2003, the average population density was 75 people per square kilometre with over 84% of the population living in rural areas. Approximately 51.4% of the population are females. Life expectancy is increasing and is now 58 years for women and 54 years for men (CDHS: 2000).

Average Population Density
(Person/Km²)

Region	2006	2021
Phnom Penh	4,969	7,769
Plains	297	390
Tonle Sap Lake	67	94
Coastal	65	22
Plateu and Mountain	23	38

Source: NIS Statistical Yearbook 2005

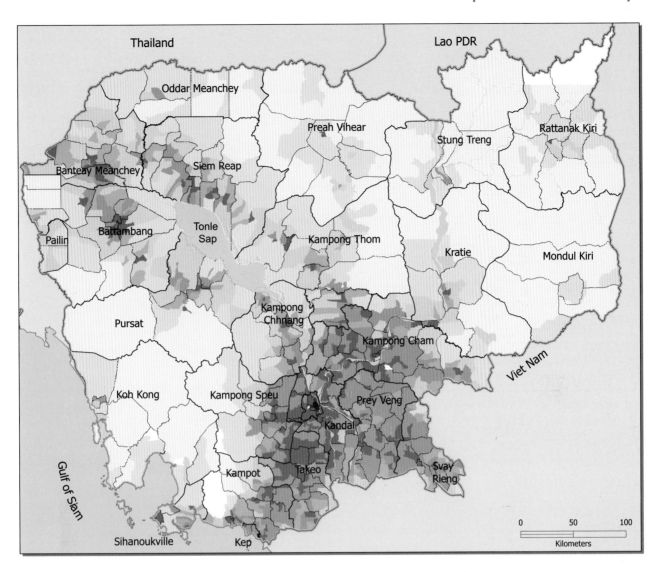

Legend

Population Density (People/Km²)

- <10
- 11 - 50
- 51 - 100
- 101 - 150
- 151 - 300
- 301 - 3,000
- 3,001 - 8,000
- 8,001 - 164,437
- No Data
- Water Body
- District Boundary
- Provincial Boundary
- International Boundary

Data Sources:
Population Density: Commune Database 2004
District, Provincial and International Boundary:
Department of Geography 2005
Water Body: JICA Dataset 2002

There is a particularly high younger population with approximately 60.8% being 24 years old or younger. The elderly population is still relatively low with 3.7% of the population over 65, however this figure is increasing. While the national population growth rate decreased from 2.4% in 1998 to 1.7% in 2006, it is still high compared to other countries in the region. The projected population for 2020 is approximately 19 million people.

Population Density

Population density is one of the key indicators of pressure placed on the environment and its associated effects on the quality of life and standard of living. The population density of Cambodia has increased considerably from an average of 37 people/km² in 1981 to 75 people/km² in 2004 and is projected to reach 112 people/km² in 2020.

According to population projections for 2006 based on the 1998 census, population density is highest in the Plains region with 297 people/km² (NIS: 2005). Population is most dense in Phnom Penh with an average of 4,969 people/Km². Next are the Tonle Sap (67 pp/km²) and Coastal regions (65 pp/km²) and finally the Plateau and Mountain region is the least densely populated (23 pp/km²). The Plains and Tonle Sap Lake regions with lower elevation and higher soil fertility have traditionally been the main agricultural areas of Cambodia. These regions also exhibit a greater socio-economic infrastructure, are more easily accessible and have lower unemployment levels. The wetlands of the Tonle Sap and Mekong River also support abundant Fisheries and provide other natural resources intrinsic to many people's livelihood strategies. The coastal region, while rich in forests and natural resources is less densely populated mainly due to poor infrastructure with the linkage between provincial centers and communes seemingly non-existent.

In 2004, about 11 % of the total population lived in the Plateau and Mountain region of the Northeast. While this region occupies approximately 38% of the total land area, it has a very low population density, mainly due to inaccessibility as this area is heavily forested with few roads. Access is further limited during the wet season when many roads are washed away. As a result of poor infrastructure there is a low level of development initiative, resulting in very few employment opportunities. In recent years there has been growing concern about the establishment of economic concessions in this area. The population density of the provinces increased unevenly during 1998-2004 with some provinces showing far greater growth than others. This indicates a need to create measures that would help to distribute the population more evenly. This could be achieved by creating industrial zones along the national routes and introducing equal conditions and opportunities across regions especially in regards to providing educational and vocational training facilities in each province.

Population Age Structure

The demographic profile of Cambodia reflects the legacy of a long draw-out period of civil strife. High mortality rates and low fertility rates during the Khmer Rouge Regime from 1974-1979, coupled with a post conflict baby boom, have contributed to a large young population. With 60% of the population 24 and younger, factors such as education, health and employment opportunities need to be addressed in order to aid development. Investments in education and health are necessary to equip the large proportion of youth with skills necessary to become productive adults and assist in the economic development of the country. As many Cambodians have a high dependency on natural resources, without greater employment opportunities for youth, there will be continued pressure on the natural environment as expanding households clear new land for agriculture and forage for forest products. An increasing elderly population also raises concerns of establishing adequate healthcare facilities and housing in order to improve the wellbeing of elderly citizens. Cambodia's elderly population lived through an exceptionally traumatic period during their adult years and one that has eroded the basis of core family support for many. Additionally, formal channels of assistance to this section of the population are virtually non-existent and need to be urgently addressed (Knodel et al: 2005).

Population Pyramid 2004

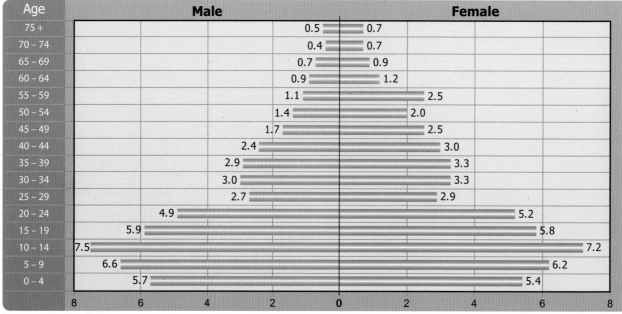

Source : UNFPA : 2005

Population Age Structure

Population Age Structure from 0 to 5 years old

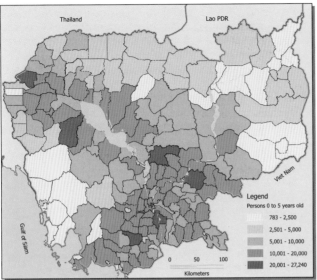

Legend
Persons 0 to 5 years old

783 - 2,500
2,501 - 5,000
5,001 - 10,000
10,001 - 20,000
20,001 - 27,240

Population Age Structure from 6 to 14 years old

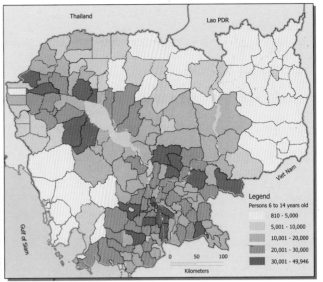

Legend
Persons 6 to 14 years old

810 - 5,000
5,001 - 10,000
10,001 - 20,000
20,001 - 30,000
30,001 - 49,946

Population Age Structure from 15 to 17 years old

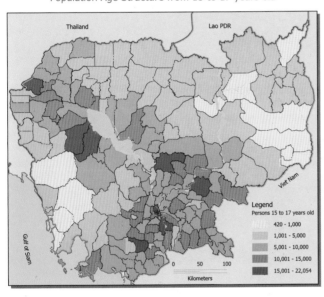

Legend
Persons 15 to 17 years old

420 - 1,000
1,001 - 5,000
5,001 - 10,000
10,001 - 15,000
15,001 - 22,054

Population Age Structure from 18 to 64 years old

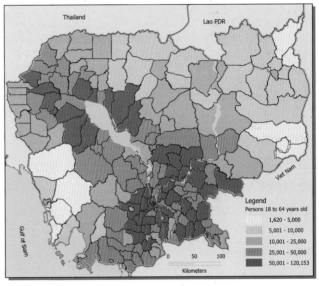

Legend
Persons 18 to 64 years old

1,620 - 5,000
5,001 - 10,000
10,001 - 25,000
25,001 - 50,000
50,001 - 120,153

Population Age Structure Over 65 years old

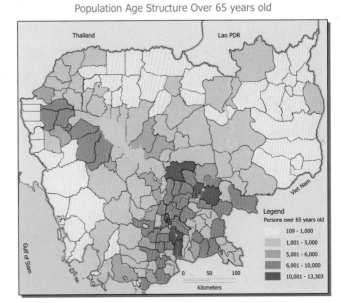

Legend
Persons over 65 years old

109 - 1,000
1,001 - 5,000
5,001 - 6,000
6,001 - 10,000
10,001 - 13,303

Legend

 Water Body

----- District Boundary

----- Provincial Boundary

----- International Boundary

Data Sources:
Age Structure: Commune Database 2004
District, Provincial and International Boundary:
Department of Geography 2005
Water Body: JICA Dataset 2002

Urban - Rural Population

In gathering data for the urban-rural population, the commune database considered all provincial headquarter towns as urban. In addition, the entire provinces of Krong Preah Sihanoukville, Kep and Pailin were treated as urban. In Phnom Penh the four districts of Doun Penh, Chamkarmon, 7 Makara and Tuol Kouk were classified as urban. All the remaining areas of the country were classified as rural. Data from the GPCC 1998 were utilized to determine the appropriate cut-off points to establish three criteria for classifying urban or rural populations. These criteria are as follows:

- Population density exceeding 200 people/km²
- Male employment in agriculture below 50%
- Total population of the commune exceeding 2000 people

Although the criteria for urban designation appear to be sound for Cambodian conditions, field visits were conducted in order to examine conditions on the ground, especially for some borderline cases in the provinces of Kampong Speu, Kampong Chhnang, Pursat, Battambang, Banteay Meanchey and Siem Reap. These field visits revealed that:

- The communes selected as urban according to agreed criteria did indeed exhibit urban characteristics
- Certain areas which exhibited urban characteristics in the field did not qualify according to the criteria used, mainly because of weaknesses in using the communes rather than the villages as the unit of analysis
- Local directors of planning had certain recommendations based on local knowledge. In some cases these suggestions were fully justified
- Discussion with commune chiefs indicated that approximate data on areas of village are available at commune offices

Application of cut-off points ran into difficulties in four provinces with a small population and/or an isolated location (Pailin, Kep, Mondul Kiri and Oddar Meanchey). Yet in each of these provinces, the provincial center was indeed a small town. Because of the need to ensure that every province contains at last one town, in these provinces the criteria were relaxed so that the provincial capital could be considered to be an urban area.

Over 84% of the Cambodian population live in rural areas, with around 9% and 7% living in Phnom Penh and other urban areas. In terms of geographic distribution, approximately 52% of the population lives in the Plains region, which covers less than 14% of Cambodia's total land area. A further 30% of the population lives in and around the Tonle Sap Lake region covering 37% of the total land area. Just over 7% of the population lives in the Coastal region (10% of total land area) and 11% live in the Plateau and Mountain region (38% of total land area).

Cambodia's urban population is principally located in Phnom Penh, Battambang, Kampong Cham, Kampong Chnnang, Siem Reap and Sihanoukville. Phnom Penh has an estimated population of 1,165 million and an annual rate of growth of about 1.7%. Regionally, the distribution of the population is concentrated in the six provinces located in the Plains region and around the capital. This area supports close to 60% of the entire population.

There are a number of social, political and economic factors influencing rural-urban migration and thus contributing to Phnom Penh's growing population density. Social factors include:

- Major educational facilities are located in Phnom Penh and a desire for higher education attracts many to the city
- A perception of a higher standard of living in Phnom Penh
- The presence of friends and relatives in Phnom Penh
- An expectation among migrants of a rise in social prestige associated with urban living

Environmental factors such as land degradation, unsuitable land use and the unsustainable use of natural resources help to create conditions that can no longer support a rural livelihood in some areas. This has also caused an increase in rural-urban migration. The economic differences between Phnom Penh and the rural areas are vast and obviously motivate many to move to the city. Other economic factors such as the existence of high population pressure on rural land, a low rate of investment in agriculture, fragmentation of land ownership, inequality in the distribution of land and food shortages also act as an influence.

Urban - Rural Population

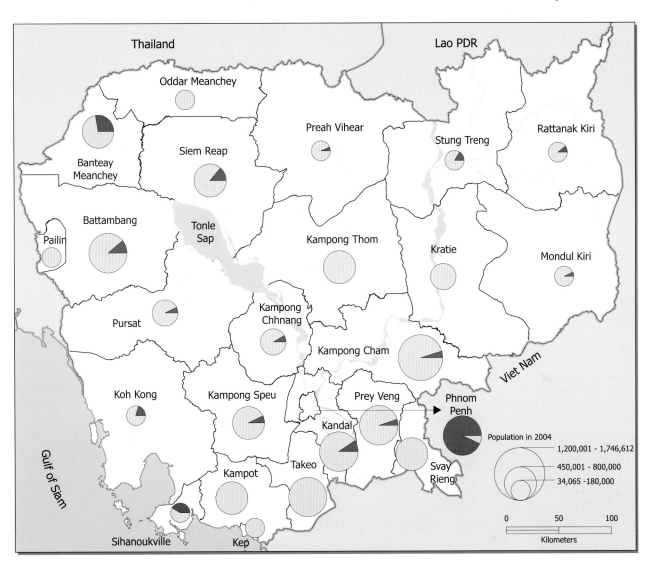

Legend

- ▓ Urban Population (%)
- ░ Rural Population (%)
- ▒ Water Body
- — Provincial Boundary
- ━ International Boundary

Data Sources:
Urban - Rural Data: Commune Database 2004
Provincial and International Boundary:
Department of Geography 2005
Water Body: JICA Dataset 2002

Urban - Rural Population

Province	Total Population	Urban Population	Rural Population	% Urban Population	% Rural Population
Banteay Meanchey	586,571	162,644	423,927	28	72
Battambang	948,706	103,058	845,648	11	89
Kampong Cham	1,746,612	83,238	1,663,374	5	95
Kampong Chhnang	444,475	35,265	409,210	8	92
Kampong Speu	690,963	49,333	641,630	7	93
Kampong Thom	624,846	3,013	621,833	1	99
Kampot	575,013	0	575,013	0	100
Kandal	1,185,791	110,562	1,075,229	9	91
Koh Kong	130,562	26,464	104,098	20	80
Kratie	285,251	0	285,251	0	100
Mondul Kiri	47,391	3,260	44,131	7	93
Phnom Penh	1,001,951	932,847	69,104	93	7
Preah Vihear	141,749	8,551	133,198	6	94
Prey Veng	1,065,550	53,726	1,011,824	5	95
Pursat	385,301	27,183	358,118	7	93
Rattanak Kiri	124,403	13,124	111,279	10	90
Siem Reap	776,978	107,084	669,894	14	86
Sihanoukville	173,904	72,580	101,324	42	58
Stung Treng	92,870	15,514	77,356	17	83
Svay Rieng	529,531	0	529,531	0	100
Takeo	881,940	0	881,940	0	100
Oddar Meanchey	144,371	0	144,371	0	100
Kep	34,065	0	34,065	0	100
Pailin	54,203	0	54,203	0	100

Boat population

The boat population refers to persons living in boats or conducting business from a boat that is on the move and therefore not registered with any local authority. The boat population is difficult to reach during the census and special arrangements are made to try and enumerate them as accurately as possible. The actual population living on boats at a fixed location are generally registered with the local authority and are therefore included in the regular household population. In 1998 the boat population was estimated to be 22 000 with 23% in Kandal, 22% in Phnom Penh, 17% in Pursat and 14% in Kompong Chhnang.

Homeless population

Homeless people are those who do not live in a dwelling but reside on the pavements, in parks and in open spaces outside pagodas or markets. In 1998 the homeless population was estimated at 20 000 with just over 22% living in Phnom Penh followed by 11% in Kampong Thom and 11.3% in Kandal. Most of the homeless population, (86.7%), live in the Plains and Tonle Sap Lake regions where urbanization and industrial growth is very high compared to other regions.

Transient population

This category of population includes those people who stayed in airports, railway stations, bus stands, harbours, ferries and in carts (as travellers), camped in a village, stayed on boats within the Cambodian territorial waters and stayed at international border posts during the night of the census. In 1998 the transient population was estimated to be 17 000 with 20% in Battambang followed by 15% in Kandal, 14.4% in Prey Veng and 7.7% in Koh Kong. Most of the transient population, (83.9%) travelled in the Plains and Tonle Sap Lake regions. The transient population circulated more in urban areas except in the Tonle Sap Lake region where about 42 % of the transient population were located in rural areas.

Population Projection

According to CIPS 2004, the fertility rate has declined substantially in the last two decades from more than 6 children per woman in the 1980s, to 4 children in 1998 to 3.3 children per woman in 2003 (Neupert: 2005). This could be attributed to developments in reproductive health, although much remains to be done to continue to improve this situation. There has also been a significant decline in infant and child mortality, although compared

to other countries in the region these are still considered high. Socio-economic development and the expansion of the provision of healthcare have not been broad enough to explain a decline in infant and child mortality. Rather, the decline may be attributed to a decline in fertility (Neupert: 2005). Experiences from other countries indicate that further declines in infant and child mortality will not be possible unless there are substantial improvements in healthcare and standard of living. In spite of a declining fertility rate, the rate of population growth will continue to be high over the next decade. This can be attributed to the population momentum which occurs when the large proportion of young people in the population reach reproductive age. It is estimated that the total population for 2020 will be approximately 19 million (NIS: 2005).

An increasing population has many implications. It affects poverty by increasing the number of dependents to income earners within the household by increasing under and unemployment and depressing wages if the increasing labour pool is not absorbed into the economy. It impacts on education outcomes by increasing the pressure on public service delivery in education. It often reflects significant gender inequality insofar as women are without reproductive choice and subject to traditional norms about female sexuality. Infant and child mortality are closely related to birth spacing and mother's age at childbirth, both of which are adversely affected by high population growth, as is the quality of health care provision. The same point applies to maternal mortality. In addition, the burgeoning young population living in very poor hygienic conditions puts undue stress on the health care system, which is unable to respond effectively. The high demand for social services strain government finance and threaten macroeconomic balances.

Rapid population growth in rural areas is likely to lead to deforestation, degradation of land, depletion of water resources and reduction in biodiversity. In urban areas it puts pressure on water and sanitation provision, and often has a negative effect on air quality. In addition, a large population is often associated with increasing conflict over land in rural areas and to social ills in urban areas such as overcrowding, spread of infectious diseases and delinquency. The challenge is to implement an effective population policy attuned to the social and cultural context of Cambodia

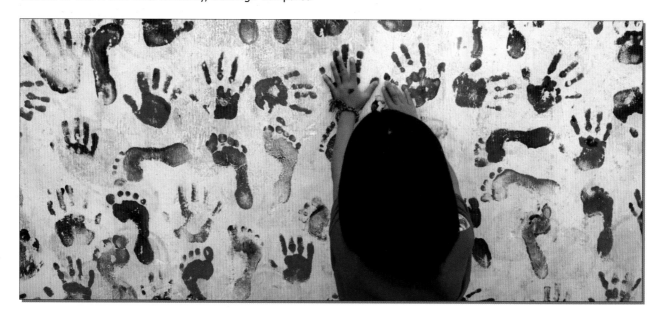

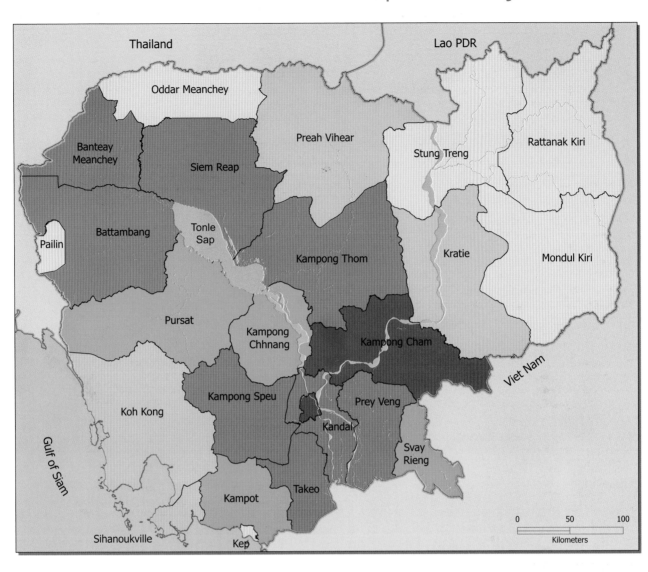

Legend

Population Projection 2020

	54,706 - 223,000
	223,001 - 500,000
	500,001 - 900,000
	900,001 - 1,585,000
	1,585,001 - 2,358,926
	Water Body
——	Provincial Boundary
━━	International Boundary

Data Sources:
Population Projection: NIS 2005
Provincial and International Boundary:
Department of Geography 2005
Water Body: JICA Dataset 2002

Population Projection

Province	2005		2020		% increase in Population
	Male	Female	Male	Female	
Banteay Meanchey	380,559	392,533	571,098	581,054	19.7
Battambang	491,652	506,188	676,369	682,076	15.3
Kampong Cham	900,010	957,490	1,154,726	1,204,200	11.9
Kampong Chhnang	246,499	266,680	368,257	381,534	18.7
Kampong Speu	353,489	376,063	505,454	521,019	16.9
Kampong Thom	329,837	351,855	447,736	463,705	14.4
Kampot	291,225	311,399	372,913	386,249	11.5
Kandal	601,990	640,516	779,921	802,791	12.0
Koh Kong	99,045	92,423	169,655	156,347	26.0
Kratie	166,559	167,202	243,444	239,281	18.2
Mondul Kiri	21,580	20,832	33,581	31,813	21.3
Phnom Penh	630,016	683,835	946,861	1,036,243	20.3
Preah Vihear	76,943	75,435	114,750	108,863	18.9
Prey Veng	493,215	551,161	583,765	639,428	7.9
Pursat	207,048	221,125	284,809	294,856	15.0
Rattanak Kiri	59,774	61,254	93,379	94,022	21.5
Siem Reap	419,362	441,852	605,609	623,823	17.6
Sihanoukville	104,042	104,963	168,171	167,015	23.2
Stung Treng	51,591	52,342	76,822	77,304	19.5
Svay Rieng	255,082	283,098	312,987	338,086	9.5
Takeo	432,811	468,069	548,225	577,124	11.1
Oddar Meanchey	49,952	47,851	74,549	69,693	19.2
Kep	18,820	18,966	30,410	29,592	22.7
Pailin	17,682	15,008	29,435	25,271	25.2

Settlement

Housing

The CIPS 2004 classifies housing into permanent, semi-permanent and temporary structures based on the construction material used for the roof and walls of the dwelling. A house is classified as semi-permanent if either the roof or walls are constructed out of temporary materials such as bamboo, thatch, grass, reeds, earth or any improvised materials. According to this classification it is estimated that 47% of residential and partly residential buildings in Cambodia are considered to be permanent. In 1998 the corresponding figure was 34.2%. Even though approximately 27% of buildings are considered to be temporary structures, the quality of housing seems to be improving in Cambodia. Phnom Penh has 91.4% permanent dwellings. In the coastal region permanent buildings predominated with an estimated 56%. The remaining three regions record a predominance of either semi-permanent or temporary housing with the Plains region recording 50.6%, the Tonle Sap region 58.3% and the Plateau and Mountain region 61% of these types of structures.

While the quality of housing has shown some improvement in recent years, this needs to continue on a greater scale. Policy intervention is required to ensure the step by step replacement of temporary structures with more permanent dwellings to decrease the likelihood of damage from annual flooding and natural disasters (NIS: 2005). In addition, construction regulations should be enforced throughout the country, even in the more remote areas.

The nuclear family, in rural Cambodia, typically lives in a rectangular house that may vary in size from four by six meters to six by ten meters. It is constructed of a wooden frame with gabled thatch roof and walls of woven bamboo. Khmer houses are usually raised on stilts as much as three meters for protection from annual floods. Two ladders or wooden staircases provide access to the house. The steep thatch roof overhanging the house walls protects the interior from rain. Typically a house contains three rooms separated by partitions of woven bamboo. The front room serves as a living room used to receive visitors, the next room is the parent's bedroom, and the third is for unmarried daughters. Sons sleep anywhere they can find space. The CIPS 2004 established that at national level about 98% of households occupied houses ranging from 1 to 3 rooms. Bigger dwellings (4 rooms or more) in urban areas accounted for 6% of urban households in 2004. The houses of poorer persons may contain only a single large room. Food is prepared in a separate kitchen located near the house and usually behind it. Toilet facilities usually consist of simple pits in the ground. Any livestock is kept below the house.

Households

The concepts of the modern household in the GPCC 1998 and CIPS 2004 refers to a group of persons who commonly live together and take meals from a common kitchen unless the exigencies of work prevented any of them from doing so. They may be a household of persons related by blood or a household of unrelated persons or having a mix of both. Examples of unrelated households include boarding houses, hotels, residential hotels, rescue homes, jails and pagodas. These are called institutional households.

The CIPS 2004 calculated a total of 2.4 million households in 2004 compared to 2.2 million households

Housing Type

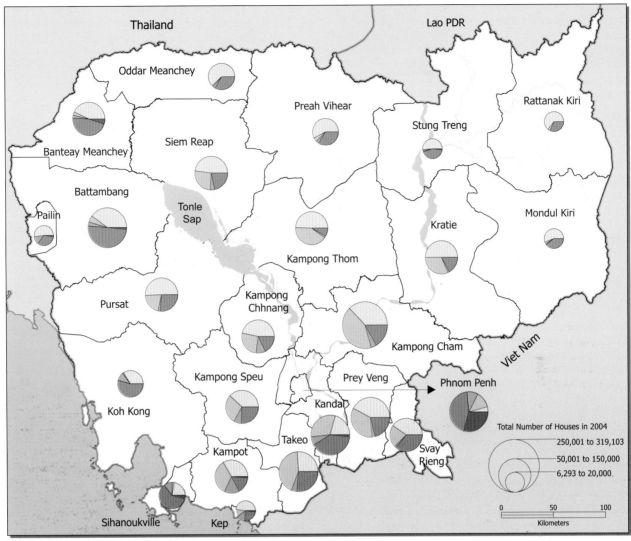

Total Number of Houses in 2004

- 250,001 to 319,103
- 50,001 to 150,000
- 6,293 to 20,000

0   50   100
Kilometers

Household Size

Legend

Household Size
- 3.6 - 4.5
- 4.6 - 5.0
- 5.1 - 5.5
- 5.6 - 6.0
- 6.1 - 8.0
- No Data
- Water Body
- ·—··—· District Boundary
- —— Provincial Boundary
- —— International Boundary

Housing Type
- Thatch Roof
- Tile Roof
- Fibro Roof
- Zinc Roof
- Concrete Roof

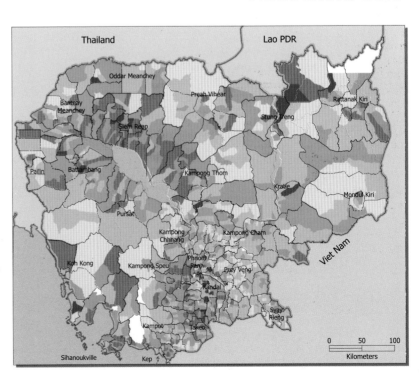

0   50   100
Kilometers

Data Sources:
Housing Type and Household Size:
Commune Database 2004
District, Provincial and International Boundary:
Department of Geography 2005
Water Body: JICA Dataset 2002

recorded in the GPCC 1998. This represents an average annual increase of 2.6% for households during 1998-2004. In 2004, 2.2 million households were located in rural areas with an above average rate of increase. These statistics would seem to support the concerns within the environmental sector that the expansion of new households is contributing to agricultural encroachment of forested areas. While expansion of households is a reasonable occurrence, without clear land resource assessments and land suitability studies, the clearing of forested areas may be unable to support productive agriculture and thus be less likely to contribute to the socio-economic development of the family. Additionally, with a large dependence on forest products for rural livelihoods, the associated forest degradation resulting form new settlements will further diminish food security and the general well being of the population.

Household Size

The average household size of regular households in Cambodia was 5.1 in 2004 with a decline of only 0.1 % from 1998 (5.2). The small difference can be attributed to a declining fertility rate coupled with increasing life expectancy keeping family size relatively stable. Poverty rate increases significantly amongst households larger than 5 persons (WB: 2006). The average real consumption rate declines in these households as they generally exhibit a higher dependency ratio - that is more children and elderly per prime age adult.

The nuclear family, consisting of a husband and a wife and their unmarried children, probably continues to be the most important kin group within Khmer society. The family is the major unit of both production and consumption. Within this unit are the strongest emotional ties, the assurance of aid in the event of trouble, economic cooperation in labour, sharing of produce and income, and contribution as a unit to ceremonial obligations. A larger grouping, the personal kindred that includes a nuclear family with the children, grandchildren, grandparents, uncles, aunts, first cousins, nephews, and nieces, may be included in the household. Ties between related families beyond the kindred are loosely defined at best.

Gender

While gender roles have been undergoing rapid change in Cambodia, gender inequalities still remain high and social attitudes and tradition deem women to be of a lower status than men (UNIFEM: 2004). Significant gender inequalities such as access to education, participation in decision making and access to paid employment have severe social and economic impacts. While there is fairly equal access to primary education, girls experience a greater drop out rate than boys as household duties and cultural expectations add more pressure in puberty. Without equal access to education, employment opportunities outside of the agricultural sector are limited for girls. Additionally, limited access to healthcare places women, and thus society, at a disadvantage. The majority of the population is employed in agriculture and more than 50 % of this workforce is comprised of women. Research also indicates that the division of labour is changing with women taking on broader roles and making greater contributions to household income (UNIFEM: 2004). Despite this, the average rate of pay for men is 33% higher than that for women. Many policies and planning strategies recognize the importance of women to economic development and therefore many tend to be gender sensitive. However, continued action is needed to foster socio-cultural practices that promote and protect the rights of women and girls (UNFPA: 2005).

Household Amenities

In 2004, the main source of drinking water for most Cambodian households were springs and rivers (28.5 %), unprotected dug wells (26.6 %), tube wells (26.3 %), piped water (8.2 %), bought water (6.7 %), and protected dug wells (3.0 %). Approximately 27.7 % of urban households and 59.7 % of rural households used unprotected dug wells and river water. In 2004, approximately 15 % of households had access to electric power and 14 % of households had access to toilet facilities. Only 11 % of the households in Cambodia as a whole had electric power, toilet facility and safe drinking water. In urban areas the number of households with all amenities was much higher at 47 % than in rural areas (5.1 %).

The distribution of household amenities is an important poverty indicator. The availability of clean drinking water and access to adequate toilet facilities also has an impact on the general health of the population. For more detail please refer to Sanitation and Access to Water in chapter 6.

Households with Amenities

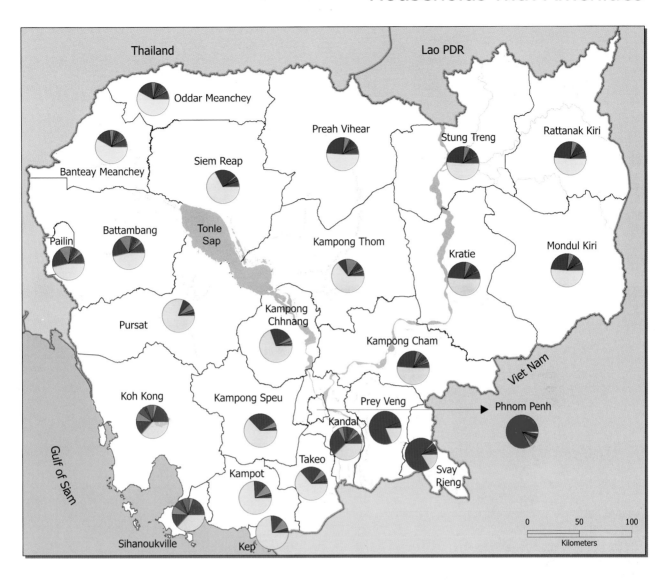

Population and Settlement

Legend

% of Households with Amenities

- ETW: Electricity, Toilet and Safe Drinking Water.
- ET: Electricity and Toilet.
- EW: Electricity and Safe Drinking Water.
- TW: Toilet and Safe Drinking Water.
- E: Electricity.
- T: Toilet.
- W: Safe Drinking Water.
- NA: No Amenities.
- Water Body
- —— Provincial Boundary
- ━━ International Boundary

Data Sources:
Households with Amenities: CIPS 2004
Provincial and International Boundary:
Department of Geography 2005
Water Body: JICA Dataset 2002

Households with Amenities (%)

Province	ETW	ET	EW	TW	E	T	W	NA
Banteay Meanchey	7.7	2.3	5.6	4.2	2.7	4.3	15.2	58
Battambang	9.9	3.3	2.5	4.5	2.2	11.9	19	46.7
Kampong Cham	5.1	2.1	3.1	4.1	3.1	4.2	27	51.3
Kampong Chhnang	2	1.7	1.3	0.8	0.9	3.2	21.9	68.2
Kampong Speu	0.6	0.5	1	2.5	0.7	5	28.1	61.6
Kampong Tho m	4.3	2.8	1.6	4.8	1.6	12.3	7.8	64.8
Kampot	2.2	0.6	0.9	2.5	0.8	8.9	11.8	72.3
Kandal	9.8	3.3	4.3	6.7	3.6	5.3	29.3	37.7
Koh Kong	20	3.5	7.8	3.1	6.6	8.4	13.7	36.9
Kratie	6.8	1.4	1.4	6.6	1.7	5.5	25.4	51.2
Mondul Kiri	6.8	1.4	1.4	6.6	1.7	5.5	25.4	51.2
Phnom Penh	81.5	3.2	6.5	1.5	0.8	0.9	3.9	1.7
Preah Vihear	6.8	1.4	1.4	6.6	1.7	5.5	25.4	51.2
Prey Veng	1.5	0.1	0.5	4.5	0.1	0.8	74.3	18.2
Pursat	2.1	0.9	0.6	1.4	2.4	6.6	7.3	78.7
Rattanak Kiri	6.8	1.4	1.4	6.6	1.7	5.5	25.4	51.2
Siem R eap	5.6	0.9	2.2	1.6	0.9	1.8	21.3	65.7
Sihanoukville	20	3.5	7.8	3.1	6.6	8.4	13.7	36.9
Stung Treng	6.8	1.4	1.4	6.6	1.7	5.5	25.4	51.2
Svay Rieng	4.7	0.1	1.5	5.1	0.2	1.4	70.9	16.1
Takeo	1.8	0.4	0.4	7.2	0.6	5.5	21.3	62.8
Oddar Meanchey	7.7	2.3	5.6	4.2	2.7	4.3	15.2	58
Kep	2.2	0.6	0.9	2.5	0.8	8.9	11.8	72.3
Pailin	9.9	3.3	2.5	4.5	2.2	11.9	19	46.7

Transport Infrastructure and Market Locations

An effective transport network helps to generate economic growth, contributes to poverty alleviation and enables regional co-operation. The improvement of rural livelihoods, in particular, are hampered by inadequate infrastructure limiting access to markets and the opportunity to increase cash flow through the supply and demand of goods. According to a study conducted by the World Bank, agro-climatic conditions and remoteness are highly correlated. Analyses of farm level productivity indicate the importance of rural infrastructure including roads and access to markets. Farms with access to markets in their villages have a 26% higher crop yield than those without (WB: 2006). The poor state of the Cambodian rural road network resulting from decades of internal conflict also limits access to social services such as health and education and economic services such as agricultural extension, and technical support. Sea port, air and cross border road linkages also open up important international markets providing the potential to further generate economic growth. Additionally, poor road infrastructure has left many provincial centers and numerous natural and cultural sites with tourism potential inaccessible to the outside world (ADB: 2005).

In 2002-2003, external assistance for the rehabilitation of 1,400 km of road network was secured (CDC: 2002). The RGC's first priority is to improve the main roads that connect Phnom Penh with the provincial centers. The second priority is to rehabilitate the roads linking adjacent provinces and connecting small communities with larger regional towns. This will improve the linkages between the three broad economic zones identified by the transport planning process (CDC: 2002). These are the tourism zone formed by the triangle of Siem Reap, Prey Vihear and Kompong Thom, the industrial zone in

the coastal region and the industrial/eco-tourism zone covering Rattanak Kirri and Mondul Kiri. A major limitation to improving the rural road network is the large number of river crossings. Many bridges have a capacity of less than 20 tons and collapses are not uncommon. The tropical climate also inhibits reconstruction with a large majority of unpaved roads washed away during the wet season.

Rehabilitation of the road network enhances important urban - rural linkages thus contributing to development. Although not enough is known about these links, it is increasingly recognized that urban and rural development is interdependent and with proper planning can be mutually supportive (Dwyer: 2003). For example, an improved road network provides the rural population with access to markets, services and capital that are mostly found in urban areas.

With careful planning, urban centers can be developed within a sub-regional network providing the rural economy and population with national, sub-regional and global markets. Thus the growth and welfare of an urban center has a direct impact on its rural hinterland. A sub-regional economic corridor providing trade and production links enhances rural development and examples of this can be seen in the development of regional centers such as Sisophon and Battambang.

Inland waterways also provide essential transport routes. This has traditionally been the principle means of travel for Cambodians and as more than a third of the population live more than 10 km from a year round road, there is still a large dependence on the waterways (MRC: 2003). The advantages of river transport are numerous

Transport Infrastructure and Market Locations

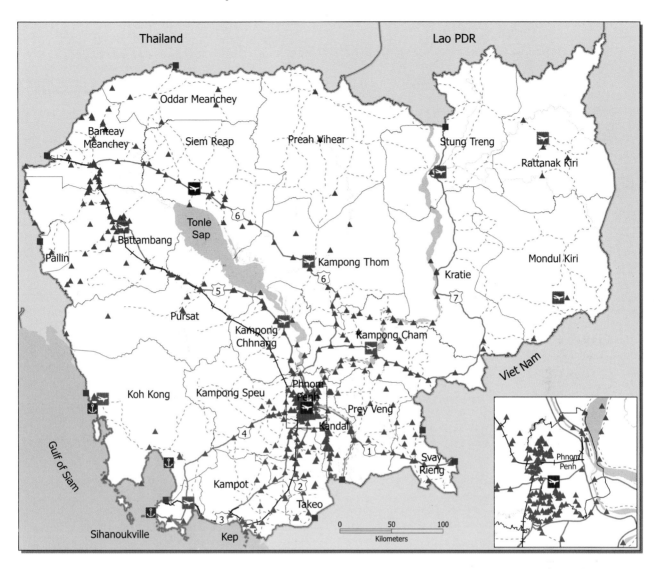

Legend

▲ Market Location

■ International Border Check Point

✈ International Airport

✈ Domestic Airport
(irregular or no service)

⚓ Harbour

-⬡6⬡- Main Roads

- - - - Secondary Roads

+—+ Railways

　　 Water Body

—— Provincial Boundary

—— International Boundary

Data Sources:
Market Locations: Commune Database 2004
Road, Railways, Airports and Habour: JICA Dataset 2002
International Border Check Point: Annual Report of
Tourism Statistics 2004
International and Provincial Boundary:
Department of Geography 2005
Water Body: JICA Dataset 2002

including providing lower travel costs to local communities. Also, the cost of building and maintaining river facilities are less than those of road and rail networks. Additionally, with careful environmental impact assessments, river transport can be more environmentally friendly with less intrusive infrastructure, a better fuel economy and less air pollution. Although the communities that benefit the most from river transport are those that have the most limited access to year round roads, boats still provide the cheapest mode of transport and thus those communities with better access to roads are still likely to depend on river transport.

Not only is this form of transport important to people living near rivers and streams, it also provides a valuable international trade route. In 2001, international trade on the Mekong River for the entire lower Mekong basin was estimated at US $4,700 million with trade into and out of Cambodia estimated at US $235 million (MRC: 2003). The seasonal variation in water depth limits the navigation of large vessels to approximately eight months of the year. The RGC's priorities for ports and inland waterways include the rehabilitation of dredgers, the rehabilitation and expansion of the deep sea port at Sihanoukville and the rehabilitation of the inland river port at Phnom Penh as well as smaller domestic river ports (CDC: 2002).

At present there are only two lines of rail running between Phnom Penh and Battambang, and between Phnom Penh and Sihanoukville via Kampot. The train service experienced severe damage during Cambodia's years of conflict and is in very poor condition. The southern line between Phnom Penh and the port of Sihanoukville needs extensive rehabilitation in order to reduce excessive operating costs to enable it to effectively compete with road transport (CDC: 2002). The viability of revitalizing the rail network needs careful consideration and at present it appears that more priority is being given to improvements in road infrastructure.

The tourism sector has grown rapidly in recent years and the development of civil aviation services are an important factor in stimulating continued growth. Tourism is a main impetus for Cambodia's economic growth. Since Cambodia re-opened its borders in 1993, tourism has grown rapidly. By 2004, the number of visitor arrivals reached more than one million and grew 50 % compared to those in 2003. The increase in arrivals is attributed to the renewed openness of the country and the maintenance of political stability since the national elections in 1998. Continued increases in tourist arrivals helped to stimulate a moderate increase in service sub-sectors such as hotels, restaurants, transport, and communications. There are now two international airports one located in Phnom Penh and one in Siem Reap. The third largest airport is being planned for Sihanoukville in order to boost beach-based tourism. Elsewhere, airports are present in nine other provinces but are undeveloped or damaged. Few of them are running, if functioning at all.

There are many obvious benefits to improved transport infrastructure. With agriculture and rural development a key priority for poverty alleviation, improved transport infrastructure allowing easier access to markets and services will have a positive impact on rural livelihoods and quality of life. The rehabilitation of transport infrastructure may also provide employment for many people. This offers tremendous potential for effective poverty-reducing income generation through public works programmes. However, consideration also needs to be given to the social affects of road building, especially in forested and highlander areas where roads may speed up land grabbing and the destruction of natural resources.

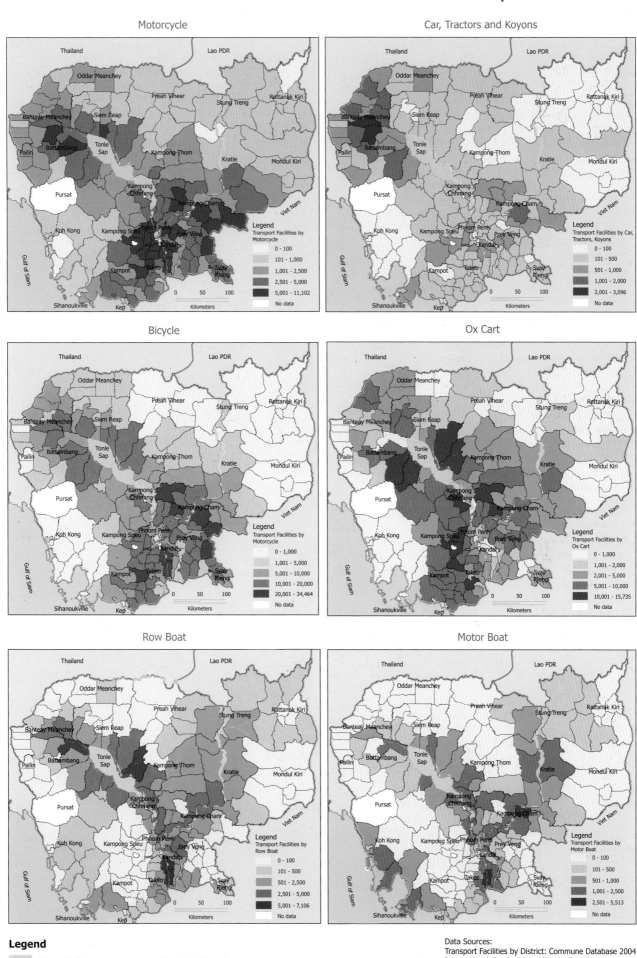

Motorcycle

Car, Tractors and Koyons

Bicycle

Ox Cart

Row Boat

Motor Boat

Population and Settlement

Legend

Water Body

District Boundary

Provincial Boundary

International Boundary

Data Sources:
Transport Facilities by District: Commune Database 2004
International, Provincial and District Boundary:
Department of Geography 2005
Water Body: JICA Dataset 2002

References

ADB. 2005. Technical Assistance Kingdom of Cambodia: Preparing the transport Infrastructure Development and Maintenance Project. Asia Development Bank. Phnom Penh, Cambodia

CDC, CRDB. 2002. Socio-economic Development Priorities and the Official Development Assistance Needs. Cambodia Development Council and Cambodia Rehabilitation and Development Board

CDHS. 2000. Cambodia Demographic and Health Survey, 2000. National Institute of Statistics, Ministry of Planning

CIPS. 2004. Cambodia Inter-Censal Population Survey 2004, General Report. National Institute of Statistics, Ministry of Planning

Dwyer, G. 2003. Rural-Urban Sub-regional Linkages Offer New Opportunities for Mekong Region. Accessed at: www.adb.org/media/Articles/2003

Knodel, J., Kim, S., Zimmer, Z., Puch, S. 2005. Older Persons in Cambodia: A Profile from the 2004 Survey of the Elderly in Cambodia. Royal University of Phnom Penh and UNFPA. Phnom Penh, Cambodia

MRC. 2003. State of the Basin Report: 2003. Mekong River Commission, Phnom Penh. ISSN: 1728:3248

Neupert, Dr R. 2005. New Demographic Estimates and updated Projections for Cambodia. National Institute of Statistics and Ministry of Planning.

NIS. 2002. General Population Census of Cambodia 1998, Final Census Results 2nd Edition. National Institute of Statistics, Ministry of Planning

NIS. 2005. Cambodia Inter-Censal Population Survey 2004, Analysis of CIPS Results Report 4, Housing and Household Amenities. National Institute of Statistics, Ministry of Planning

NIS. 2005. Statistical Yearbook 2005. National Institute of Statistics, Ministry of Planning. Phnom Penh Cambodia.

UNFPA. 2005. Cambodia at a Glance: Population, Gender and Reproductive Health

UNIFEM, WB, ADB, UNDP and DFID/UK. 2004. A Fair Share for Women: Cambodia Gender Assessment. UNIFEM, WB, ADB, UNDP and DFID/UK. Phnom Penh, Cambodia. ISBN: 1-93287-00-5

World Bank. 2006. Cambodia Halving Poverty by 2015? Poverty Assessment Report

Natural Resources

Forest Resources

Cambodia's forests play two major roles. They provide important ecological functions such as ecosystem preservation, biodiversity conservation and the protection of soil and water resources (CDRI: 2006a). They also play a significant role in contributing to the socio-economic development of the country. Over 84% of Cambodians live in rural areas with a large proportion of this population dependent on forest resources for both consumption and income generation. Timber products are used as the main source of fuel and for construction materials with NTFPs such as resin, rattan, edible fruits and vegetables, bush meat and medicinal plants also contributing to diverse livelihood strategies. The urban population also benefits from forest resources and related employment possibilities, most notably associated with the processing of timber products (IFSR: 2004). Cambodia's forests face many pressures including small and large scale logging, the encroachment of agriculture and an increasing population, all of which have contributed to varying degrees of forest degradation. Recent trends show that there is a change in interest from forest products to forest land, shifting the focus from forest degradation to deforestation (Turton: 2004).

During the 1990s, the main form of forest management was the establishment of large scale commercial logging concessions. The RGC has acknowledged the failure of this system and is currently exploring alternative management techniques. These need to take into account the economic importance of forests to local livelihoods. Many commentators have identified the dangers of a management vacuum before changes in forest management approach become more established. Cancelled forest concessions fall into this grey zone with no clear definition of management (Miller: 2004).

A variety of maps and datasets have been produced showing vegetation types and the extent of forest cover in Cambodia however there are discrepancies in the forest cover percentages between these. The wide variety of forest cover figures can be attributed to factors such as incomparable data generation methods, lack of background knowledge on the analyst's part and lack of funds or time (MRC: 2003). For more detailed information, please refer to *Forest Trends*.

The selection of Forest Resource maps in the atlas intends to give an overview of the forestry sector in Cambodia including information on vegetation types, trends, non timber forest products and management approaches. Explanations of the methodology used and limitations in regards to data collection are given in the appropriate sections throughout the chapter.

Terrestrial Vegetation and Landuse Patterns

The Ministry of Environment's Biodiversity and Protected Areas Management Project has produced the Terrestrial Vegetation map as part of the National Protected Areas Gap Analysis Project. This map is based on the recent, national-level digital land cover map produced by the Japanese International Cooperation Agency (JICA) in association with the Department of Geography (Ministry of Land Management, Urban Planning and Construction) and the Ministry of Public Works and Transport. This map was produced through manual interpretation of LandSat and SPOT satellite imagery and conventional aerial photos acquired between 1997 and 2002.

In several cases, landcover categories used in the JICA map were adapted and/or augmented with data from additional sources, such as photos from targeted aerial

Terrestrial Vegetation and Landuse Patterns

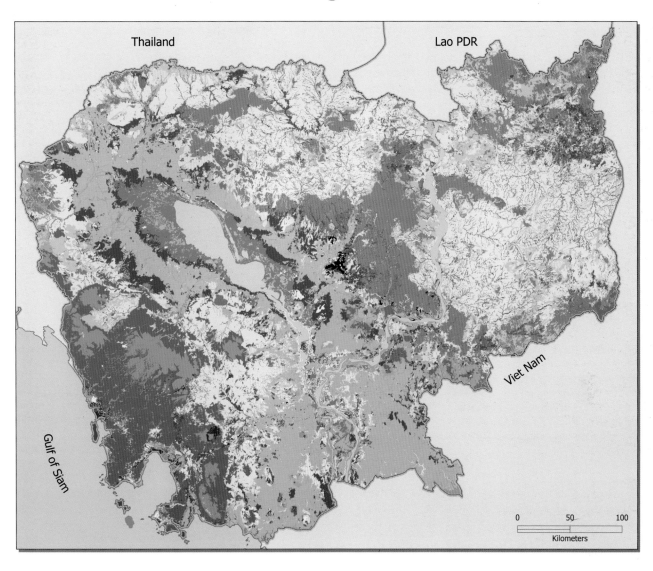

Thailand

Lao PDR

Viet Nam

Gulf of Siam

0   50   100
Kilometers

Legend

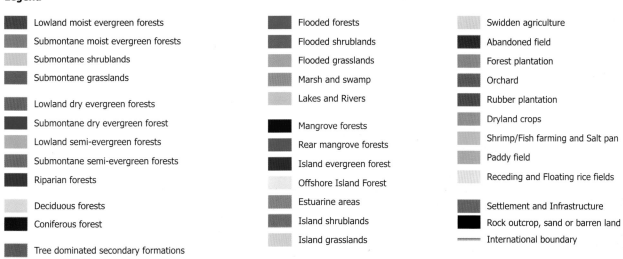

Lowland moist evergreen forests

Submontane moist evergreen forests

Submontane shrublands

Submontane grasslands

Lowland dry evergreen forests

Submontane dry evergreen forest

Lowland semi-evergreen forests

Submontane semi-evergreen forests

Riparian forests

Deciduous forests

Coniferous forest

Tree dominated secondary formations

Bamboo dominated secondary formations

Lowland shrublands

Lowland grasslands

Flooded forests

Flooded shrublands

Flooded grasslands

Marsh and swamp

Lakes and Rivers

Mangrove forests

Rear mangrove forests

Island evergreen forest

Offshore Island Forest

Estuarine areas

Island shrublands

Island grasslands

Swidden agriculture

Abandoned field

Forest plantation

Orchard

Rubber plantation

Dryland crops

Shrimp/Fish farming and Salt pan

Paddy field

Receding and Floating rice fields

Settlement and Infrastructure

Rock outcrop, sand or barren land

International boundary

Data Sources:
Terrestrial Vegetation
and Landuse Patterns: BPAMP, MoE
International Boundary:
Department of Geography 2005
Water Body: JICA Dataset 2002

surveys carried out in 2004 and 2005, to increase the resolution and, in some cases, the accuracy. Specific modifications included using information on climate patterns to separate the moist areas of Southwest Cambodia from the drier, more seasonal Northern and Eastern regions, and using elevation to separate vegetation types to capture documented patterns of distinctiveness in submontane and lowland areas.

Main Pressures on Forest Resources

Logging

In the early 1990s, in order to attract foreign private-sector investment, commercial logging concessions were introduced. The first concession was awarded in 1994 and between 1994 and 1998 logging concessions were granted to thirty six companies covering approximately 7 million ha (CDRI: 2006b). The process of the delineation of the concessions and negotiation of their terms was done without any reliable resource assessment, even though the commercial viability of the concessions depended on the nature and extent of the standing timber (Fraser: 2000). A lack of transparency in forest concession allocation and the negotiation process, limited management plan preparation, an inadequate legal framework and limited capacity of government institutions to control the concession system resulted in over-exploitation and over-processing of forest products in the forest concessions. Furthermore, the traditional user rights of local communities in accessing forest resources for NTFPs and non-extractive forest values were violated by the concessions (McKenny et al: 2002).

In 2000, in an attempt to improve sustainable forest concession management, the government signed a Development Credit Agreement with the International Development Association of the World Bank to support a Forest Concession and Control Pilot Project. The project provided assistance to the Forestry Administration in its efforts to strengthen its institutional capacity to manage, monitor and regulate forest concession operations. A significant component of the project was to implement forest concession reforms requiring forest concessionaires to prepare Strategic Forest Management Plans (SFMPs) consistent with international standards.

With the forestry sector reform on January 1, 2002, the RGC imposed a moratorium on logging activities in forest concessions until adequate SFMPs were developed. In 2006, the moratorium is still in place. With the failure to produce effective management plans many forest concessions have been cancelled. Other concessions, due to unsustainable harvesting, are no longer economically viable for the concessionaires. In 2003 nine concessions were requested to submit SFMPs to the independent reviewer Forest Resource Management (FRM). At this time FRM recommended that 6 concessions could continue if their SFMPs were further improved and three concessions had operations suspended for 15 to 20 years. In 2005, further independent review of FRM's findings recommend continuation of only 2 to 3 concessions with revised SFMPs.

The associated improved infrastructure that results from commercial logging has meant that the more isolated primary forests of Cambodia are becoming accessible. Recent trends show that these areas are becoming more likely to be settled allowing for greater pressure on forest products and the encroachment of agriculture. For more detail please refer to *Forest Disturbance*.

Fuelwood Collection

The Cambodian Inter-censal population survey calculates that 84% of people rely on fuel wood and 5.5% rely on charcoal, for cooking (NIS: 2005). This roughly translates as 6, 968, 000 m³ of mainly dead fuel wood collected annually (IFSR: 2004). While the supply of fuel wood satisfies the national demand, the existence of fuel wood deficient areas has led to the development of active fuel wood and charcoal markets. Charcoal production is particularly damaging as it relies on the collection of green wood. In provinces such as Kampong Speu, charcoal constitutes the main income earning livelihood strategy with producers claiming it is more profitable than agriculture (Turton: 2004). While evidence indicates that fuel wood and charcoal production enhance the economic situation of producers, the effect of small scale wood collection on forest degradation should not be underestimated.

Agricultural Encroachment

Increasingly, attention is being given to the establishment of large scale agricultural concessions throughout Cambodia. The main objective of these is to raise revenue for the state with the rationale that large scale agribusinesses have the ability to increase inputs and thus improve productivity. Reliable information on the exact number of agricultural concessions remains sketchy, although the Ministry of Agriculture, Forestry and Fisheries have recently published data listing 37 operational economic concessions covering 791, 170 ha and a further 5 concessions with contracts pending covering an additional 46, 754 ha (www.maff.gov.kh 2006). Agri-business may hold some benefits, however, the failures of the logging concessions need to be acknowledged in the implementation of these areas. The transparent allocation of sites should only gain approval after management plans, land suitability and resource assessments are analysed. Additionally, agri-businesses need to enhance local economic growth by providing employment, technical education for capacity building and encouraging community participation. Please refer to Economic Land Concessions map page 93.

Population Growth

Cambodia has a fairly high population growth rate of 1.7%, with a projected population of 19 million in 2020 (NIS: 2005). Although the population growth rate has declined in recent years, it will continue to be high in rural areas due to higher fertility rates. As demographic pressures increase, agricultural encroachment accelerates as people search for new land. This may be a result of new household formation, in migration or the expansion of land due to poor agricultural productivity. If newly cleared land does not support productive agriculture due to poor soil fertility, there is a danger of ongoing deforestation, forest degradation and poverty as people continually look for more arable land and further rely on natural resources to ensure against low agricultural yields (Dümmer: 2004).

Impacts of Forest Change

The ongoing forest changes occurring throughout Cambodia have severe implications to the sustainability of natural resources. Deforestation and forest degradation in watershed areas and the clearing of flooded forests for paddy farming have contributed to a decrease in the natural size of floodplain habitats. This

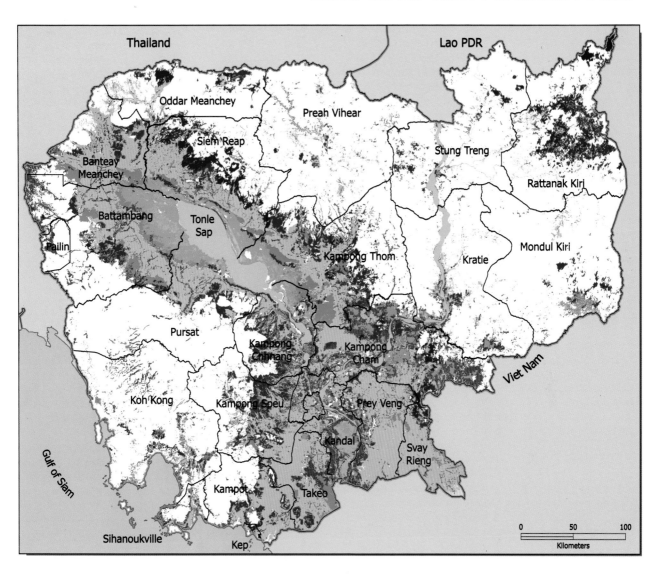

Legend

Land Cover	Ha
Total LCNFA	7,168,424

	Land Cover	Ha
	Paddy field	3,163,000
	Field crop	372,600
	Swidden agriculture	349,700
	Village garden crop	198,300
	Receding and Floating rice fields	194,000
	Rubber plantation	88,300
	Infrastructure	18,100
	Orchard	8,800
	Bamboo	32,224
	Abandoned field covered by grass	861,600

	Land Cover	Ha
	Abandoned field covered by shrub	1,094,000
	Flooded grassland	173,500
	Flooded shrub	533,200
	Marsh and swamp	44,600
	Sand bank	7,500
	Barren land	27,200
	Rock outcrop	1,800
	Water Body	
	Provincial Boundary	
	International Boundary	

Data Sources:
Land cover: JICA Dataset 2002
International and Provincial Boundary:
Department of Geography 2005
Water Body: JICA Dataset 2002

has a direct negative impact on aquatic and terrestrial habitats including species diversity, migration and spawning / nursery areas. It also has an impact on the quality and quantity of water in downstream areas. It is estimated that 12-15% of the Mekong River flow was reduced during the 1980s with approximately 240,000 ha of the regulatory flooded land around the Tonle Sap Lake no longer submerged during the wet season (NIS: 2003). Although accurate and substantial data and information are lacking, the observations made by fish researchers clearly indicate a change in fish species composition favouring small low value fish species, and the disappearance of migratory large fish species.

Forests provide a buffer to filter water and hold soil in place. In watershed areas, when forests are destroyed, natural disasters such as peak floods and soil erosion increase during the wet season, and minimum flows decrease during the dry season. This decreases agricultural productivity and further reduces the amount of arable land, resulting in fewer land use options and shorter economic life for investments in the agricultural sector. Productivity losses in turn increase pressure on the remaining natural forest areas

The National Committee on Disasters Management (NCDM) stated that in 2001, 995 communes in 24 provinces were flooded, affecting 945,665 people with a mortality of 62 (NCDM: 2004). 150,118 ha of rice fields were damaged. It is reported that 175 bridges and many other areas of infrastructure were also flooded and damaged. The total loss due to flood and drought in 2001 was USD 36 million, in 2002 USD 34 million and in 2004 USD 93.3 million (NCDM: 2004). In addition, ARD (1998) warned that severe overexploitation of natural resources was causing declining standards of living in rural communities and forcing people to relocate to other areas. This can lead to a breakdown of cultural and traditional diversity, leading to social friction.

Deforestation has already caused severe shortages of fuel wood for households. Fuel wood in some communities can only be obtained 20km from the household, mainly in high population density areas such as the region surrounding the Tonle Sap Lake. This results in higher labour costs for limited return. As mentioned above, the alteration of aquatic habitats has a direct effect on fisheries production on which a large proportion of the population rely for protein needs and income generation (refer to *Fisheries* for greater detail). Factors related to rural poverty that increase deforestation and degradation include chronic fuel wood shortages, poor standards of nutrition and health and high underemployment and unemployment. O'Brien (1999), warned that because the life of Cambodians traditionally depend on rice production and fish harvesting for food and on wood energy for fuel, deforestation is causing negative impacts not only on the environment but also on the agricultural sector and public finances.

Protecting the Forest Environment

With the forestry sector reform in 2002, the Forestry Law was established as the legal instrument governing the forestry sector. The forest law identifies three types of forest areas; protection areas, production areas and conversion areas (Miller: 2004). To effectively implement the forestry law, the governmental forestry agency was restructured into the Forestry Administration, delegating more functions and resources to local offices with the intention of enabling effective law enforcement and management of concession systems. With the acknowledged failures of the concession system, including over-exploitation of forest resources and little contribution to rural development, new management approaches need to be identified. Many commentators suggest more locally based forest management models to help protect local user rights and promote rural poverty alleviation (CDRI: 2006b).

It can be argued that community led forestry has been an unofficial tool of forestry management in Cambodia for centuries as those dependent on forest resources for their livelihood have sustainably managed the forests in the past. However, as an official tool of forest management, CF has only been recognized in the last decade and has largely been driven by support from NGOs. For more information please refer to *Community Forestry*.

More recently, attention is being given to partnership forestry which is based on a partnership between state and communes in terms of developing commune forest plans. The principle behind this is that communes would have an incentive to protect forest resources and put pressure on the state to prevent illegal logging (CDRI: 2006b). Community forestry would then become a part of the overall commune forest plans. While there are currently no legal provisions for this type of management technique it certainly fits with the RGC's ongoing focus on decentralization. It should be noted that the implementation of any new system is not without complications and as such needs to be closely monitored.

Effective forest management will help to improve food security, preserve customs and traditions and ensure the sustainability of agriculture, forestry and fisheries, thus helping to bring about a reduction in poverty. To further develop the forestry sector, reliable national and local forestry development plans need to be agreed upon and effective management mechanisms for implementing and monitoring the plans need to be developed. Additionally, local peoples land rights need to be secured through land titling. This will enable the clear demarcation of forest estates so that future conflicts over rights of forest management can be avoided (CDRI: 2006 b). Forest management constraints including capacity building, motivation and lack of incentives need to be solved. Finally, the national and local judicial systems need to be improved to enforce forestry laws.

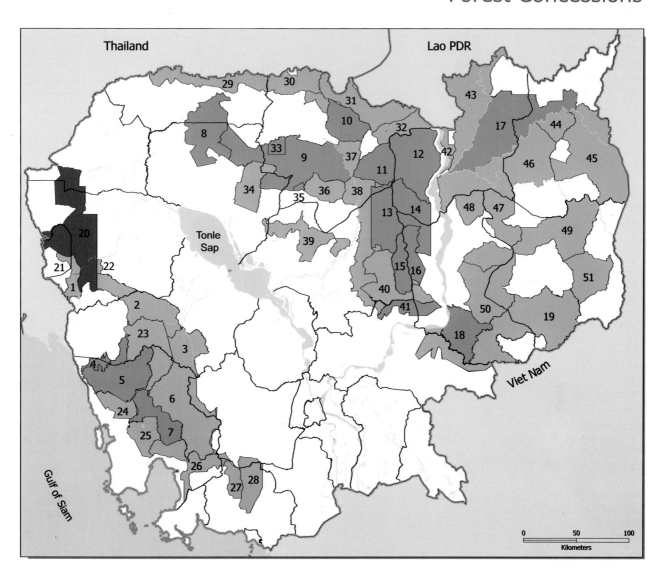

Legend

■ Bamboo concession

■ Timber concession

■ Terminated timber concession

■ Water Body

— Provincial Boundary

— International Boundary

Note: Current timber concessions status undetermined.

Data Sources:
Forest Concession: IFSR 2004
International and Provincial Boundary:
Department of Geography 2005
Water Body: JICA Dataset 2002

Forest Concessions

	Concession		Concession
1	You Rysaco West	27	Cambodia Timber Product
2	You Rysaco East	28	Long Day
3	Super Wood	29	Geometric
4	TPP Koah Kong	30	BLP
5	Silverroad Pursat	31	Chung Shing North
6	Samling Koah Kong	32	Lan Song Preah Vihear
7	Silverroad Koah Kong	33	TPP Koah Keh
8	Samrong Wood	34	Mekong
9	TPP Siem Reap	35	TPP Preah Khan Temple
10	Cherndar Plywood	36	Lan Song
11	Timas Preah Vihear	37	Super Land
12	Pheapimex Stung Treng	38	Mieng Lyheng
13	Colexim	39	Lan Song Preah Vihear
14	Everbright	40	GAT Kampong Thom/Kratie
15	Pheapimex Kampong Thom	41	Timas
16	Pheapimex Kratie	42	Pacific Craft
17	Pheapimex Rattanakiri	43	Changling Lumber
18	Casotim	44	Hero Taiwan
19	Samling	45	Thai Boonroong
20	Pheapimex Bamboo	46	North Easten Forest
21	P.T. Maharani	47	King Wood
22	P.T. Maharani	48	King Wood 2
23	GAT	49	Thai Boonroong
24	GAT Koah Kong	50	Chung Shing South
25	Wood Tree Peanich	51	Thai Boonroong Mondolkiri
26	Talam		

Source: IFSR 2004

Forest Trends

Estimates from the 1976 Mekong Secretariat forest cover map, which is based on Landsat images, show that approximately 75% of Cambodia was covered by forests at that time (including wood and shrubland). The MRC 1997 map shows that 58.6% forest cover remained at that time and the Forestry Administration calculated 61% of forest cover in 2002. There is debate over the accuracy of these figures, complicated by the variety of ways in which forest cover has been assessed over the years. The fact remains that Cambodia still has some of the most substantial relative forest cover in the region, although the rate of forest change is clearly increasing. Between 1997 and 2002 gross forest cover decreased by approximately 5% or 1% per annum (IFSR: 2004). Between 2002 and 2005, forest cover declined at a rate of 2% (CDRI: 2006c). Perhaps more importantly, the shrinking forest area has been accompanied by a reduction in forest quality characterized by a significant fall in commercial stems per unit area.

There are three official national datasets calculating forest cover for 1993, 1997 and 2002. Comparisons of this data make it difficult to determine the true extent of deforestation and degradation as the categorization system of vegetation types changed between 97 and 2002 with the 2002 data using fewer categories. Additionally, the status of the 'wood and shrubland' category is inconsistent, with the data from 93 and 97 categorizing this as non-forest whereas it's included as 'other forest' in the 2002 data. There are also different definitions of what constitutes a forest in relation to crown cover (20% compared to 10%) and the lack of aerial photographs further complicates interpretations. Thus, the acknowledged inaccuracies and limitations of these datasets make it difficult to accurately assess trends in forest cover. However, a variety of studies in the forestry sector indicate that trends in forest changes accelerated during the period from 97 to 2002 and further increased between 2002 and 2005.

The objective of the selection of forest cover maps presented in the atlas is to provide a guide to forest trends over the last 40 years with the inclusion of the Mekong Secretariat map enabling the trends to be tracked over a longer time period. With consideration given to the limitations of the data already mentioned, the maps provide a useful estimation of forest changes with the major areas of deforestation clearly evident. The national average rate of deforestation does not reflect the extent of forest loss in localized areas, particularly for those provinces rich in forest resources. For example,

Deforestation:

'The conversion of forest to another landuse or the long term reduction of the tree canopy cover below the minimum 10% threshold.'

Forest Degradation:

'Changes within the forest which negatively affect the structure or function of the stand or site, and thereby lower the capacity to supply products and/or services.'

Source : CDRI Policy Briefs 2006c.

provincial level data in Rattanak kiri province established that between 1996 and 2002, the area of evergreen forest declined by 138, 000 ha or more than 10% of the provinces total forest cover (CDRI: 2006c). Thus there is a high concentration of deforestation and degradation occurring in the high value primary evergreen forests.

According to the Independent Forest Sector Review (2004), forest loss from 1991 to 1997 was primarily concentrated on the boundary between agriculture, particularly in the lowland areas, and the major forest blocks. Loss of flooded forest was also evident. In contrast, recent trends indicate that the establishment of new roads has enabled easier access to more isolated locations and primary forests. Forest losses since 1997 have been concentrated in the following key areas (IFSR: 2004):

- Deciduous and semi-evergreen areas of the far Northwestern region
- Semi-evergreen and evergreen forests of the basaltic soils in Rattanak kiri
- Evergreen forests along the newly repaired roads in the coastal hinterland
- Evergreen forests associated with areas of good soil along National Route #4
- Deciduous forests across Northern and Northeastern Cambodia, though some of this apparent change probably reflects improvements in the mapping of natural grasslands
- Flooded forests associated with the Tonle Sap Lake, though some of these apparent changes may also partially reflect improvements in the mapping of natural grassland

The main factors contributing to deforestation and forest degradation in Cambodia include commercial logging, illegal logging (both large and small scale), large scale agricultural concessions, fuel wood collection, shifting cultivation and the settlement of new villages. Secondary measures include forest fires and infrastructure development (MRC: 2003).

Forest Disturbance

While the debate continues over the extent of forest cover in Cambodia, there is no definitive statement on the condition of the forests (IFSR: 2004). Identifying the quality of Cambodia's forests helps to determine their future use and value in relation to the sustainability of the remaining natural resources including land, fisheries and agriculture. The well documented importance of the forests for livelihoods in Cambodia should not be underestimated and includes the dependence on firewood and charcoal and NTFPs such as bush meat, resin and medicinal plants. Analysis of the socio-economic importance of such resources makes it clear that a reduction in forest quality is detrimental to the RGC's goal of rural poverty alleviation and improved food security.

Given the strong evidence from various sources that roads, logging tracks and villages have a direct link to forest exploitation, the Independent Forest Sector Review (2004), developed a Forest Disturbance model with the objective of determining the level of degradation of Cambodia's forests. The model is based on the assumption that all forest areas within 5km of villages and/or 1.5km of mapped roads and tracks are subject to

Forest Cover 1976

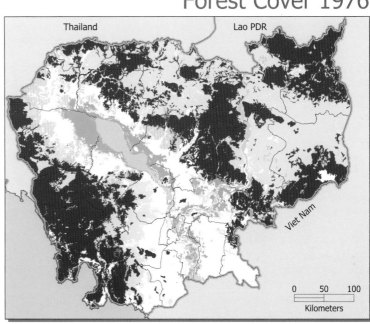

Legend	Ha
Evergreen forest	6,887,491
Deciduous forest	4,814,512
Coniferous forest	7,410
Inundated	939,242
Mangrove forest	95,776
Orchards and Plantation	93,746
Woodland and shrub	1,021,956
Total Forest	**13,860,133**
Total Non Forest	**4,287,775**
—— Provincial Boundary	
—— International Boundary	
Water Body	

Forest Cover 1997

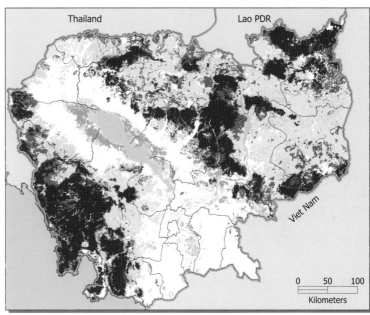

Legend	Ha
Evergreen (dense, disturbed and mosaic)	3,990,535
Mixed (dense, disturbed and mosaic)	1,505,520
Deciduous (including mosaic)	4,281,861
Inundated	335,307
Mangrove	72,968
Forest regrowth	374,716
Forest Plantation	82,472
Total Forest	**10,643,379**
Woodland and shrub	2,059,470
Other non forest	**5,455,386**
Total Non Forest	**7,514,856**

Forest Cover 2002

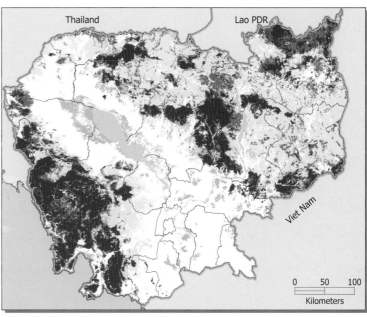

Legend	Ha
Evergreen forest	3,720,506
Semi-Evergreen	1,455,190
Deciduous forest	4,833,861
Other forest	1,094,727
Total Forest	**11,104,284**
Total Non Forest	**7,056,388**

Note:
To account for the overestimation of deciduous forest and underestimation of non forest, a 15% adjustment must be applied to total forest area to obtain a final figure of 10,379,000 ha of forest.

Note: Original categorization of data includes Wood/Shrubland as non forest in 1997 and as other forest in 2002.

Data Sources:
Forest Cover 1976: Mekong Secretariat
Forest Cover 1997: MRC
Forest Cover 2002: FA
International and Provincial Boundary :
Department of Geography 2005
Water Body: JICA Dataset 2002

degradation. As many roads and tracks have not been mapped, the results of the model may be considered a conservative estimate.

The Forest Disturbance model indicates that approximately 55 % of the forest area, (34 % of total land area) has some, to heavy, degradation. It is estimated that 45% of forests within protected areas are disturbed and 50% of forests within concessions are disturbed, some heavily. The extent of 'less disturbed' forest is in the order of 25 - 30% (IFSR: 2004).

While previous trends indicated that most forest disturbance was primarily located on the periphery of agricultural areas, pressures on the less disturbed forests have continued to increase. This is mainly due to population growth (a projected 19 million in 2020 NIS: 2005) and the establishment of new roads. Post 1997 many new villages have been established within or very close to forests. Two factors appear to influence the establishment of these new villages - the lack of clear land tenure of both private and state owned land and the proximity to roads and markets.

Of concern is that many villages are being established in areas of low soil fertility and where a low annual rainfall and/or an extended dry season mean that prospects for agricultural productivity are uncertain. In such areas the land becomes degraded relatively quickly enforcing the people to move on in order to improve their living conditions and ensure food security. This results in a cycle of deforestation and degradation.

Approximately 33 % of the population lives within a distance of 5 km of a forest - semi evergreen, evergreen, deciduous or other forests (Dümmer: 2004). Most of these forests are already slightly to heavily degraded but offer opportunities for management options such as rehabilitation, Community Forestry and joint forest management. The Independent Forest Sector Review (2004) argues that a large proportion of land remains outside the legally recognized areas of concessions, protected areas and community forestry management with no clear legal claim or formal management and is thus susceptible to uncontrolled land use.

In order to arrest the increasing trends of deforestation and forest degradation throughout Cambodia, land resource assessments must continue and be made accessible to local communities. Land resource assessments based on land suitability provide a useful tool for land users/planners to determine the best land management techniques including identifying areas suited to different uses. This requires matching the conditionality of the land (climate, soil, vegetation etc,) with the requirements of the purpose. The options considered can be limited by cultural and socio economic factors, or extended by incentives such as irrigation and drainage possibilities (Dümmer: 2004).

By identifying the limitations and options in a particular area the land user/planner can then calculate the benefits of forest change in the short and long term. The decision of what to do with the land should fit within a framework of sustainable land use management and this does not always equate with highest productivity.

The effectiveness of land resource assessments is partly based on the proper collection, storage and distribution of quality data. As forest management moves towards a more participatory and community based approach, the effective use of such assessments are intrinsically linked with the accessibility of this data to local people. Widespread use of land resource assessments needs to be supported at different levels including provincial and district offices to ensure balanced decision-making on the future of Cambodia's forests.

Uncontrolled land use affects the livelihood conditions of many communities as their dependencies on natural resources are still strong. Secure and sufficient access to land and resources are crucial to raise income levels and provide livelihood options for those who depend on these resources on a daily basis, especially where alternative options do not exist. It is apparent that a clear central policy, improved property rights and an appropriate incentive framework to support land allocation is necessary or the opportunistic settlement process will continue and in many places forest areas that have little chance of providing a productive livelihood will continue to be cleared.

Forest Disturbance

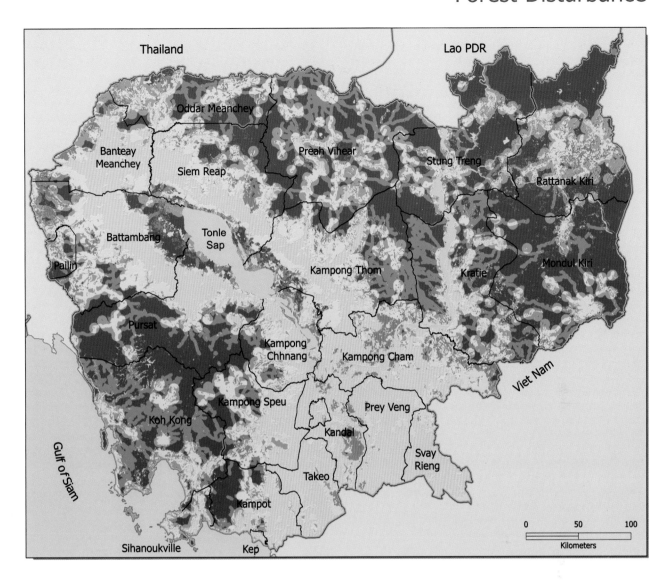

Legend

•	Village Location 1997	
·	Village Location 2001	
	Agriculture 1997	22%
	Cleared land 97-02	8%
	Other non-forest	11%
	Forest disturbed by Village and Roads	10%
	Forest disturbed by Villages	9%
	Forest disturbed by Roads	11%
	Less disturbed forest	27%
	Water Body	2%
-----	Roads	
———	Provincial Boundary	
———	International Boundary	

Note: Forest disturbance calculated using a model.

Data Sources:
Forest Disturbance: IFSR 2004
Village location 1997: Census
Village location 2001 and Roads:
Level one survey
International and Provincial Boundary:
Department of Geography 2005
Water Body: JICA Dataset 2002

Village Locations

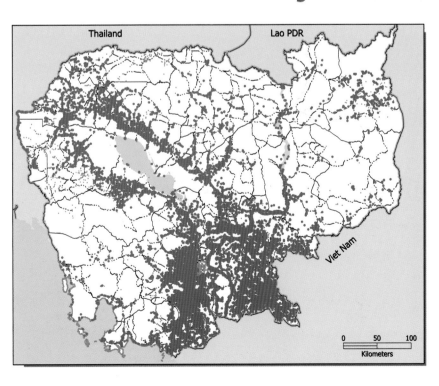

Non Timber Forest Products

The importance of non timber forest products (NTFPs) to the livelihood strategies of many Cambodians is widely recognized. However, the actual value of these products within the total value of a house hold's economic activities, is more difficult to determine. Identifying this figure will help to calculate the economic consequences of continued forest change to rural livelihoods. The Cambodian Development Research Institute (CDRI) has been conducting ongoing research with the aim of determining the direct and indirect value of Cambodia's forest resources in order to assist in the RGC's development goals of poverty reduction, environmental sustainability and economic growth.

In the past, forest management in Cambodia has conventionally been based on the value of the commercial worth of its timber. This approach largely ignores the value of both timber and NTFPs to rural livelihoods such as the use of timber for fuel and construction materials and the use of NTFPs for food, medicinal purposes and income generation. Recent economic data and the knowledge that previous management approaches have done little to contribute to rural development signify the importance of including ongoing research into NTFPs and its application to future forest management plans. Additionally, the long held belief that NTFPs provide food security in times of hardship underestimates the true value of this resource (Turton: 2004).

Calculating the Value of NTFPs

Research conducted by CDRI calculates the actual economic value of NTFPs based on data collected from household surveys carried out in 504 homes in four different provinces (Kratie, Mondul kiri, Pursat and Kampong Cham). Information on the cash and subsistence value of non-timber forest products was collected based on the total amount of forest products collected, traded and used for consumption per year. The valuation was based on market prices. Additional data on the total value of consumption and income of other livelihood activities, such as farming, livestock, employment and other business was gathered in order to compare these with the value of NTFPs. In order to compare the characteristics of NTFP use and value between different income groups of the population, the households were divided into two income categories: medium and low. The division was based on a participatory assessment by the villagers and included characteristics such as the size of land holdings, number of livestock and the extent of rice sufficiency throughout the year.

Rural Livelihoods and NTFPs

Rural people have a number of different livelihood strategies, including collection of NTFPs, rice farming, up-land farming, livestock, home gardens, employment and small business. In this context, the total value of a rural household's livelihood is made up of agricultural activities, off-farm income, other business and collection of NTFPs. The total household livelihood value includes cash income as well as the value of produce consumed and used in the household.

The results of the survey established that NTFPs dominated in their contribution to livelihood strategies of these households compared to all other activities. This is true of both the medium and low income groups (Figure: 2). These results dispute the notion that NTFPs mainly provide a safety net in times of hardship and clearly establish the fact that they play an intrinsic role in the lives of those surveyed.

Analysis of the data collected concludes that NTFPs contributed to 42% of the total household economic activities for the low income group and 30% for the medium income group. This was calculated as an absolute figure of US $280 contribution to the economic activities of low income households per year and US $345 for medium income households. Another important fact about the difference between the two income categories was highlighted during the study. Analysis showed that the better off households capture a larger absolute value from forests than the poorer households. This means that while the poorer group has a greater dependence on NTFPs, the monetary value of these resources was lower than in the better off households. This shows an important differentiation in the proportion of the NTFP value that is converted to cash income or used for consumption between the two income categories.

Considering the general lack of official market channels for NTFPs and local products, it is surprising that such a large proportion of the products collected from forests by both income categories is actually traded and marketed. This could be an indication of the potential for further market development of certain products at local, national, and perhaps international levels.

Implications of NTFPs to Forest Management

The main finding of the research study provides evidence of the high value of NTFPs to the livelihood strategies of those households surveyed. Given that approximately 33% of the population lives within 5 km of a forest, the study provides a good indication of the absolute value of forest resources to the well being of many Cambodians. The study also shows that the total value of collected forest products that are sold, traded or otherwise exchanged for cash is surprisingly large. This underlines the importance of NTFPs in the rural economy as a commodity group that is not only used as a "safety net". Thus, the overall importance of NTFPs to the well being of rural Cambodians should play a key role in future forest management plans to ensure that the already precarious livelihoods of many rural Cambodians is not further limited by restricted access to forest resources and the services they provide.

Value of Forest Resources

Figure 1: Illustration of the Components of the Total Economic Value of Forests

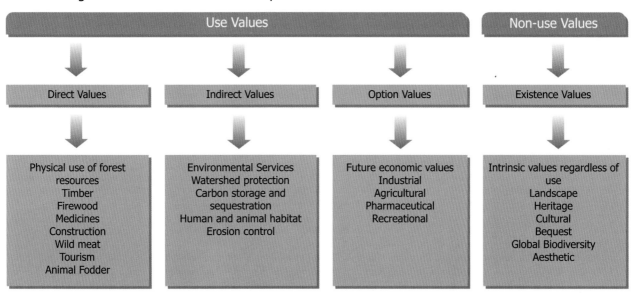

Use Values			Non-use Values
Direct Values	Indirect Values	Option Values	Existence Values
Physical use of forest resources Timber Firewood Medicines Construction Wild meat Tourism Animal Fodder	Environmental Services Watershed protection Carbon storage and sequestration Human and animal habitat Erosion control	Future economic values Industrial Agricultural Pharmaceutical Recreational	Intrinsic values regardless of use Landscape Heritage Cultural Bequest Global Biodiversity Aesthetic

Figure 2: Distribution of Total Livelihood Values for Farm and Off-Farm Activities and NTFP Collection in Low and Medium Income Category Households

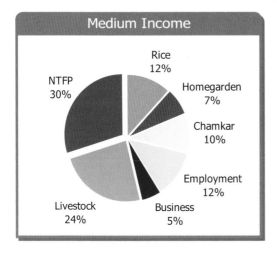

Medium Income

Rice 12%
Homegarden 7%
Chamkar 10%
Employment 12%
Business 5%
Livestock 24%
NTFP 30%

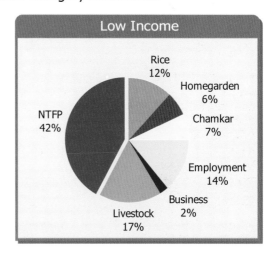

Low Income

Rice 12%
Homegarden 6%
Chamkar 7%
Employment 14%
Business 2%
Livestock 17%
NTFP 42%

Resin Collectors, Tumring

Community Forestry

Community Forestry (CF) is a form of forest management that empowers local people to manage forest resources in a sustainable way. A wide range of activities can be classified as CF including the establishment of communal forests for firewood and local timber use, community protection and management of existing forest areas, the planting of trees in communal areas and incorporating trees on farms. This wide range of initiative is reflective of the differing needs of communities in differing provinces and the goals and financial resources of the NGOs involved. Objectives may be focused on specific timber and forest resources, needs for local communities or on broader environmental regeneration and protection work.

While NGO driven community led forestry management has been in place in Cambodia for some time, it has only been recognized as a form of forestry management by the RGC relatively recently. The Community Forestry sub-decree, approved in December 2003 is an important step in recognizing the importance of Community Forestry (CDRI: 2006b).

In Cambodia the first Community Forestry project was established in 1992. This involved 500 ha of degraded forest at Prey Ler in Takeo province. In 2002, areas under CF management represented 0.7% of Cambodias total forest area suitable for CF management (Fichtenau et al: 2002). According to the Forestry Administration, by 2004 there were 274 CF initiatives in Cambodia, covering a total area of 218,647 ha, approximately 2% of forested areas. These CF are located in 19 provinces covering 76 districts in 157 communes or 614 villages throughout the country.

Typically, forest resources closest to villages tend to be the most degraded, as a result, these are the areas where many of the intensive community based programmes are focused (Miller: 2004). It must be noted that many of the Community Forestry sites are still at an early stage of development.

Only limited Community Forestry initiatives are shown on the accompanying map due to a lack of official raw data at commune level. In early 2004 the Community Forestry Office (CFO) was established within the FA and at present this office is gathering information from various projects in order to improve the CF database. This is expected to be completed in 2006. There has been some fragmentation in data collection as different NGOs provide support to many different CF initiatives. The government has been working closely with these groups to establish CF locations, number, status, the process of establishment, management plans and what products are being harvested. It is anticipated that this information will help to build a framework in which to develop a National Community Forestry Programme.

The Forestry Administration has reported widespread potential interest in establishing Community Forestry areas, calculating that since 2002 the number of communities involved in initiatives has increased by over 200. FA approval is required in order to establish a formally recognized CF and local FA officers assist these communities by providing technical assistance. Additionally, local communities can seek technical assistance from the numerous NGOs involved in CF.

Community Forestry members elect a committee from within the community to represent them for a term of five years. The agreement to manage the CF area covers a term of 15 years and if the community manages the forest according to the management plans this may be renewed for an additional 15 year period. However, if the community is not managing the area the agreement can be revoked before the 15 year time period.

The potential benefits of Community Forestry are:

* A stable supply of forest products for the community to ensure livelihoods and food security
* Land security for CF areas
* Protection of watersheds and moderation of climate in the surrounding area
* A secure habitat for wild plants and animals
* A possibility to attract tourists
* Protection of spiritual sites

Community Forestry can be an important tool for both poverty alleviation and forest conservation, although in order to achieve this in the Cambodian context a number of factors need to be addressed. If the future target for Community Forestry is to achieve self sufficiency, identifying economic and legal conditions must be a priority. According to the Independent Forest Sector Review (2004), a good resource base and secure, expected revenue flows for the community are necessary. This may be achieved with clear incentives to the local people in relation to future benefits and the involvement of CF committees in decision making to enable them to effectively manage their resources.

Natural Resources

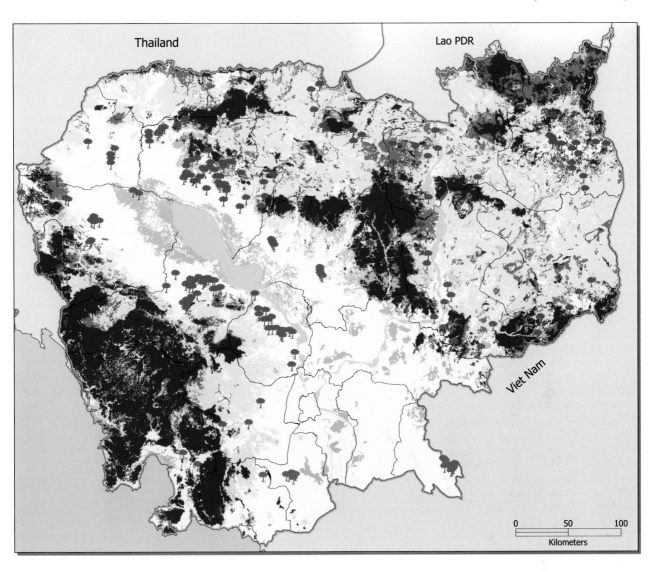

Thailand

Lao PDR

Viet Nam

| 0 | 50 | 100 |

Kilometers

Legend

🌳 Community Forestry

⬛ Evergreen forest

⬛ Semi-Evergreen Forest

☐ Deciduous forest

⬜ Other forest

☐ Non forest

☐ Water Body

— Provincial Boundary

━ International Boundary

Data Sources:
Community Forestry: FA 2005
Forest cover 2002: FA
International and Provincial Boundary :
Department of Geography 2005
Water Body: JICA Dataset 2002

Gene-Ecological Zonation

Gene-ecological zonation is a cost-effective tool to organize and prioritize action plans for the conservation and use of important native tree species. Even though genetic information on most wild plant species is lacking, it is possible to locate and protect distinctive population types on the basis of their present-day preference for natural environments.

> **A gene-ecological zone is an area that exhibits uniform ecological conditions and limited degrees of gene flow between surrounding regions.**

Each gene-ecological zone should be defined in a manner that reflects the genetic similarity of plant populations, yet it should also be large enough to be of practical use.

Creation of the Gene-Ecological Zonation System

The Gene-Ecological Zonation System was created from a variety of national environmental data-sets, and interpolated with datasets from Thailand, Laos PDR and Vietnam. The information most directly relevant to the processes of natural selection in the context of plant populations was emphasised, including:

- Annual rainfall (using 200 and 600mm range classes)
- Period of dry months (<40 mm rain-fall/month)
- Temperature of the coldest month (<16.5 degrees Centigrade)
- Geological distribution of basalt, sand-silt stone, alluvial deposits, gneiss and schist, and complex sub strates
- Soil fertility (low, medium and high)
- Vegetation and land use (agricultural lands, shrub land, deciduous forest, evergreen forest and inundated/mangrove forests)

This information, presented on separate maps of the same scale, was overlaid electronically using Arcview software. The results can be viewed and analysed using Arcexplorer GIS.

Uses of the Gene-Ecological Zonation System

The Gene-Ecological Zonation System serves a variety of objectives in forest gene conservation:

- **Gene Conservation Planning:** identification of unique habitats in which ecologically typical varieties of specific timber trees can be permanently conserved.

- **Seed Sources:** establishment of seed production zones in native forests for the sourcing of seed for local planting needs.

- **Planning of Planting Material Sources:** quantitative and qualitative assessments of seed source sites for the planning of future needs and plans for forest improvement on a long-term basis.

- **Plant Breeding:** assessment of local genetic types for use in plant breeding programs (i.e. improvement of domesticated varieties).

- **Distribution Potential:** establishment of productive seed-source sites for the sale and dissemination of planting material at a national or international scale.

Seed sources most appropriate for use are those located within the same gene-ecological zone as the tree planting site. However, the gene-ecological zonation system is a model that serves as a guideline, and cannot replace a forester's pragmatic decisions on the choice of seeds for planting programmes. It is further recommended that the gene-ecological zonation system and data-bases be used to assist land-planners in assessing the geographical distributions and ecological preferences of high priority native tree species and other plant species.

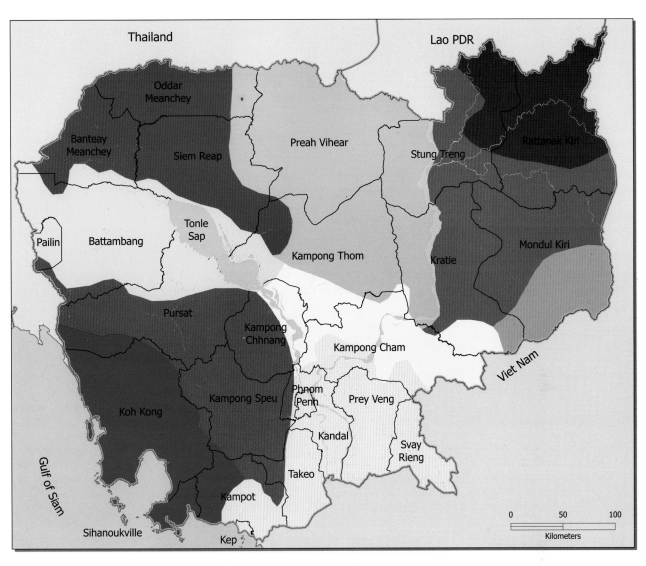

Legend

Gene-Ecological Zones

- Coastal Cardamoms
- Northern Cardamoms
- Tonle Sap Floodplain
- Northwestern Lowlands
- LowerMekongFloodplain
- Eastern Mekong Basin
- Central Annamites
- Redlands
- Central Lowlands
- Southern Annamites

- Water Body
- Provincial Boundary
- International Boundary

Data Sources:
Gene-Ecological Zones: CTSP, FA
International and Provincial Boundary:
Department of Geography 2005
Water Body: JICA Dataset 2002

Conservation of Indigenous Tree Species

The roles of natural forests are vast in contributing to poverty reduction, sustainable livelihoods, national economic development, biodiversity and environmental conservation. While the traditional focus of forest management towards timber production is important in raising government revenues for national economic development it often overlooks the broader roles and values of forest resources. As the livelihoods of the majority of rural Cambodians are dependent on access to forest products, especially for food, fuel wood, small-scale timber harvesting, resin tapping, fodder, traditional medicines and other non timber forest products, conservation of the forests directly contributes to food security and standard of living for a large proportion of the population. The natural forest also provides environmental services and functions in relation to the prevention of soil erosion, the retention of water, and conservation of biodiversity and natural heritage. Well managed forests and functions enhance production and sustainability within other sectors, most obviously in agriculture.

Indigenous Species
Indigenous trees are in high demand due to the high quality and high value of timber from luxury species (the highest value species classification); and the high value of other species within community livelihoods.

Vulnerable and Threatened Species
Rapid degradation and loss of the forest resource base results in diminishing access and low value forest products. Several indigenous tree species are now listed as vulnerable or endangered, and in particular, many populations are threatened. For the future, this means that genetic resources of many economically, and potentially valuable, indigenous tree species will be reduced, and therefore, quality planting materials will be lost.

Forest Gene Conservation
The RGC, through the Forestry Administration and the Cambodia Tree Seed Project embarked on forest gene conservation in 2001. This involved identifying target species and their populations in a carefully planned network of designated and managed gene conservation areas, which in the future will also serve as seed sources. Thirty six seed sources, comprising 20 endangered tree species have been established to date (please refer to table of Seed Sources Sites in the appendix).

This work is critical in ensuring potential economic and environmental benefits for both the rural population and the national economy. It ensures the future use of indigenous tree species, whether in meeting commercial (timber, forest plantations), livelihood (agro-forestry, living fences, home gardens, fuel wood), or environmental (watershed protection, erosion control) objectives.

The Use of Quality Seed
The importance of using quality seed for tree planting is evident in the genetic quality of the trees which they produce. The significance of this is clear in total economic valuations, as the use of quality seed can be expected to result in a considerably higher value than that from unknown, or inferior, origin. Also, seedlings from quality seeds are faster growing and healthier, with desired form, thereby attracting higher prices in the market, or higher fruit/fodder production, which increases income potential.

Seed Source Sites

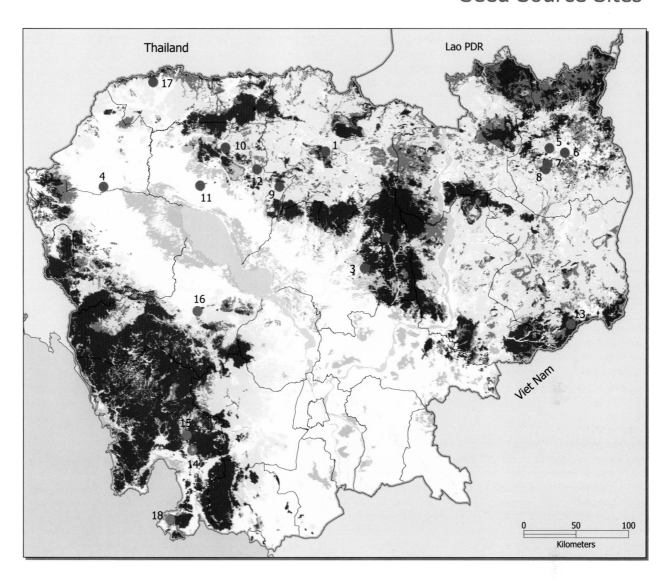

Thailand

Lao PDR

17

10
1
5
6
7
8
4
12
9
11

2
3

16

13

15
14

Viet Nam

18

0   50   100
Kilometers

Legend

● Seed source sites

■ Evergreen forest

■ Semi-Evergreen Forest

Deciduous forest

Other forest

Non forest

Water Body

—— Provincial Boundary

—— International Boundary

Note: Refer to appendix for
Seed Source location, indigenous
species and number of mother trees.

Data Sources:
Seed Source: CTSP, FA
Fover Cover 2002: FA
International and Provincial Boundary :
Department of Geography 2005
Water Body: JICA Dataset 2002

Protected Areas

A traditional means for pursuing wildlife conservation is the establishment of protected areas in which human activities are prohibited or controlled with a view to safeguarding particular species or species' habitats. More recently the creation of protected areas has been conceived as part of a 'national system', or preferably in the framework of an international network. This enables the overall objectives of biodiversity protection to be more effectively pursued, an express requirement of the Convention on Biological Diversity, which among the obligations for *in situ* conservation lists the creation of a system of protected areas. A protected area is important not only for the survival of its flora and fauna, but also for economic and social reasons. Recent advances in economic techniques reveal the significant public benefits of protected areas including both private and public economic benefits, significant health values and their importance as a key educational resource.

History of Protected Areas in Cambodia

A protected area is an area of land or sea dedicated to the protection and maintenance of biological diversity and of natural and associated cultural resources which are managed through legal or other effective means (IUCN: 1994). The first protected area in Cambodia was Angkor Archaeological Park. Declared in 1925, it established a 10,800 ha area surrounding the Angkor temples.

Prior to 1957, approximately one third of the country was subjected to some form of inventory and classified into 173 forest reserves and six wildlife protection areas. The 173 forest reserves constituted about 3.9 million hectares and were designated primarily for forest production. The six wildlife reserves consisted of approximately 2.2 million hectares set aside for the management of wildlife resources, particularly large mammals.

On the 1st November 1993, the Royal Decree for 'Protected Areas' was issued for the Ministry of Environment to lead, manage, plan and develop a protected areas system to ensure the protection of the land, forests, wildlife, wetlands and the coastal zone.

There are 23 areas covered by this decree totaling 3,273,200 ha or 18% of Cambodia's total area. In 1999 three Ramsar sites were formally acceded signifying the global importance of Cambodia's wetlands. The total area of these sites is 54,600 ha with about 38% of this overlapping the established protected areas.

Between 1996 and 2002, the Forestry Administration established eight protected areas primarily aimed at wildlife conservation, watershed management and gene pools. These areas cover a total of 1,346,225 ha or 7.5% of the country. The Department of Fisheries also makes a great effort to establish conservation zones as fish sanctuaries in both freshwater and marine areas for key species such as dolphins, dugongs, sea turtles, coral reefs and sea grass. Therefore, the total protected areas officially cover up to 26% of the country under the jurisdiction of the MoE and MAFF.

Achievements of Protected Area Management

The protected areas system in Cambodia is based on the IUCN categories and objectives. This system is considered an essential tool for *in-situ* conservation providing benefit to biodiversity and the environment. Of the total number of protected areas in Cambodia, 24 are under management of the MoE and 8 are under management of MAFF. The main achievements to date in relation to these protected areas are as follows:

- Establishment of the Protected Areas with boundary demarcations and management infrastructures.
- Legislation and management framework: policy formulation, laws and MEAs, law enforcement and procedures, managerial infrastructures, human resources, facilities and allocation of resources for each protected area.
- Development: strategy, action plan, management plan and protected areas management guideline.
- Co-management: community based natural resources management through the establishment of the Community Protected Areas, Community Forestry and Community Fisheries.

Summary of Cambodia's Protected Area System

Category	Main Management Objectives	Management Responsibility	Number of Protected Areas	Total Area (Km²)
National Park	Conservation of biodiversity, ecosystem conservation and recreation.	MoE	7	7,751
Wildlife Sanctuary	Conservation of biodiversity, scientific research and wilderness protection.		10	19,161
Protected Landscape	Conservation of biodiversity and of specific natural and cultural features.		3	1,018
Multiple Use Area	Conservation of biodiversity, sustainable use of resources in natural ecosystems.		3	4,210
Ramsar Site	Protection of internationally significant wetlands.		1*	149
Subtotal MoE			**24**	**32,289**
Protected Forest	Conservation of biodiversity, genetic resources and wildlife habitant.	MAFF	8	14,860
Marine Protected Area	To manage and protect threatened species and habitants in the marine realm.	MAFF - DoF*	1	696
TOTAL			**33**	**47,845**

* One of the 3 Ramsar sites lies completely within a Multiple Use Area and one is partially contained within a Wildlife Sanctuary and a National Park. The non-overlapping area of Koh Kapi and the entire area of Stung Treng Ramsar Site are included here.
* Koh Sdach Marine Protected Area status uncertain.
Source: Lacerda et al: 2005

Protected Areas and Protected Forests

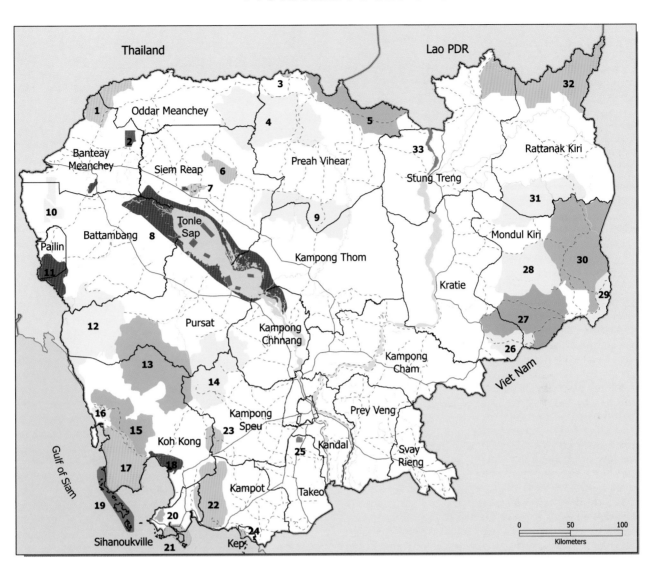

Thailand

Lao PDR

1 — Oddar Meanchey
3
4
5
2
Banteay Meanchey
Siem Reap
6
Preah Vihear
33
Stung Treng
Rattanak Kiri
7
9
31
10
Battambang
8
Tonle Sap
Mondul Kiri
Pailin
11
Kampong Thom
Kratie
28
30
29
12
Pursat
Kampong Chhnang
27
26
13
Kampong Cham
Viet Nam
14
15
16
Kampong Speu
Prey Veng
17
23
Koh Kong
25
Kandal
Svay Rieng
18
Kampot
19
22
Takeo
20
Sihanoukville
21
Kep

Gulf of Siam

0 | 50 | 100
Kilometers

Natural Resources

Legend

- Crane Sanctuary
- Marine Protected Area
- Multiple Use Area
- National Park
- Protected Forest
- Protected Landscape
- Wildlife Sanctuary
- Zoo
- Biodiversity Conservation Area
- Fish Sanctuaries
- Ramsar

- Water Body
- Main Roads
- Secondary Roads
- Provincial Boundary
- International Boundary

No.	Name	No.	Name
1	Banteay Chhmar	18	Dong Peng
2	Ang Trapeang Thmor	19	Koh Sdach
3	Preah Vihear	20	Kbal Chhay
4	Kulen Promtep	21	Ream
5	Preah Vihear	22	Bokor
6	Phnom Kulen	23	Kirirom
7	Angkor	24	Kep
8	Tonle Sap Bioshpere Reserve	25	Phnom Thmau Zoo
9	Boeng Per	26	Snoul
10	Roniem Daun Sam	27	Seima
11	Samlaut	28	Phnom Prich
12	Phnom Samkos	29	Phnom Nam Lyr
13	Central Cardamom	30	Mondulkiri
14	Phnom Aural	31	Lomphat
15	Southern Cardamoms	32	Virachey
16	Peam Krasop	33	Stung Treng
17	Botum Sakor		

Data Sources:
Protected Areas: MoE
Protected Forests: FA, MAFF
Main Roads, Secondary Roads and Water Body:
JICA Dataset 2002
International and Provincial Boundary:
Department of Geography 2005

Geology

Cambodia is geologically composed of three major facies and lithological structures:

- The **Triassic** and **Liassic** 'ancient gulf' covering large areas in the East
- The **Jurassic-Cretaceous** continental sandstones forming the main highlands in the West
- The **Quaternary basin** which occupies the whole central plain of the country between both older structures.

Further geological studies prove a series of sedimentary formations extending from the very old *Pre-Cambrian* age at the base to *Cretaceous* at the top while the whole profile is affected by successive tectonic activity. *Tertiary formations*, of which outcrops are very limited on the continent, form a thick layer offshore and seem to be an important target for oil and gas exploration.

From the base upward, the hard rock stratigraphy shows the oldest formation to be of *Precambrian* age and consisting of high grade metamorphic rocks namely gneiss, quartzite and amphibolite. These are found in two areas in the Northwest and Northeast of Cambodia. The solitary *Cambrian* argillite proved by the presence of a fossil of trilobite, is found in NE Cambodia. Other formations consisting predominantly of high metamorphic quartzites are considered to be of *Cambrian-Silurian* age based only on stratigraphic correlation, proven by French geologists. Another series of lower metamorphic quartzite are found in SW Cambodia and considered to be *Cambrian-Upper Silurian.*

The *Devonian-Carboniferous* formation is composed of a heavily folded but unmetamorphosed series of sandstone and shale covering large areas in the North, Northwest and West. Two Upper Carboniferous to *Permian* and *Upper Permian* limestone series are found in Cambodia. The first series, consisting of limestone and dolomite, partially metamorphosed to marble, are found in Stung Treng province. The second series consists of pure limestone, with some cherts in its lower parts, are found mainly in Southwestern and Northwestern Cambodia. Sandstone formed in near shore areas is found in Northeastern Cambodia and is considered to be of *Upper Carboniferous-Triassic* age.

The undifferentiated Triassic formation, composed of a sandstone-shale series containing some volcanic elements, are widely found in the form of isolated hills and mountain ranges in Takeo, Kampong Speu and other parts of the country. Lying above the Triassic sandstone series is the so-called "Red Terrane" of *Lower-Middle* Jurassic age consisting of red sandstone, siltstone and marl of a brackish depositional environment. The topmost and youngest hard rock known in Cambodia is the series of sandstone and claystone of *Upper Jurassic age* that forms the important massifs of Damrey, Kravanh, Kulen, Dangrek and some small isolated hills in Central and Eastern Cambodia.

Thick *Paleogene* and *Neogene* formations are found offshore and beneath the Tonle Sap Lake, while small outcrops are found in very limited areas in the Northeastern province of Stung Treng. Finally, *Quaternary formations*, composed of eluvial and alluvial sand, silt and clay, covers very large areas of Central Cambodia. In some regions along the Mekong River, the depth of the *Quaternary formation* reaches up to 200 meters.

Magmatic activities, which happened in four phases namely *Lower-Middle Paleozoic, Permian-Triassic, Late Triassic* and *Cretaceous-Paleogene*, resulted in intrusions of granite, granodiorite and other intrusive rocks found in different locations in Cambodia. The predominant volcanic rocks are rhyolite and dacite which occurred in different eruption phases namely *Cambrian-Silurian, Ante-Permian, Triassic* and *Jurassic-Cretaceous.* Andesitic lava was formed during the eruption phase of Permian and Jurassic-Cretaceous and is observed in the central North of Cambodia. The youngest volcanic eruption in the *Late Neogene-Early Quaternary* phase resulted in the occurrence of mafic basaltic plateaus in Kampong Cham, Kratie, Mondul Kiri and Rattanak kiri. Thick Paleogene and Neogene formations are found offshore and beneath the Tonle Sap Lake, while small outcrops are found in very limited areas in the Northeastern province of Stung Treng. Finally, *Quaternary formations*, composed of eluvial and alluvial sand, silt and clay, covers very large areas of central Cambodia.

Time Units of the Geologic Time Scale					Development of Plants and Animals
EON	ERA	PERIOD		EPOCH	
Phanerozoic	Cenozoic	Quaternary		Holocene 0.01	Humans develop
				Pleistocene 1.6	
		Tertiary		Pliocene 5.3	"Age of Mammals"
				Miocene 23.7	
				Oligocene 36.6	
				Eocene 57.8	
				Paleocene 66.4	Extinction of dinosaurs
	Mesozoic	Cretaceous	144	"Age of Reptiles"	and many other species
		Jurassic	208		First flowering plants. First birds.
		Triassic	245		Dinosaurs dominant.
	Paleozoic	Permian	286	"Age of Amphibians"	Extinction of trilobites and many other marine animals. First reptiles. Large coal swamps. Amphibians abundant.
		Carboniferous	Pennsylvanian 320		
			Mississippian 360		
		Devonian	408	"Age of Fishes"	First insect fossils.
		Silurian	438		Fishes dominant, first land plants
		Ordovician	505	"Age of Invertebrates"	First fishes. Trilobites dominant.
		Cambrian	570		First organisms with shells.
proterozoic	2,500	Collectively called Precambrian, comprises about 87% of the geologic time scale			First multi-celled organisms.
archean	3,800				First one-celled organisms.
hadean	4,600				Age of oldest rocks. Origin of the earth.

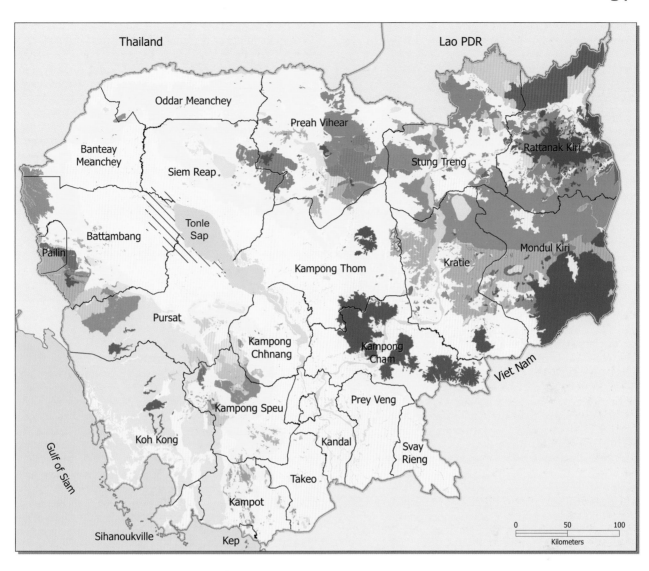

Legend

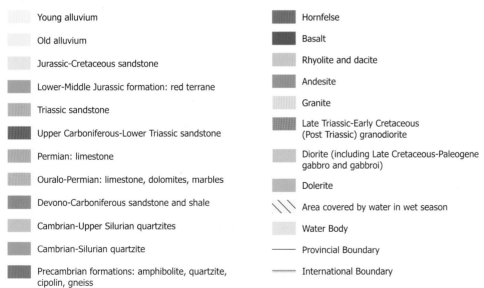

Young alluvium	Hornfelse
Old alluvium	Basalt
Jurassic-Cretaceous sandstone	Rhyolite and dacite
Lower-Middle Jurassic formation: red terrane	Andesite
Triassic sandstone	Granite
Upper Carboniferous-Lower Triassic sandstone	Late Triassic-Early Cretaceous (Post Triassic) granodiorite
Permian: limestone	Diorite (including Late Cretaceous-Paleogene gabbro and gabbroi)
Ouralo-Permian: limestone, dolomites, marbles	Dolerite
Devono-Carboniferous sandstone and shale	Area covered by water in wet season
Cambrian-Upper Silurian quartzites	Water Body
Cambrian-Silurian quartzite	Provincial Boundary
Precambrian formations: amphibolite, quartzite, cipolin, gneiss	International Boundary

Data Sources:
Geology: Department of Geology, MIME
International and Provincial Boundary:
Department of Geography 2005
Water Body: JICA Dataset 2002

Mineral Resources

The periods during which minerals are formed are called Metallogenic epochs. In Cambodia, four such epochs are known. These are the Devonian-Carboniferous, Carboniferous-Permian, Jurassic-Cretaceous and Cenozoic epochs which resulted in the formation of 133 mineral deposits which can be divided into four groups: Metallic, Non-metallic, Gemstone and Fuel minerals.

Metallic Minerals

Sixteen iron deposits composed of magnetite and hematite are concentrated mainly in Northern provinces, including Stung Treng, Preah Vihear, Oddar Meanchey and Battambang. Most of the deposits are of skarn type having a late Triassic age and have an iron content of up to 68% in some places. In the Phnom Deck iron deposit, the iron ore is estimated to be about 5-6 million tons. Three manganese occurrences of lateritic type with 11-26% manganese content are found in the Chhep district of Preah Vihear. Two bauxite deposits are known in Battambang and Mondul kiri. The most important is that of Mondul kiri, where lateritic bauxite with high alumina content varying from 25-35% covers large areas on the basaltic plateau of Sen Monorom and O Reang districts. Base metals containing zinc, lead, copper and other accessory sulfide minerals are found in twelve places in various provinces. Gold is one of the main commodities of Cambodia. A total of 19 gold deposits and occurrences are known in the country and 7 of them have been discovered accidentally by farmers during the gold rush of the eighties. Some of the deposits were actively mined in the past and are considered to be exhausted. New locations are being mined by locals and causing severe environmental damage. Silver has been found along with gold in some of the gold deposits located in Oddar Meanchey and Kampong Speu. Other metallic minerals of high economic value are found in Cambodia including molybdenum, tin, chromium, antimony, tungsten. Unfortunately, there are no systematic studies carried out and their potential remains unknown.

Non Metallic Minerals

Non metallic minerals include both industrial minerals and construction materials. Several non metallic minerals are being exploited and play an important role in the development of the country. Phosphate minerals, or high quality phosphorite of Karst type are found associated with limestone in Southwestern and Northwestern Cambodia. Some quarries have been opened in the past to mine these minerals to supply local fertilizer factories. Silica sand is the raw material for the fabrication of glassware. Nine pure beach sand deposits with high silica content of up to 99.5 % covers the coastal area from Sihanoukville to Koh Kong. Despite its important economic value, the exploitation of this sand must be undertaken in a careful way to avoid environmental impacts to the coast and its surrounding ecology. With its large flood plain, Cambodia possesses a high potential of clay minerals, in particular those which are used for brick and tile production. However, only six clay deposits in Kampong Chhnang, Kampong Cham (Prek Kak), Kampot (Chakrey Ting), Siem Reap (Phnom Krom) and Pothisat (Trasey) have been studied for their quality and approximate reserve. The sole dolomite deposit, located in the Thalaboriwat district of Stung Treng, has been mined in the past to supply the glass factory in Phnom Penh. Most of the limestone deposits found in Cambodia consist of a high content of $CaCo^3$ suitable for cement and lime production. In some areas limestone is mined and used as road ballast without studying its chemical properties resulting in a waste of limestone materials.

The mineral zircon is being mined in Rattana kiri in rich deposits on the basaltic plateau of Banlung and Bokeo districts. High quality zircon gems are selected for jewelry during the mining process, while low non-gem quality crystals that can be used as a source of industrial zircon, are abandoned in the tailing. Two occurrences of graphite have been reported in Kampot. Fluorite minerals are found in quartz veins cutting across the granite in the Chheu Kach granitic massif in the Ba Phnom district of Prey Veng.

Gemstones

Among gems found in Cambodia, the corundum (Sapphire and Ruby), are the most important. Several deposits of high quality corundumare are found associated with red soil weathered from basaltic rocks. Three main areas are known for corundum including Pailin-Samlot, Chamnop-Chhnuon and Thmar Baing. Amethyst of a purple and violet colour is exploited from Phnom Chi granitic massifs of Sandan district, Kampong Thom and Kon mum in Rattanak kiri. Crystals of yellowish green peridot are reported to be exploited in Mondul kiri from the alluvium in the vicinity of the Nam Lyr granitic massif located near the border of Vietnam. Black meteorite glass is found in Kampong Thom, Stung Treng and Rattanak kiri. The exact location of these deposits is unknown. Important deposits of ornamental stone including pagodite, jet, and agate are found in Pursat and Strung Treng.

Fuel Minerals

Occurrences of fuel minerals, including anthracite, coal, lignite, peat, petroleum and gas are found in Cambodia and exploration of these continues. A few incidences of anthracite are reported in the North in Preah Vihear and Oddar Meanchey, however information on the geological setting of these deposits is not available. Coal and lignite are found in different geological formations, but the most important coal deposits are of Lower-Middle Jurassic Red bed formations covering large areas in Kratie, Rattanak kiri, Stung Treng, Preah Vihear and Oddar Meanchey. Large deposits of peat are found in the Chantrea district of Svay Rieng. Geological and geophysical investigations in the early 1990s revealed some probable petroleum basins in Cambodia and gas and oil deposits offshore.

Construction Materials

Several rock types, namely granite, basalt and sandstone as well as laterite, sand and gravel suitable for construction materials are important in Cambodia. Among them the most appreciated crushed stone is exploited from sandstone quarries of Triassic age in Takeo and Kampong Speu. Sand and gravel are exploited from the Mekong River in Stung Treng, Kratie, Kampong Cham, Kandal and Prey Veng.

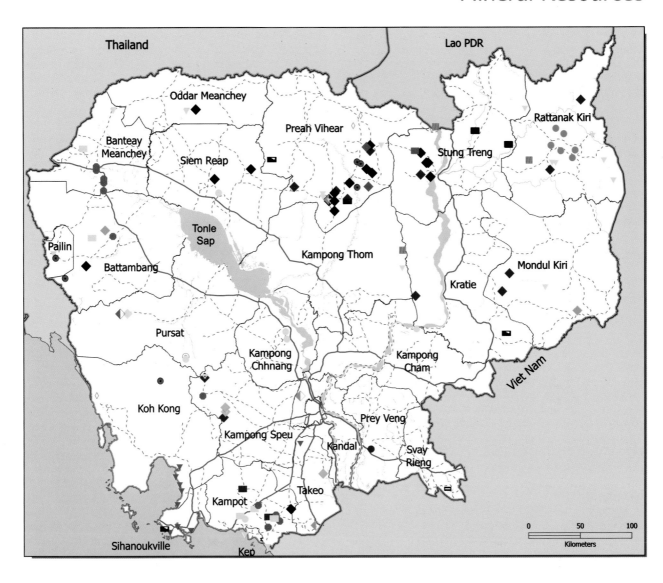

Legend

Mineral Resources, Number of deposits

METALLIC

- ◆ Iron, 18
- ◆ Manganese, 2
- ◈ Antimony, 1
- ◈ Molybdenum, 3
- ◈ Tungsten, 1
- ◈ Chromium, 1
- ◈ Tin, 2
- ◈ Aluminium, 2
- ◆ Base metals, 12
- ▽ Silver, 3
- ▽ Gold, 19

NON METALLIC

- ● White clay and clay for cement, 6
- ● Fluorite, 1
- ◼ Graphite, 2
- ◻ Limestone, 5
- ◼ Dolomite, 1
- ● Phosphate, 11
- ▼ Silica, 9
- ● Zircon, 7

GEMSTONES

- ● Corundum, 6
- ▦ Amethyst, 3
- ◇ Jet, 4
- ◎ Pagodite, 1

FUEL MINERALS

- ◼ Coal, 2
- ▱ Lignite, 4
- ▭ Peat, 1

Water Body

—— Main Roads

----- Secondary Roads

—— Provincial Boundary

━━ International Boundary

Data Sources:
Minerals and Symbology: Department of Geology, MIME
International and Provincial Boundary:
Department of Geography 2005
Water Body: JICA Dataset 2002

Energy Resources

After restoration of order in Cambodia the RGC has followed a program focused on rehabilitation and development of the basic infrastructure, including energy supply and exploration of energy resources, with the aim of improving socio-economic conditions and aiding development. Currently over 84% of primary energy consumption is based on fuel wood with only around 13% of rural households having access to grid-quality electricity services (NIS: 2005). However, rural electrification in Cambodia is increasing at a surprising rate in many districts and provinces, serviced by a government coordinated electrification program. The basis for this progress is a ready market for the sale of electricity by local entrepreneurs. The state electricity companies alone cannot meet the increasing electricity demand, especially for the rural population. Renewable energy technologies (RETs) will be the most appropriate way to meet the energy demand in rural and remote areas, especially in off-grid areas.

While Cambodia has indications of oil, gas and coal deposits and the potential for hydropower, there is an urgent need to assess the extent of these energy resources. Other renewable energy sources, such as biomass, solar power and mini hydro, are being investigated and in some instances these are currently being used. In order to provide sufficient electricity to Cambodia, there must be further diversification of energy sources. There also needs to be intensified exploration of natural gas deposits and the development of renewable sources of energy.

Energy Supply
At present, the electricity supply in Cambodia is fragmented into 24 isolated power systems centred in provincial towns and cities. All are fully reliant on diesel power stations. Per capita consumption is only about 48 kWh per year and less than 15% of households have access to electricity (of these 54% are urban and 13% rural). The private sector consumes 0.5% of electricity, the service sector 40% while the industrial sector consumes 14%. The supply requirements are projected to increase on average by 12.1% per year, and the peak load is expected to reach up to 1,000 MW in 2020.

The largest system is in Phnom Penh, which accounts for 70% of the country's electricity consumption, with a peak demand of 80 MW, and an available capacity of 129.2 MW (EDC 74.5 MW, IPPs 54.7 MW). The peak demand is estimated to increase to 649MW in 2020. The total installed capacity for provincial towns is estimated at about 50 MW with the size ranging from 300kW to 5 MW, and the peak demand is expected to increase to 342 MW in 2020.

Due to the small size of generation dependent on high cost imported oil, the lack of a high voltage transmission system and big losses in distribution, the price of electricity in Cambodia is the highest in the region. According to data from 2000, the average tariff is about 14.6 US Cents / kWh in Phnom Penh, and 25 to 50 US cents / kWh in remote areas.

Two types of licensees generate electricity in Cambodia. Independent Power Producers (IPP) generate and sell bulk power to suppliers and Consolidated Licensees generate power for supply through their distribution systems. Another source is importation from neighbouring countries.

Power Development
Electricity is very important for the improvement of living standards and for agricultural and small-scale industrial development in rural areas. As a reflection of this the government has set the goal of raising the access rate to reliable, affordable grid-quality electricity to 70% of rural households by 2030.

Rural Electrification comprises the provision of electricity services needed in rural areas for basic household demand (lighting, television and fans) and the basic village demand (public lighting and electricity supply to community centers, health clinics, schools) and local businesses. However, the long-term goal may be exceeded by the possibility of electricity supply over the next 30 years. In the mid-term, there is a need to develop a 10-year target (2010) of 25% of households to be connected.

Interconnection
The Interconnection Master Plan for electricity and natural gas will be established through the ASEAN Power Grid (APG) and the Trans Asean Gas Pipeline crossborder projects. This will develop an efficient power supply, facilitate economic generation and transmission of electricity, enhance security of power systems and provide opportunities to private investment for future energy trading among ASEAN member countries.

Most of the power plants will be located in the Southwest, Northeast and along the coastal areas of the country. The grids located in the Southwest are a high priority due to agro-industries operating in the area. These power plants will be connected to the grid interconnecting Thailand, Cambodia, Viet Nam and Lao PDR. The projected transmission grids are expected to be completed by 2010. In the short term, the power supply will be based on power imported from Viet Nam to Phnom Penh and from Thailand to Northwestern Cambodia.

Oil and Gas
All commercial fuels in Cambodia are imported in the form of LPG, gasoline, diesel and other petroleum products. An average of 900,000 tons per year was imported from 1998-2000, an increase of approximately 700,000 tons per year since 1985. So far, wells suitable for a commercial scale have not been found in Cambodia, although explorations continue. At present Thailand seems to be the most likely gas supplier to Cambodia, however, with a small demand for natural gas, combined with the construction costs of the pipeline, this may not be a viable option. Another option is for the supply of natural gas from Viet Nam to a power station in the Mekong Delta. In order to secure the supply of natural gas and thus improve the supply of energy to industry, which is necessary for capital investment, Cambodia needs to be connected to the Trans ASEAN gas pipeline.

Projected National Transmission Grid and Potential Hydropower

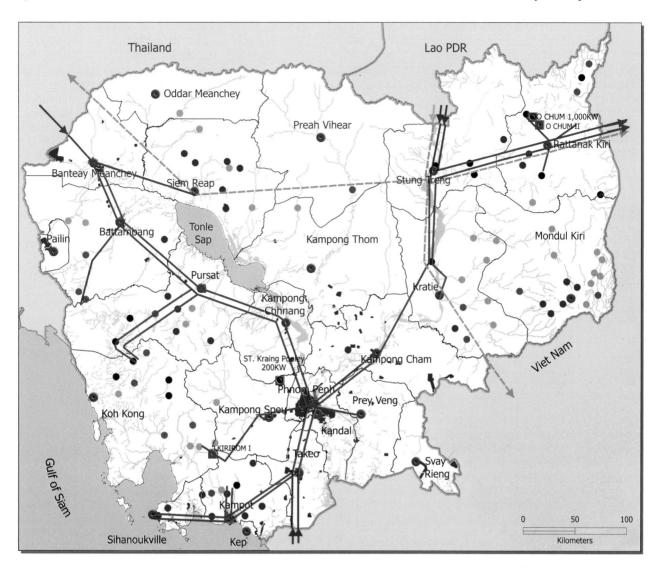

Legend

- ▣ Hydropower Station in Operation
- ● Proposed Hydropower Sites
- ● Proposed Small Scale 500 - 10,000 KW
- ● Proposed Medium Scale 10,000 - 50,000 KW
- ● Proposed Large Scale more than 50,001 KW

- ◉ Provincial Center
- ■ Area of Electricity
- —— Transmission Line 115 KV
- —— Proposed Transmission Line 220 KV
- - - - Proposed Interconnection Grid
- 100KW Installed Capacity

- ▨ Water Body
- —— River
- —— Provincial Boundary
- —— International Boundary

Data Sources:
Electricity and Hydropower Data: MIME 2005
International, Provincial Boundary and Provincial Center:
Department of Geography 2005
River, Water Body: JICA Dataset 2002

Hydropower

In 1995 the hydropower potential of Cambodia was estimated to be 10,000 MW and could therefore play a significant role in the long-term development of energy supply. In some parts of the country, micro hydropower may provide opportunities for electrification and thus decrease the dependence on fuel wood. However, hydropower needs technical and financial support in order to complete feasibility studies. At present only two mini-hydropower plants are in operation: in Rattanak Kiri, O Chum II with the installed capacity of 1000 kW has been operating since 1993 and in Kirrirom a mini-hydropower operation which began in 2002. There are also privately owned micro hydropower plants in the Northern provinces with installed capacity ranging from 1 kW to 50 kW. All proposed hydropower plants producing over 500kw require an Environmental Impact Assessment (EIA).

Solar Energy

There is considerable potential for solar power in Cambodia. International organizations have installed demonstration photovoltaic systems in some health rehabilitation centers. Solar Home Systems (SHS) are a good solution for low income rural households. With an investment cost of US$40 per household, these systems can provide energy at approximately 24.4 US cents/KWh.

Biomass and Biogas

Biomass energy plays a major role in satisfying the rural demands of energy in Cambodia. Besides fuel wood, agro-industrial residues, such as rice, sugarcane, maize and cattle excreta, are also available as fuel. Biomass is also used in the industrial sector for copra drying and system generation, and rice husks in bakeries, brickworks and other commercial establishments. However, no reliable estimates of the amount of biomass energy consumption are available and a study needs to be conducted for this purpose.

Wind Energy

The potential of wind energy in Cambodia has not yet been assessed. Due to the inconsistency of wind patterns, a hybrid generation system with a base operating system of diesel or micro-hydro is ideal. Mechanical wind pumps are probably the best choice for using wind energy as the annual average wind speed is less than 4 m/s. It is possible that small wind power systems or individual household wind power systems may be applicable in some areas, particularly along the Southwest coast close to the Cardamom Mountains or in the highlands along the Viet Nam border.

Coal

There is need for an inventory and feasibility study of coal deposits in Cambodia. There have been reports of coal deposits in Kampot, Kampong Thom, Kratie, Stung Treng and Battambang provinces. One deposit, in Stung Treng province has been identified with an estimated reserve of around 7 million tons.

Wood Energy

Fuel wood has played a crucial role in traditionally meeting the energy needs of Cambodia and is likely to continue to be an important energy resource for many years to come. Its use is no longer confined only to rural households and traditional commercial activities. Fuel wood use is also growing in many urban areas and within different industrial and commercial activities. There is a need to develop a better understanding of the environmental impacts of fuel wood use and to develop policies to replace it with other forms of renewable energy. There is also a need to increase the efficiency of fuel wood. Improving stoves has the potential to decrease wood use by up to 50%. Wood energy development needs to be addressed through inter-ministerial co-operation. This co-operation should examine the current status of forestry, energy and environmental policies in order to identify the strengths and weaknesses of each in relation to wood energy development.

Main Source of Light in Rural Areas

Fuel Source	Percentage of use
Grid electricity	8%
Generator	1%
Kerosene	70%
Candles	0.2%
Battery	17%

Source: NIS Statistical Year Book 2005

Fuel Wood Use

Wood Energy

1 family burns 2.12 kg of charcoal/day

Total families burning charcoal = 5.1% or 122,000 families
Total Charcoal needed = 258 tons/day or 94,403 tons/year

1 family burns 2.78 kg of fuel wood/day
Total families burning fuel wood = 91.2% or 2,179,985 families

Total fuel wood needed = 6,060 tons/day 2,212,031 tons/year

Source: Cambodian Fuel Wood Saving Project: http://www.cfsp.org.kh

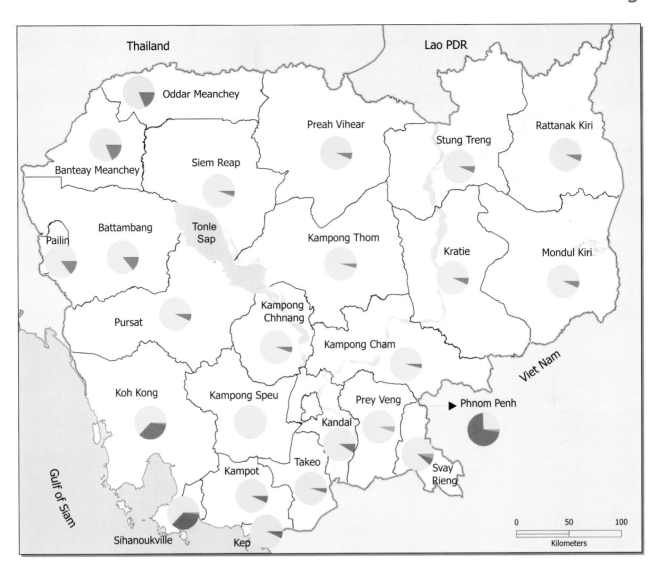

Legend

Household Fuel

Firewood

Charcoal

Kerosene

Gas

Other

Water Body

——— Provincial Boundary

——— International Boundary

Note: Percentage of Fuel Wood
Use < 1% not repersented in pie chart.

Data Sources:
Fuel Wood Use: CIPS 2004 and 1998 Census, General
Report and Provincial Report, NIS, Ministry of Planning
International and Provincial Boundary:
Department of Geography 2005
Water Body: JICA Dataset 2002

Fuel Wood Use (%)

Province	Firewood	Charcoal	Kerosene	LPG	Other
Banteay Meanchey	81.2	16.4	1.1	1.0	0.3
Battambang	84.8	12.8	0.4	1.4	0.6
Kampong Cham	95.3	2.4	0.6	1.6	0.1
Kampong Chhnang	93.8	4.5	0.6	1.1	0
Kampong Speu	98.7	0.6	0.3	0.3	0.1
Kampong Thom	94.9	4.4	0.1	0.5	0.1
Kampot	91.3	6.8	0.9	0.4	0.6
Kandal	90.3	5.8	0.7	2.7	0.5
Koh Kong	62.4	28.2	0.7	6.8	1.9
Kratie	92.4	6.6	0.2	0.8	0
Mondul Kiri	92.4	6.6	0.2	0.8	0
Phnom Penh	25.5	30.1	0.7	41.2	2.5
Preah Vihear	92.4	6.6	0.2	0.8	0
Prey Veng	93.1	0.5	0.6	0.6	5.2
Pursat	92.6	5.8	0.3	1.1	0.2
Rattanak Kiri	92.4	6.6	0.2	0.8	0
Siem Reap	93.1	3.8	0.9	1.8	0.4
Sihanoukville	62.4	28.2	0.7	6.8	1.9
Stung Treng	92.4	6.6	0.2	0.8	0
Svay Rieng	88.3	3.9	0.3	3.0	4.5
Takeo	94.6	3.5	0.5	1.2	0.2
Oddar Meanchey	81.2	16.4	1.1	1.0	0.3
Kep	91.3	6.8	0.9	0.4	0.6
Pailin	84.8	12.8	0.4	1.4	0.6

References

Asia Development Bank. 2004. Cambodia: Country Environmental Analysis. Asian Development Bank

Associates in Rural Development. 1998. Forest policy Transition Paper for Cambodia, Final Draft. Department of Forestry and Wildlife. Phnom Penh, Cambodia

Ashwell, D. 1997. A National Biodiversity Prospectus: A Contribution Towards the Implementation of the Conservation on Biological Diversity with Particular Emphasis upon Cambodia's Terrestrial Ecosystems. IUCN, Phnom Penh, Cambodia

CDRI 2006a. The Value of Forest Resources to Rural Livelihoods in Cambodia. Cambodia Development Resource Institute Policy Brief. March 2006, Issue 2

CDRI. 2006b. Forest Management Options in Cambodia. Cambodia Development Resource Institute Policy Brief. March 2006, Issue 4

CDRI. 2006c. Trends and Dynamics of Deforestation and Forest Degradation. Cambodia Development Resource Institute Policy Brief. March 2006, Issue 1

DFW. 2002. Guidelines for Sustainable Forest Management in Cambodia. Department of Forestry and Wildlife, Forestry Administration, Ministry of Agriculture, Forestry and Fisheries, Phnom Penh, Cambodia

Dümmer, I. 2004. Information and Knowledge Based System for Land Suitability Analysis in Cambodia. A Paper Prepared for the Land Resource Assessment Forum (14-17 September 2004)
Accessed at: www.danida-cambodia.org

Fraser, T. 2000. Cambodian Forest Concession Review Report, 2000. Department of Forestry and Wildlife, and Asian Development Bank, Phnom Penh, Cambodia

Fichtenau, J., Ly Chou Beang, Nup Sothea, Dy Sophy. 2002. An Assessment of Ongoing Community Forestry Initiatives in Cambodia - Implications for the Development of a Forestry Extension Strategy. Accessed at: www.mekonginfo.org

Forestry Administration. 2003. Cambodia: Forestry Statistics 2002. Forestry Administration, Phnom Penh, Cambodia

Forestry Administration. 2005. Cambodia: Forestry Statistics 2004. Forestry Administration, Phnom Penh, Cambodia

ICEM. 2003. Regional Report on Protected Areas and Development. in Cambodia National Report on Protected Areas and Development, Review of Protected Areas and Development in the Lower Mekong River Region. Indooroopilly, Queensland, Australia

IFSR. 2004. Independant Forest Sector Review. Royal Danish Embassy Development Cooperation Section and Forest Administration, Phnom Penh, Cambodia. Accessed at: www.cambodia-forest-sector.net/docs-part2.htm

Lacerda, L., Schmitt, K., Cutter, P., Meas, S. 2005. Management Effectiveness of the System of Protected Areas in Cambodia using WWF's RAPPAM Methodology. BPAMP, Department of Nature Conservation and Protection, Ministry of Environment

Mckenney, B., Yim C., Prom, T. and Evans, T. 2004. Focusing on Cambodian's High Value Forest: Livelihood and Management. Cambodia Development Research Centre, Phnom Penh, Cambodia

Miller, F. 2004. The Silvicultural Status, Growth and Productivity of Cambodia's Forests. in The Independent Forest Sector Review, Part II Current Context, Forest Sector in Cambodia. Phnom Penh, Cambodia

MoE. 2002. Cambodia National Environmental Action Plan 1998-2002. Ministry of Environment, Phnom Penh, Cambodia

SOER. 2004. State of Environment Report 2004. Ministry of Environment, Phnom Penh, Cambodia

MoE. 2005. Identification of Important Conservation Areas in Cambodia. National Assessment. Ministry of Environment, Phnom Penh, Cambodia

MRC. 2003. State of The Basin Report: 2003. Mekong River Commission. Phnom Penh. ISSN: 1728:3248

NCDM. 2004. Natural Disasters Status in Cambodia 2004. Report, National Committee on Disasters Management, Phnom Penh, Cambodia

NIS. 2005. Statistical Yearbook 2005. National Institute of Statistics, Ministry of Planning, Phnom Penh, Cambodia

O'Brien, N. 1999. Environmental Concepts and Issues - A Focus on Cambodia. Ministry of Environment, Phnom Penh, Cambodia

Prom, T. and McKenney, B. 2002. Natural Resources and Rural Livelihoods in Cambodia: A Baseline Assessment. Cambodia Development Resource Institute. Working paper 28. Phnom Penh, Cambodia

Prom, T. and McKenney, B. 2003. Trading Forest Products in Cambodia. Challenges, Threats and Opportunities for Resin. Cambodia Development Resource Institute. Working paper 28. Phnom Penh, Cambodia

Sloth, C. Khlok Bottra and Heow Kim Sreng. 2005. Non-timber Forest Products: Their Value to Rural Livelihoods. in Cambodia Development Review October-December 2005

Turton, C. 2004. Livelihoods and Forest Resources. in The Independent Forest Sector Review, Part II Current Context, Forest Sector in Cambodia. Phnom Penh, Cambodia

Water Resources

The Mekong River

Extending 4,800 km in length from the Himalayan Mountains in China and meandering across Myanmar, Thailand, Lao PDR, Cambodia and Viet Nam before discharging into the South China Sea, the Mekong is the longest river in Southeast Asia and one of the world's largest river systems. With a total drainage area of 795,000 km² it has an estimated annual discharge of over 500 billion m³ (MRC: 2003).

Cambodia's Mekong forms part of the Lower Mekong sub region and comprises distinctive features and a variety of habitats including headwaters characterized by sandy gravel bars, long tracts of deep pools up to 100m in depth, numerous rapids, tributary streams, and extensive meandering plains. As it enters Cambodia from Lao PDR in the Northeast, the Mekong exhibits a lower gradient with numerous tributaries and islets. The main river channels sustain water all year round with a 10 meter depth variation between the wet and dry seasons.

Deep pools are formed in the fast flowing channels of large rivers and maintained by a scouring high flow during the wet season. In Cambodia, this feature is located just below the Khone falls and stretches South almost to Kratie. Many rapids emerge in the dry season along this section of the river. Small islands and sandbars are also common on this stretch of the Mekong and its tributaries including the Se San, Sre Pok and Se Kong as they are formed by natural deposition during the seasonal high river flow. A unique type of flooded forest occurs on sandy islands and isolated rock outcrops. These are characterized by almost horizontal growth as vegetation resists prolonged submersion and strong water currents.

A fluvial lowland with high natural levees, broad floodplains and extensive backwater swamps, many of which remain flooded throughout the dry season, is formed downstream of Kratie. From Kampong Cham Southward, the vast fertile plain of the Mekong delta begins and extends into Viet Nam. The delta covers some 65, 000 km². Downstream of Phnom Penh the Mekong delta is formed by both the Mekong and Bassac Rivers (MRC: 2003).

Ecological and Biological Significance

One of the fundamental aspects of the Mekong River system is its seasonal variation in flow and flood and its relationship with the Tonle Sap Lake, which presents significant ecological and socio-economic implications. The Mekong water levels and flows are lowest in April and May and highest in September and October. Many water bodies become isolated and the smaller tributaries tend to dry out by the end of April. With the start of the monsoon rains in late May, the river revives its flow and attains its greatest level in September or October. The Tonle Sap Lake flows Southeast and into the Mekong at its confluence in Phnom Penh, however, in the wet season (May to October) the Mekong waters rise overflowing its banks and feed into the Tonle Sap River reversing its flow back into the Tonle Sap Lake. This causes the Great Lake to swell to more than twice its size during the wet season. As the Mekong's peak pulse is passed, the Tonle Sap Lake discharges back into the Mekong. The physical characteristics of the Mekong basin and its seasonal flow patterns feature as important environmental functions and flood control.

The rich biodiversity of the Mekong River and its basin are of significant conservation value. The river, its

Upper and Lower Mekong Basin

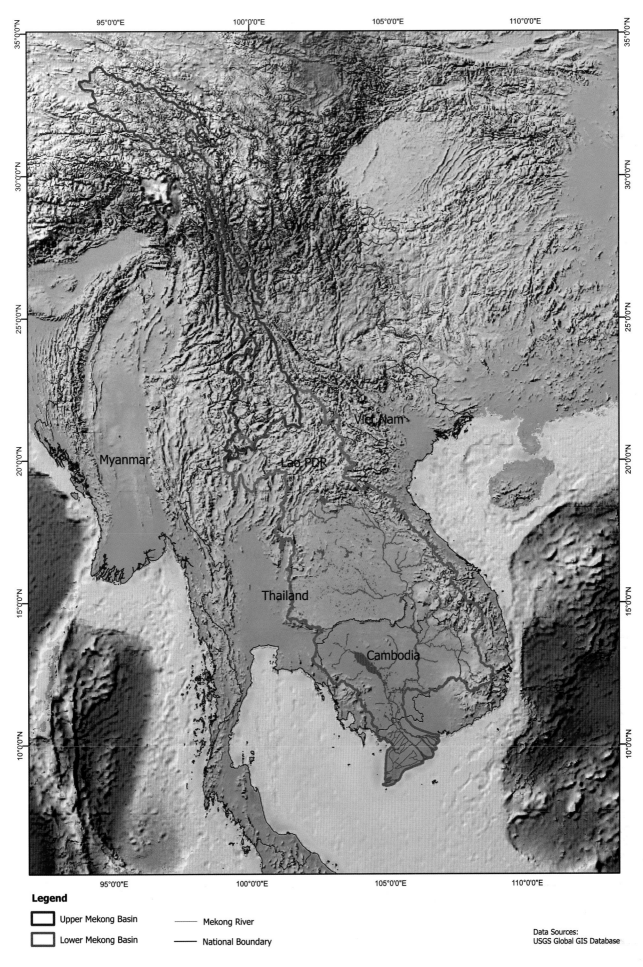

Legend

☐ Upper Mekong Basin	—— Mekong River
☐ Lower Mekong Basin	—— National Boundary

Data Sources:
USGS Global GIS Database

Note: This map is a digital elevation model.

tributaries and associated wetland habitats support many unique ecosystems and a wide array of globally-threatened species with over 1,300 species of fish inhabiting the whole Mekong system. Over 850 species have been estimated to occur in the Lower Mekong basin of which 456 species have been identified and 179 (40%) are known to be endemic.

The many deep pools upstream of Kratie, the flooded forests of the Tonle Sap Lake and the stretch of the Mekong between Kratie and the Khone Falls are known to provide refuge and spawning grounds for many important species. Over 100 fish species are believed to migrate between the Tonle Sap and upstream of the Mekong and across the Khone Falls. Two fish species, globally recognized as critically endangered, occur in the Lower Mekong basin.

The Mekong and its low gradient tributaries are important for distinctive guilds of riverine bird species. There are also 20 species of turtles and terrapins reported in the Lower Mekong Basin, ten of which are listed in the IUCN Red list. Numerous other wild fauna and flora are found to have significant conservation value, however these are largely not yet identified.

Livelihood and Economics

Annual flooding of the Mekong inundates floodplains and swamps forests enriching the soil with nutrients and providing feeding and spawning grounds for its highly diverse fisheries. Biodiversity in the Mekong is also fundamental to the viability of natural resource-based rural livelihoods of a population of 55 million people living in the Lower Mekong Basin. This is equivalent to more than 90% of the population of the entire Mekong Basin, and about one third of the total population of Cambodia, Lao PDR, Thailand and Vietnam combined. In Cambodia, over 90% of the entire population, varying from 110-500 persons per km^2, live in the Mekong Basin (MoE: 1999). Phnom Penh, a city of over one million people, is located on the confluence of the Mekong, Tonle Sap and Bassac rivers and extends into the associated wetlands.

Local people fish in the main channels of the Mekong and its river system throughout the year, using a wide array of fishing gear including gill nets, cast nets, and hooked lines. While the male members of the family fish, female members take charge of fish processing on the site, including salting, sun-drying, and smoking fish. Most people fish to supplement their crops and others also forage for non-timber forest and wetland products including birds, insects, and edible leaves for food, grass for mats and roofing and firewood.

The Mekong and its tributaries also provide water for drinking and irrigation and serves as an important route for transport. According to the Ministry of Public Works and Transport, the total length of navigable waterways is 855 km in the dry season and 1,544 km in the wet season (Neou et al: 2005). The potential for hydropower production has been projected for Cambodia. The Mekong also provides significant potential for income generation through eco-tourism and other recreational activities.

An economic valuation in Veun Sean, in the Stung Treng Ramsar site reveals that the value of the Mekongs wetland resources are estimated at about 13 million Riel ($3,200) per household per year, of which the average contribution from fisheries resources is 1.7 million Riel ($425) per household per year (MWBASUP: 2005). Much of this value is derived from income earned from selling fish, which is used mainly to purchase food, particularly rice. The cited values for households in Veun Sean come from a range of resources including fish and aquatic animals, plants, water birds, reptiles, and through activities such as fishing, washing, cooking, drinking, transportation, construction, collection of traditional medicines, irrigation, floodplain rice farming and recreation.

Major Watersheds

Three major watershed regions can be distinguished in Cambodia, including the Mekong, Tonle Sap and the Coastal area covering 42%, 44% and 14% of the country's land area. To the East, Cambodia's watershed covers the entire Northeast plateau of the three Mekong tributaries, the Sekong, Se San and Sre Pok. It extends southward to cover Chhlong and Kampong Cham, and the Bassac area. To the Northwest, it includes the catchment of the Tonle Ropov and Prek Thnot in the Southwest but excludes that of Stung Chinit. Major watersheds of the Tonle Sap include the Southern slopes of Dangrek, the Eastern slope of the Korat plateau in Thailand, and the Northern slope of the Cardamom Mountains. The Southern slope of the Cardamom Mountains and Elephant Ranges form the coastal watershed.

A classification aimed at giving an indication of the sensitivity of watersheds with regard to water degradation, mainly by soil erosion, was developed for the countries in the Mekong Basin. On the basis of the topography of the landscape including slope, elevation, landform, and variable forest cover, five watershed classes were defined:

- Class 1: Protected Forests
- Class 2: Commercial Forests
- Class 3: Agro-Forestry
- Class 4: Upland Farming
- Class 5: Lowland Farming

Population Density of Wetland Areas

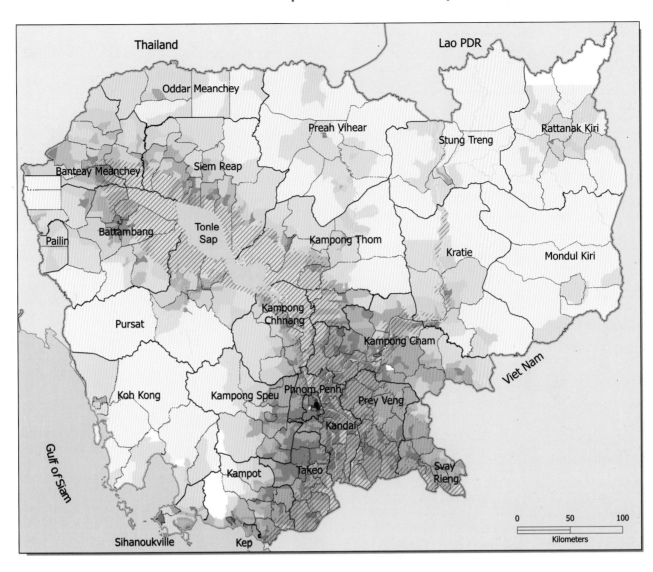

Thailand

Lao PDR

Oddar Meanchey

Preah Vihear

Stung Treng

Rattanak Kiri

Banteay Meanchey

Siem Reap

Battambang

Tonle Sap

Kampong Thom

Kratie

Mondul Kiri

Pailin

Pursat

Kampong Chhnang

Kampong Cham

Viet Nam

Koh Kong

Kampong Speu

Phnom Penh

Prey Veng

Kandal

Gulf of Siam

Kampot

Takeo

Svay Rieng

Sihanoukville

Kep

0   50   100

Kilometers

Legend

Population Density Person/Km²

▒	<10	No Data
▒	11 - 50	▨ Wetlands
▒	51 - 100	Water Body
▒	101 - 150	----- District Boundary
▒	151 - 300	—— Provincial Boundary
▒	301 - 3,000	═══ International Boundary
▓	3,001 - 8,000	
■	8,001 - 164,437	

Data Sources:
Population Density: Commune Database 2004
Wetlands: Department of Geography and UNESCO
International, Provincial and District Boundary:
Department of Geography 2005
Water Body: JICA Dataset 2002

Wetlands

Attempts have been made to define wetlands in the Cambodian context as areas where soils are hydric and inundated on an annual or semi-annual basis and where plants are able to tolerate inundation for over six weeks (RGC: 2000). However, according to the Ramsar Convention, Wetlands are "...areas of marsh, fen, peatland or water, whether natural or artificial, permanent or temporary, with water that is static or flowing, fresh, brackish or salt, including areas of marine water, the depth of which at low tide does not exceed six meters" (UNESCO: 1994).

According to this definition, 30% of Cambodia is covered by wetlands (MoE: 1999). These can be categorised into four main wetland regions:

- The Mekong River - 468 km in length.
- The Tonle Sap Lake - between 2,500 km^2 and 13,000 km^2 depending on the season.
- The Stung Sen - about 3,000 km^2
- The Southwest coastal wetlands of Koh Pao and Stung Kep

Hydrological patterns of the Mekong River and the Tonle Sap Lake and the relatively flat landscape characterise the features and extent of wetlands in the country. Flood water from the Mekong River and the Tonle Sap catchment in the monsoon months causes inundation converting extensive lowlands in the middle of the country into enormous open water systems. At low water levels in the dry season, wetlands are featured by smaller and more isolated open water systems consisting of river channels and many lakes, with vast areas of marsh and swampland frequently located in their periphery. Flooded forests are a common feature of wetland habitats, particularly of the Tonle Sap floodplain and the Bassac marsh.

Numerous streams flow from the Cardamom and Elephant Ranges into the coastal watershed. Their associated deltas and lagoons form major types of coastal wetlands including mangrove forests, mudflats, coral reefs and sea grass beds. Rice paddies, aquaculture ponds, including reservoirs and irrigation systems, are some of the man-made wetland types occurring in Cambodia.

The Value and Importance of Wetlands

Howe et al. (1991) identified a range of benefits provided by wetlands including:

- Services such as flow regulation, prevention of saline water intrusion, protection from natural forces, sediment removal/storage, nutrient removal/storage, toxicant removal/storage, energy production and transport.
- Goods such as water supply and provision of natural products, such as fish, woods and NTFPs.
- Other benefits: source of genes, significance for conservation, recreation/tourism, social-cultural benefits, research and education and contribution to the maintenance of existing natural systems.

Wetlands are as important for national economy as they are for local livelihood. In regards to productivity, Cambodia's inland waters contain one of the world's most productive inland fisheries. Approximately 4 million people depend on inland fishing for their livelihoods as either their primary or secondary source of income and employment. When associated activities are considered, this figure probably increases to more than 50% of Cambodia's 13.5 million inhabitants as wetlands provide water for agriculture and animal production including fisheries.

Threats to Wetlands in Cambodia

Human activities place pressure on wetlands through activities such as wetland conversion for other uses, non-sustainable harvesting of natural products and pollution. Wetland conversion is increasingly a threat. As in many countries, wetlands in Cambodia have been reclaimed and are lost to urban development, as is the case in Phnom Penh. A significant amount of Cambodia's wetlands have been lost to agricultural production, particularly rice fields, shrimp farming and salt pans. For instance, the total area of rice fields in the country has increased substantially from 1.735 million ha in 1988 to 2.3 million ha in 2003-2004 (MAFF: 2004). In 1994, 840 ha of shrimp farms were established in Koh Kong, most of which occurred on lands cleared of mangrove forest (CEPA: 2001). Mastaller (1999) reported that post 1970s, large-scale expansion of salt farms in Kampot and Kep caused a loss of 3,500-4,000 ha of mangrove land to salt pans. Construction of dams causes significant change to the hydrology of river systems and to the seasonal flooding cycle of wetlands and leads to the loss or decrease in wetland areas and functions.

Point source of pollution to wetlands comes from industry and urban sewage. Regardless of the relatively small amount of raw sewage, its direct discharge into the environment without primary treatment raises concerns over pollution loads in associated waters. Non-point source of pollution stems primarily from agricultural production, in which pesticides and fertilizers have been inappropriately used and the tail water is discharged into water bodies (Neou et al: 2005).

Wetland Management in Cambodia

Management of Cambodia's wetlands falls under a number of sectoral agencies with policies and laws specific to their mandates and coordination amongst them is particularly poor (Mam: 2004). At least three sectoral agencies have major authority and legal framework for wetland management including the Ministry of Agriculture, Forestry and Fisheries, the Ministry of Environment and the Ministry of Water Resources and Meteorology. The Cambodia National Mekong Committee (CNMC) has the primary role of coordinating the planning and management of water resource use.

Cambodia contains wetlands of international significance covering 30% of its territory. Three sites are designated Ramsar sites established in 1999. These include the middle stretch of the Mekong River North of Stung Treng (14,600 ha), Boeng Chhmar and its associated river system and floodplain (28,000ha) and the coastal wetland of Koh Kapik and its associated islets (12,000 ha). By acceding into the convention, Cambodia has a number of commitments including following the Ramsar convention framework and guidelines for wetland conservation and an obligation to foster communication and promote international co-operation in wetland conservation.

Wetlands and Catchment Areas

Water Resources

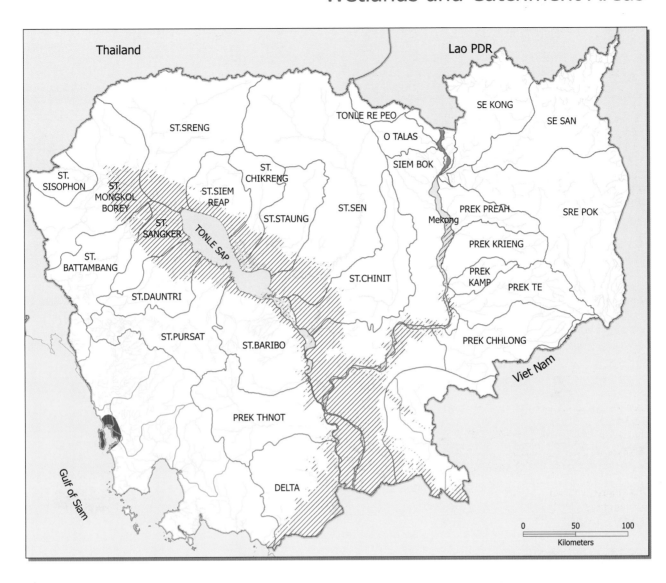

Legend

/////// Mekong (over 2,000,000ha of floodplains)
and Tonle Sap Wetlands
(total inundation 1,500,000 ha)

▓ Stung Kaoh Pao and
Stung Kep Estuaries: 30,000 ha

▓ Ramsar

░ Water Body

—— Mekong Watershed

— Other Watershed

⋯ River

—— International Boundary

Note:

ST.= Steung

Watershed created by GIS Method (Catchment Area)
using contour lines from GIS dataset 2002.

Data Sources:
Wetlands: ASEAN Regional Center for
Biodiversity Conservation
Catchment, Flooded Area: MRC 2002
Discharge: JICA Dataset 2002
International Boundary:
Department of Geography 2005
Water Body: JICA Dataset 2002

No.	Catchment	Area in ha	No.	Catchment	Area in ha
1	DELTA	1,368,359	15	ST. CHIKRENG	275,309
2	O TALAS	151,084	16	ST. CHINIT	677,297
3	PREK CHHLONG	538,176	17	ST. DAUNTRI	352,952
4	PREK KAMP	116,209	18	ST. MONGKOL BOREY	857,470
5	PREK KRIENG	322,450	19	ST. PURSAT	597,503
6	PREK PREAH	233,143	20	ST. SANGKER	235,848
7	PREK TE	416,268	21	ST. SEN	1,624,541
8	PREK THNOT	666,619	22	ST. SIEM REAP	305,535
9	SE KONG	567,619	23	ST. SISOPHON	178,809
10	SE SAN	739,387	24	ST. SRENG	1,036,918
11	SIEM BOK	950,327	25	ST. STAUNG	437,131
12	SRE POK	1,286,404	26	TONLE RE PEO	92,211
13	ST. BARIBO	607,850	27	TONLE SAP	303,291
14	ST. BATTAMBANG	436,270			

The Tonle Sap Biosphere Reserve

Biosphere Reserves are areas of terrestrial and coastal ecosystems promoting solutions to reconcile the conservation of biodiversity with its sustainable use. They are intended to fulfil three basic functions including conservation, development and logistic functions. The Tonle Sap Lake was designated a Biosphere Reserve upon approval for its inclusion in the World Network of Biosphere Reserves by the International Coordinating Council for UNESCO's Man and Biosphere (MAB) reserve programme in 1997. The designation reflects the importance of the Tonle Sap Lake ecosystem for its ecological functions and for supporting socio-economic development and the maintenance of associated cultural values.

The Royal Decree in 2001 on the creation and management of the Tonle Sap Biosphere Reserve (TSBR) emphasizes the three aforementioned functions of the biosphere reserve and the identification of three core areas, one at Prek Toal (21,342 ha) in Battambang Province and the other two areas, Boeng Chhmar (14,560 ha) and Stung Sen (6,355 ha), which are located in Kampong Thom Province. A buffer zone located in between and surrounding the three core areas extends

541,482 ha, which itself is subsequently surrounded by vast areas of floodplain covering approximately 899,600 ha.

The unique hydrological cycle of the Tonle Sap and vast areas of flooded forest and shrubs create a rich biodiversity of fish, reptiles, birds, and mammals and this forms the basis for its designation as a Biosphere Reserve. Two core areas, Prek Taol and Beoung Chhmar in particular, are the most productive fishing grounds and support large colonies of water birds, with the former serving as nesting, and the latter feeding grounds. Distinct and least disturbed flooded forests are found in the third core area, the Stung Sen. It is reported that about 1.2 million people live in the floodplain of the Tonle Sap Lake, of which 25% live on floating villages. The Tonle Sap Lake provides an important source of protein and supports employment, primarily in fishing and farming (Azimi et al.: 2000). Thuok and Sina (1997) estimated that 88% of 170 villages located in and surrounding the lake depend on fishing and its related activities. The TSBR also saves large urban centers and vital infrastructure from inundation.

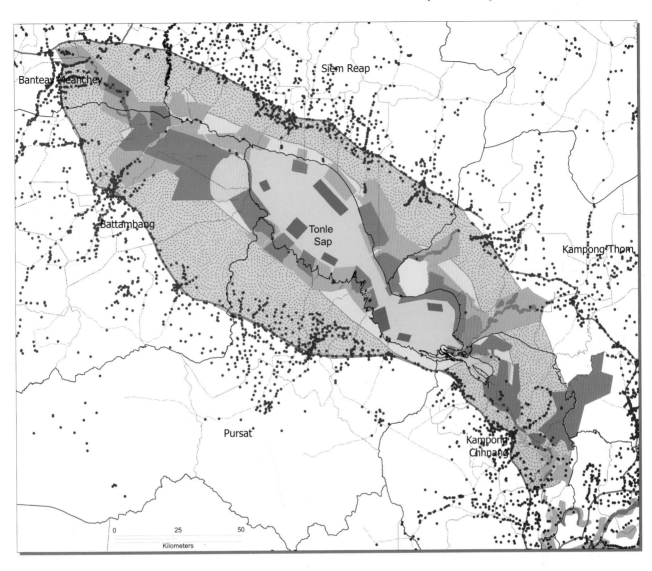

Legend

Tonle Sap Biosphere Reserve

- Boeng Chhmar Core Area
- Prek Toal Core Area
- Stung Sen Core Area
- Buffer Zone
- Transition Zone
- Tonle Sap
- Fish Sancturies

Fishing Lot

- Existing Filshing Lot Area
- Released Fishing Lot Area

- • Village Center
- —— Main Roads
- ---- Secondary Roads
- ---·--- District Boundary
- —— Provincial Boundary

Data Sources:
Tonle Sap Biosphere Reserve:
Department of Natural Resource Assessment
and Environment Data Management
Fishing Lots: MAFF 2001
Fish Sancturies: DoF, MAFF 2004
Provincial, District Boundary and Village Center:
Department of Geography 2005
Main Roads, Secondary Roads: JICA Dataset 2002

The Tonle Sap Bioshpere Reserve

- UNESCO Biosphere Reserve
- Largest wetland in the Mekong Sub region
- 2,500-3,000 km² in the dry season
- 1,000-15,000 km² in the wet season
- Depth: 1 meter in dry season and up to 10 meters in wet season

Population
- Approximately 1158 villages
- Home to 4 109 137 residents
- Density: 80 people/km²

Productivity
- Fish catch: > 40,000 ton per annum

Threats
- Over fishing
- Destructive fishing practices
- Flooded forest exploitation
- Land conversion
- Dams
- Pollution

The Coastal Zone

The coastal zone (CZ) of Cambodia extends for 435km and consists of estuaries, bays and 64 islands of various sizes. Most of the coastal population is concentrated in Sihanoukville where urban services and employment opportunities are available and in Kampot, where good soil conditions and access to water enables rice culture. Cambodia does not yet have a complement of coastal and marine environmental policies. As development pressures are rapidly mounting there is an urgent need for safeguards to be put in place that will allow economic development while ensuring the sustained quality of coastal and marine environments and the resources they provide. A starting point for this is to conceptualize the CZ as being made up of two interrelated systems, the ecological system and the socio-economic system.

The Ecological System
Coastal Fisheries
During the past decades fish catch has increased dramatically, but Catch Per Unit (CPU) has declined owing to an increase in population. This puts more pressure on natural resources and their ecosystems. The marine fishery has increased from 7,247 tons in 1986 to approx. 55,000 tons in 2003 (MAFF: 2004). However, there has been a decrease in some provinces of high value fish leading to a decrease in revenue.

Mangrove Forests
Fragile mangrove ecosystems play an essential role in the survival of some fish species and other marine organisms serving as spawning or nursery grounds. Mangroves also play an essential role in protecting the coastline, acting as a self-maintenance buffer zone against storms, strong winds and currents thus reducing coastal erosion. Mangroves were logged in the 1990s for charcoal production, urbanization, coastal development, salt farms and development of intensive shrimp aquaculture. The change in mangrove distribution in the CZ is based on data derived from FA forest cover 1993, 1997 and 2002 and the JICA land use maps. These indicate a reduction of 17% since the 1990s, a high rate compared to the annual total forest cover deforestation rate of 1.7% (IFSR: 2004).

Sea Grass Beds
Stretches of shallow, protected coastal waters are suitable habitats for sea grasses providing cover for juvenile fish and nursery grounds. They are vulnerable to impacts from degradation of water quality and destructive fishing practices. The change in water quality is a result of increased siltation due to logging, increased use of fertilizer and pesticides in the coastal agricultural areas and discharge of domestic and industrial wastewater.

Coral Reefs
The present distribution and quality of coral reefs is difficult to ascertain. Coral reef surveys were conducted in some coastal waters during the Environmental Management in the Coastal Zone project and coral checks are made annually by DoF. Based on available data it is estimated that most coral reefs are found in Kampot and Koh Kong with coral reefs also reported from almost all areas around islands off the coast. Around 70 coral species are found in Cambodian waters and these habitats are home to many different fish species. The main threats to coral habitats are over-fishing, illegal fishing practices, harvest of coral for trade and degradation of water quality.

Pollution
Marine water is currently being polluted from various sources such as waste from industries and crafts, urban areas, water transportation and ports. Sewage from all four coastal provinces/municipalities is discharged without treatment and as a result solid waste is a major problem. The estimated quantity of waste generated and dumped into water bodies at coastal provincial and municipal centers is 88 tons per day (MoE, CZM: 2002).

The Socio-Economic System
Villagers in 75% of coastal settlements have met food shortages. This is mainly due to natural disasters such as insects, storms, high winds, and a long dry season in recent years. In addition, coastal communities also lack infrastructure. The shortage of drinking water along the coast is related to the problem of inadequate rural infrastructure. Many households in Cambodia's coastal villages lack a regular and stable income. Many fishermen are unable to fish more than 10-15 days/month because of the lack of safety at sea and the incidence of natural disasters such as storms. Land and sea tenure is an extremely contentious issue throughout Cambodia. High-ranking officials and rich investors easily seize land for investment and development outside proper channels. These issues pose a problem for CZM as there does not appear to be any traditional sea tenure and the rights of access to natural resources needs to be addressed.

Port Development
The RGC's goals for Sihanoukville originally planned for economic development through the rebuilding of urban growth, tourism, port expansion and industry. The port expansion may contribute to the economy by providing a main hub for maritime transport, which should, in turn, attract manufacturing industries. Port construction and port operation will impact on water quality, coastal hydrology, sea floor contamination, marine ecology, air noise, waste management and visual quality.

Urbanisation
Investment in Sihanoukville will lead to rapid urban growth as the rural population seek better opportunities provided by tourism and associated services. The urban infrastructure is currently insufficient to meet the requirement of even the existing population. Without appropriate investments, the environmental quality of this town will degrade.

Industrialization
The industrial development zone established in Sihanoukville includes petrochemical production to exploit recently confirmed oil and gas reserves in the Gulf of Siam, food processing based on the local fisheries in the area, timber processing and re-manufacturing. These industries pose potential damage to the environment. Salt farming in Kampot and Kep is riddled with conflicts about land tenure. The original farms replaced mangrove areas and salt farms are currently expanding into the remaining areas. There is some suggestion that rice farms next to salt production areas are adversely affected by increased salinity. Oil and gas exploration is a recent phenomenon and there is no infrastructure for receiving oil or gas in Cambodia. There is neither oil spill contingency plans nor clean up capacity.

The Coastal Zone

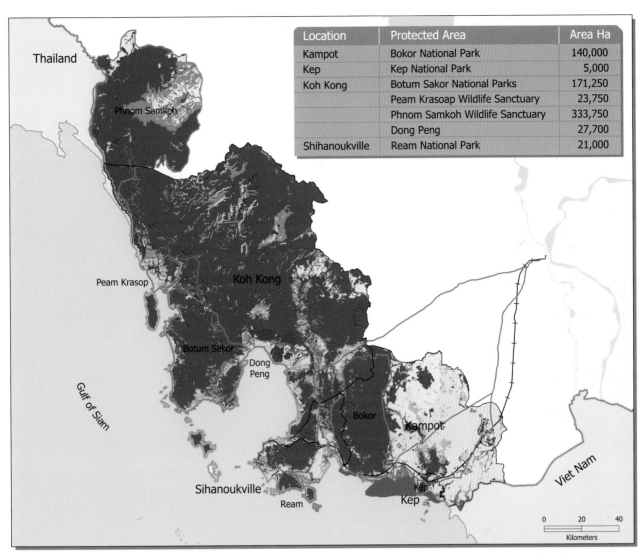

Location	Protected Area	Area Ha
Kampot	Bokor National Park	140,000
Kep	Kep National Park	5,000
Koh Kong	Botum Sakor National Parks	171,250
	Peam Krasoap Wildlife Sanctuary	23,750
	Phnom Samkoh Wildlife Sanctuary	333,750
	Dong Peng	27,700
Shihanoukville	Ream National Park	21,000

Legend

- Mangrove cover 2002
- Mangrove cleared since 1997
- Sea Grass
- Coral Reef
- Bamboo and Secondary forests
- Evergreen forest
- Mixed forest - evergreen and deciduous species
- Deciduous forest
- Grassland
- Woodland and Shrubland
- Marsh and swamp

- Abandoned field
- Paddy field
- Settlement
- Shrimp/Fish farming and Salt pan
- Other
- Water Body
- Protected Areas
- Main Roads
- Railway
- Provincial Boundary
- International Boundary

Data Sources:
Mangrove and Protected Areas: CZM, MoE 2005
Coral Reef and Sea Grass: UNEP (drafted 2004)
Landuse: JICA Dataset 2002
International and Provincial Boundary :
Department of Geography 2005
Water Body: JICA Dataset 2002

Fisheries

The staple diet of Cambodians is rice and the second most important food is fish contributing more than 75% of animal protein in the diet. An additional dietary function of fish is its importance as a source of calcium and vitamin A, especially for the rural poor. Many Cambodians eat fish every day in one form or another: fresh, salted, smoked or Prahoc, a traditional fish paste. The consumption rate is rather high compared to the region, and very high globally. On average, the countrywide consumption rate is 65.5 kg/capita/year (Van Zalinge et al: 2003). Rich fish resources are found in the Great Lake, the Tonle Sap, Mekong and Bassac rivers and their floodplains, and in coastal areas.

Every year, a combination of subsistence, middle-scale and large-scale commercial fishing harvests produce 300,000-430,000 tons of freshwater fish. This production ranks fourth in the world and is worth approximately $US 300 million contributing to about 12% of the GDP, exceeding rice production (Hortle et al: 2004). This illustrates the importance of fresh water fish capture in the daily life of people, their employment as well as the national economy. For many Cambodians, fish and aquatic products constitute their main source of food and additional household income, especially during the rainy season (Ahmed et al: 1999). A household survey in the fishing dependent communes of 8 provinces with a total population of 2.4 million people found that only about 4% of households are engaged in one way or another in large-scale fishing, while 9% are involved in middle-scale and 87% in family fishing activities (Ahmed et al: 1999).

Production
Cambodia experienced a decline in production for the fishing season of 2003-04 reporting total inland fish production at about 250,000 tons (MAFF: 2004). This consisted of 106,400 tons of family fisheries, 75,500 tons of rice field fisheries and 68,100 tons of middle and large scale fisheries. Marine fisheries production contributed an additional 55,000 tons. The highest fish production by

Definitions of Cambodian Fisheries

Fishery	Definition
Small Scale Fisheries	May be operated at anytime in open-access fishery domains and in family-scale fishing areas, in fishing lots during the closed season or in marine fisheries. Only small scale fishing gear is permitted.
Middle Scale Fisheries	May be operated only in the open-access inland or marine fishery domains by using middle-scale fishing gears. These are licensed and may only operate during the fishing season from 1 Oct to 30 June.
Commercial Fisheries	May be operated only in fishing lots of inland or marine fishery domains by using industrial fishing gears. These are licensed through an auction system for a 2-year lease and may only operate during the fishing season.

Small Scale and Marine Fish Production

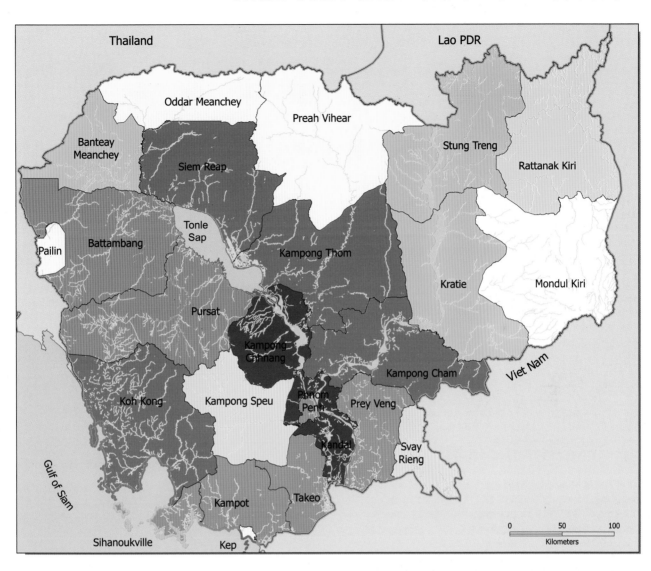

Legend

Small Scale Fish Catch

100 - 200 T	No Data
201 - 500 T	Water Body
501 - 2,500 T	Provincial Boundary
2,501 - 5,000 T	International Boundary
5,001 - 9,000 T	
9,001 - 12,000 T	
12,001 - 15,000 T	

Marine Fish Catch

620 T
5,980 T
21,000 T
28,200 T

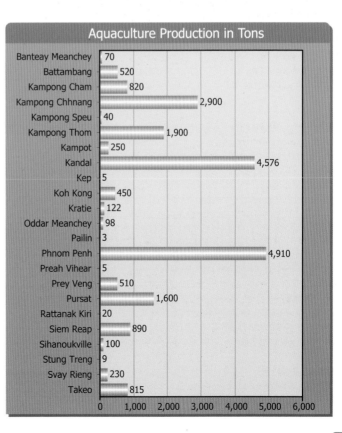

Aquaculture Production in Tons

Province	Tons
Banteay Meanchey	70
Battambang	520
Kampong Cham	820
Kampong Chhnang	2,900
Kampong Speu	40
Kampong Thom	1,900
Kampot	250
Kandal	4,576
Kep	5
Koh Kong	450
Kratie	122
Oddar Meanchey	98
Pailin	3
Phnom Penh	4,910
Preah Vihear	5
Prey Veng	510
Pursat	1,600
Rattanak Kiri	20
Siem Reap	890
Sihanoukville	100
Stung Treng	9
Svay Rieng	230
Takeo	815

Data Sources:
Fish Production:
Agricutural Statistics 2003-2004, MAFF 2004
International and Provincial Boundary:
Department of Geography 2005
Water Body: JICA Dataset 2002
Note: Provincial data only available

family scale fishing ranged from 7,501-9,377 tons in Siem Reap and Kandal provinces. The second highest family scale fish production, ranged from 3,501-7,500 tons and occurred in Pursat, followed by Battambang in the range of 2,501-3,500 tons. These provinces are rich in public fisheries such as released fishing lot areas, lakes, streams, swamps and reservoirs where only family scale fishing is permitted. The lowest production ranged from less than 250 tons and occurred in Preah Vihear and Oddar Meanchey in the upland areas.

Another form of family fishing is rice field fisheries which range from 25-62 kg/ha. These are important to rural livelihoods as they provide a source of protein and enhance food security when crop yields are low. They may also generate an additional income to people not in the fish domain area. Rice field fisheries include aquatic species that migrate into rice field ecosystems during the flooded season such as fish, crabs, shrimps, frogs, beetles, snails and aquatic plants.

Siem Reap and Kampong Chhnang have the highest fish production from commercial scale fisheries with an estimated 11,001-12,350 tons. This is followed by Pursat and Kandal which produce 5,501-11,000 tons and Battambang which produces 5,400 tons. These provinces still contain many fishing lots and have open access to fishing grounds suitable for middle scale fisheries. Presently, Kratie and Stung Treng produce approximately 1000 tons from middle scale fisheries, although there are numerous subsistence fishers in these areas. In Banteay Meanchey only a small area of fishing lots remain.

Koh Kong has the highest marine fish production at approximately 28,200 tons, followed by Sihanoukville at 21,000 tons, Krong Kaeb at 5,980 tons and Kampot province which produces 620 tons of marine catch (MAFF: 2004). This is generally related to the size of coastal area for each province.

Even though fish and aquatic products are important resources for subsistence and household income, the living standards of fishing communities have changed very little over the last few decades. Most of the fishers live in extreme poverty and are becoming poorer because of the declining yields per fisher from year to year. A possible reason for this decline could be that many believe that fish resources are renewable and common property for all and thus over fishing is common. Also, some fishermen operate using fishing methods such as dynamite, electricity and poisons. These practices have caused negative impacts on the environment resulting in the rapid depletion of fish resources. This decline in fish supply leads to unemployment and further poverty for many.

As an increased number of small scale fishers operate alongside commercial scale operations, the conflicts between these have accelerated. This situation is becoming more and more unfavorable for subsistence farmer-fishers. Abuse of power, inequity in benefit distribution and deprivation from access to fishing grounds have led to severe conflicts and dissatisfaction from thousands of people living along the Mekong River floodplain and around the Tonle Sap Lake (Chan & Nao: 2002). To help solve this issue, the RGC has initiated policy reforms in fisheries management aimed at dealing with the fisheries conflicts among those stakeholders. This involves a participatory management approach encouraging Community Fisheries. Community Fisheries provide opportunity for people to participate actively in the management of fisheries resources and achieve the goals of protection, conservation, development and sustainable use and management of fisheries resources to aid poverty alleviation.

Aquaculture

Aquaculture can provide economic opportunities especially to people in regions remote from rivers and wetlands thus enhancing food security. The raising of catfish and snake head in cages and pens originated in the Great Lake and it is now widespread throughout the country. Another form of aquaculture is pond culture of river and exotic species. Rice field aquaculture is still limited in Cambodia but is gradually being recognized by farmers as an important source of protein, supplementary income generation and as a source of fertilizer for rice crops. Aquaculture provides fish supply for domestic consumption and some high value species are exported to Thailand, Viet Nam, Singapore, Hong Kong and Malaysia. Shrimp farming was favourable in the coastal areas between 1988 and 1991 but disease outbreaks and pollution collapsed shrimp farming in 1999. Other forms of aquaculture in the coastal area include seaweed, finfish and crab fattening.

Status of Scientific Knowledge on Fish and Fisheries in Cambodia

- Information on fish growth is available for only 8 % of fish species, diet is known for only 6 %, and information on reproduction is available for just one fourth of these species. There is no information about the ecology, population dynamics and population genetics of most fish species.

- The relationship between diversity, density and extent of floodplain vegetation or habitats and fish stock or catch has never been quantified.

- The scientific assessment of the catch of subsistence fisheries (roughly one-third of the total catch) is based on household consumption studies led in 1995-1996. There has been no field-based update of the scientific assessment of the catch of the mobile gear and lot fisheries (about one quarter and one-fifth of the total fish catch respectively) in the past 10 years. Rice field fisheries (a quarter of the catch) have never been scientifically assessed on a large scale.

- The dai fishery is the only fishery currently monitored; it represents only 4 to 5% of the overall fish production and is specialized, targeting long distance migrant species.

- The estimates of the number of persons who earn their livelihood from fishing and their socio-economic conditions are also very sketchy. These estimates were also made in 1995 and this source is quoted ad infinitum or updated using guesstimates of trends

Source: Kurien J. et al : 2006.

Fishing Lots

During the French colonial period from 1872 to 1886 fishers protested the exclusive lot exploitation by the French protectorate. Following that protest in 1889 the French authority made a slight reform of fisheries and kept about 7 % of the lot areas for subsistence fishing (Touch: 2001). Since that time the management of fishing lots has been based on bureaucratic and exclusive

Fish Production and Fishing Lots

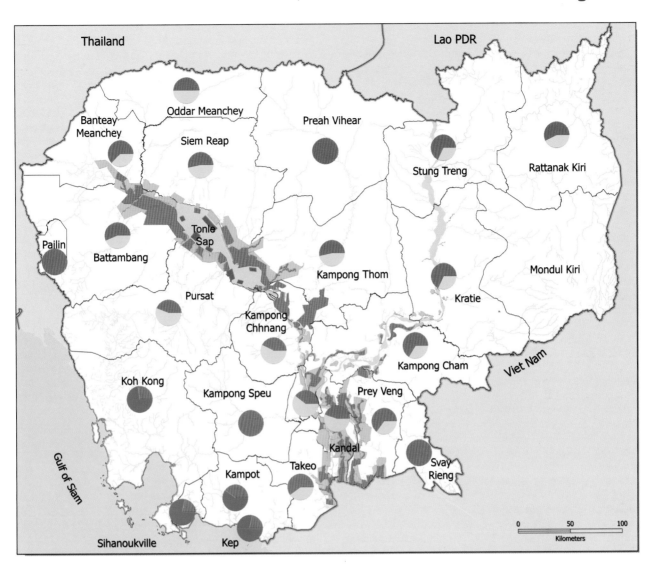

Legend

- Small Scale fish catch
- Commercial fish catch
- Marine Fish Catch

Fishing Lots

- Existing Fishing Lot Area
- Released Fishing Lot Area
- Fish Sanctuaries
- Water Body
- Provincial Boundary
- International Boundary

Data Sources:
Catch Fish: Agricultural Statistics 2003-2004
Fishing Lots: MAFF 2001
International and Provincial Boundary:
Department of Geography 2005
Water Body: JICA Dataset 2002

PROVINCE	SMALL SCALE FISH CATCH	COMMERCIAL FISH CATCH	MARINE FISH CATCH
Banteay Meanchey	2,000	1,200	-
Battambang	8,000	6,250	-
Kampong Cham	12,000	6,100	-
Kampong Chhnang	13,000	17,400	-
Kampong Speu	500	NA	-
Kampong Thom	10,000	8,800	-
Kampot	4,000	NA	6,045
Kandal	15,000	18,500	-
Koh Kong	11,000	NA	29,549
Kratie	2,500	1,200	-
Mondul Kiri	NA	NA	-
Phnom Penh	5,000	7,500	-
Preah Vihear	100	NA	-
Prey Veng	4,000	2,200	-
Pursat	9,000	11,400	-
Rattanak Kiri	400	300	-
Siem Reap	11,000	9,800	-
Sihanoukville	5,000	NA	18,211
Stung Treng	2,500	1,200	-
Svay Rieng	500	NA	-
Takeo	4,000	2,700	-
Oddar Meanchey	200	200	-
Kep	200	NA	737
Pailin	100	NA	-

access rights. Many believe this management regime has resulted not only in the deterioration of the socio-economic conditions of the fishing community, but also the gradual depletion of fisheries resources. However, some commentators would argue that lot fisheries with their restricted access and inbuilt incentive for leasees to conserve the resource base are much more attuned to resource conservation than are open access fisheries. Alternatively, the fishing lot management system has the potential to be exploited as each lot is allocated at auction on a two year cycle. Thus leaseholders may show little regard for sustainability of resources.

In each fishing lot, there have been some open-access areas for small scale fishing, however, during recent years lot leaseholders have deprived local communities from access to those areas. At times the lot armed guards would confiscate fishing nets, traps and row boats of subsistence fishers. Some fatal incidents have occurred in this conflict of interest. In 2000, the RGC declared the need for structural and spatial fisheries reform for the entire country to ensure more fishing grounds for subsistence fishing to help alleviate poverty among rural farmer-fishing communities and to reduce conflicts (Chan & Nao: 2002). Approximately 56% of fishing areas were released from fishing lots. In these areas, management by local users organized as Community Fisheries (CF), government technical agencies and other related stakeholders, were encouraged to ensure Fisheries Co-management. In total the area set aside by the reform for local communities is 536, 302 ha or 56 % of the total lot area of 953,740 ha in 12 provinces. Thus the lot area remaining is 417,438 ha. The lots worth less than Riel 30 million were abolished and kept for subsistence fishing. In addition to the release of the fishing concessions, an exemption of fishing fees was granted from all middle-scale fishing to help alleviate the pressures (Chan & Nao: 2002).

Immediately after the policy reforms, communities located within or adjacent to released fishing lot areas perceived positive impacts on their livelihoods through:

- Easier and more secure access to fisheries resources
- Reduced costs due to the lifting of license fees on middle-scale fishing
- Improved income
- Improved food security

Access to fishing areas has improved, but there are concerns regarding the sustainability of the benefits that this improved access has allowed, particularly for poorer groups who are increasingly suffering from the high levels of competition seen on newly opened fishing areas (PRIAC: 2004). Without an adequate management plan, there is the threat of on going habitat destruction. High value fish species are most vulnerable to habitat destruction as their reproductive cycles are typically longer. In contrast, low value fish species are more resilient to fishing pressures and as a result make up a greater proportion of the fish catch. This has an effect on the value of the fish catch per unit especially in relation to labour efforts of the fishers. Therefore it is important that Community Fisheries share the benefits, responsibilities and roles for the sustainable uses of fisheries resources and management.

Community Fisheries

The Community Fisheries Development Office (CFDO) was established in 2001 to facilitate and coordinate the urgent need for organizing Community Fisheries. After the fisheries reform, open access areas were substantially extended. However, before Community Fisheries became organized many opportunistic fishers using illegal and destructive methods attempted to fish in the open access areas and in fish sanctuaries. In addition, the flooded forests in Takeo, Kandal, and Prey Veng were encroached and cleared for agricultural purposes. To help curb this situation and to sustainably conserve and protect the natural resources through a participatory approach, Community Fisheries needed to be organized as soon as possible around the areas set aside for subsistence fishing. After more than four years of consultation with all related stakeholders from the grassroots to national level the sub-decree for Community Fisheries was fully approved in 2005. However, the guidelines of Community Fisheries such as by-laws, the agreement of Community Fisheries fishing grounds, and management plans are still being finalized. In 2001, the Government established a series of guidelines for the development of Community Fisheries as an interim measure. As a result, many Community Fisheries were established and acknowledged prior to 2005.

The Sub Decree defines Community Fisheries as a group of persons holding Khmer citizenship who live in or near the fishing area who have taken the initiative to improve their own standard of living by voluntarily using and processing fisheries resources sustainably and thus helping to contribute to socio-economic improvements and poverty alleviation.

The objective of organizing Community Fisheries is to:
- Implement the RGC policy in fishery management to guarantee equitable distribution of benefits from fisheries resources to all inhabitants.
- Empower local communities in a participatory fisheries management scheme as part of administrative reform for good governance through decentralization.
- Facilitate the community to gain knowledge on fisheries and to encourage the responsibility and capacity to sustainably manage the fisheries.
- Build the capacity of the community to attract funds from national and international sources.
- Provide the opportunity for both genders to participate in any decision making that may affect their livelihood. These decisions form the basis for self-reliance and responsibility.
- Facilitate communication between communities in experience, technical know-how and information sharing.
- Build and guarantee a permanent structure for the management and protection of fisheries resources especially the abolishment of anarchy in fishing and provide sustainable fisheries management plans. (Chan & Nao: 2002)

According to the CFDO, there are currently almost 388 Community Fisheries established in Cambodia for both inland and coastal areas. The monitoring and evaluation of Community Fisheries is carried out at both provincial and municipal levels. To date, evaluation suggests that the implementation of Community Fisheries has reduced illegal fishing and conflicts in these areas. Also, there are claims that fish production is improving in Community Fisheries where there are fish sanctuaries. Many fishers have understood the concept of participatory fisheries resource management through the implementation of Community Fisheries.

Community Fisheries

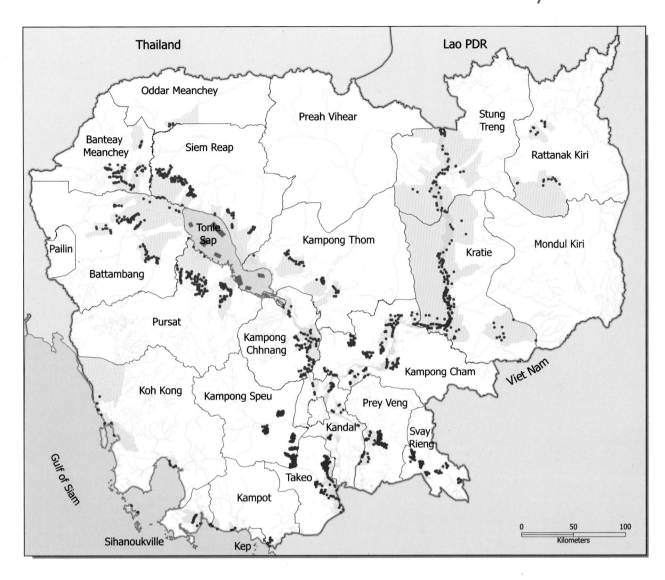

Legend

- Village Centers
- Community Fisheries
- Fish Sanctuaries
- Water Body
- —— Provincial Boundary
- —— International Boundary

Data Sources:
Community Fisheries: DoF, MAFF 2005
International and Provincial Boundary:
Department of Greography 2005
Water Body: JICA Dataset 2002

COMMUNITY FISHERIES

Province	Number of Districts	Number of Communes	Number of Villages	Number of Community Fisheries
Banteay Meanchey	4	10	65	16
Battambang	4	15	41	35
Kampong Cham	9	18	23	16
Kampong Chhnang	4	11	44	44
Kampong Speu	4	8	9	9
Kampong Thom	4	7	17	17
Kampot	2	3	8	7
Kandal	4	10	19	17
Koh Kong	4	6	6	6
Kratie	4	27	51	51
Mondul Kiri	NA	NA	NA	NA
Phnom Penh	3	9	13	1
Preah Vihear	1	1	4	2
Prey Veng	3	9	31	23
Pursat	4	11	33	22
Rattanak Kiri	4	6	NA	5
Siem Reap	6	16	116	14
Sihanoukville	NA	NA	21	12
Stung Treng	5	14	51	51
Svay Rieng	3	7	9	9
Takeo	NA	NA	88	21
Oddar Meanchey	3	3	12	3
Kep	1	1	1	1

Water Quality

There are enough renewable sources of fresh water available in Cambodia for everybody to have plenty, with approximately 35,000 m³ of water per person per year at the current population (Gleick: 1998). So while the quantity of water available is not an issue, the quality of this water is something that needs careful attention as not all water is fit for drinking (or other purposes) without some form of treatment.

Just like water itself comes in many different forms (rain water, surface water and ground water) so does water contamination. The biggest risk to health comes from microbial contamination: disease causing bacteria, viruses and other micro-organisms. Usually, the risk of microbial contamination of ground water is much smaller than that of surface water.

A risk is also posed by chemical contamination with compounds such as arsenic, fluoride or nitrate. Not all chemicals in water cause disease, but some may make the water taste bad enough that people stop using it, and switch to another source which may be of worse microbial quality. This happens for example with iron and manganese, both of which can be found in Cambodia's ground water. In this way, even chemicals that do not pose a direct risk to health may still end up causing health risks indirectly.

The effects of microbial contamination are usually immediate, while problems caused by chemical contamination are chronic; they take a long time to appear, and may be hard to get rid of. Children, older people and people with a weakened immune system are most likely to be affected by water of low quality. Every year many people die, and many working days are lost through disease caused by a combination of drinking water of bad microbial quality, not having enough water close to the home, not using a latrine, and not practicing simple hygiene behaviors such as hand washing with water and soap.

In Cambodia, most people prefer to use rain water. Surface water is also popular, in spite of its risks to health. There are large numbers of communal tubewells, which were mostly provided by external agencies. Currently more families invest in their own family well, and in a growing number of small towns and large villages it is becoming possible to get a private connection to a piped water supply.

While generally speaking the ground water of Cambodia is of good quality, from a chemical perspective it poses bigger challenges than the surface water (Feldman and Rosenboom: 2001). Ground water in certain areas of the country contain chemicals that are of concern to public health. Most of these occur naturally, although the elevated nitrate levels found in some places may be a result of human activity, such as from pit latrines or fertilizers. The biggest risk to health comes from the occurrence of inorganic arsenic in a number of areas along the major rivers. After drinking water with arsenic for a number of years, people can develop a disease called Arsenicosis which eventually results in death. Microbial contamination can be treated by boiling, adding chlorine to the water or using a home treatment system like a ceramic water filter. Chemical contamination is usually harder to treat and the most common step would be to look for a different source of safe water.

Cambodia has national drinking water quality standards, which set down the maximum allowable concentration of many chemicals. For example, drinking water cannot contain more than 0.05 mg/l of arsenic. Drinking water quality is an area of growing attention, and many measurement and mitigation programs are being implemented by UN agencies, NGOs and others, often in cooperation with the Ministry of Rural Development or the Ministry of Industry, Mines and Energy. These programs aim to identify the scale of any water quality issues, develop alternatives, and address the problems at the source or in the home.

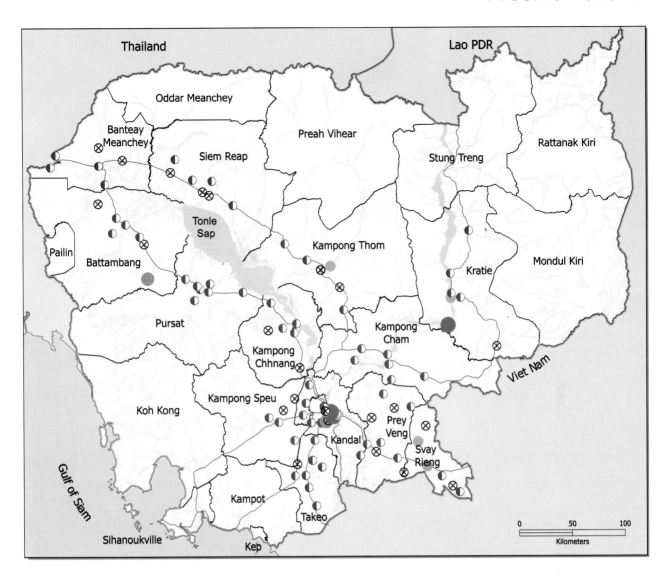

Thailand

Lao PDR

Oddar Meanchey

Banteay
Meanchey

Siem Reap

Preah Vihear

Stung Treng

Rattanak Kiri

Pailin

Battambang

Tonle
Sap

Kampong Thom

Kratie

Mondul Kiri

Pursat

Kampong
Chhnang

Kampong
Cham

Viet Nam

Koh Kong

Kampong Speu

Kandal

Prey
Veng

Svay
Rieng

Gulf of Siam

Kampot

Takeo

Sihanoukville

Kep

0   50   100
Kilometers

Legend

⊗ Below Detection Limit

◐ <= 10 Ug/l

● 11-50 Ug/l

● 51-100 Ug/l

● >100 Ug/l

Province not sampled

Sampled province

Water Body

— Main Roads

— Provincial Boundary

— International Boundary

Data Sources:
Arsenic Hazard: point data from Feldman
and Rosenboom 2000, Arsenic risk map UNICEF 2004
International and Provincial Boundary:
Department of Geography 2005
Water Body: JICA Dataset 2002

References

Ahmed M., Hap N., Ly V. and Santos R. 1999. Fish Consumption Patterns in Major Freshwater Fisheries Provinces of Cambodia. Naga, The ICLRAM Quarterly, Vol. 22, 2: 27-31

CEPA. 2001. Mangrove Resource Study in Cambodia. Culture and Environment Preservation Association with Financial Support by the Netherlands Committee for IUCN. Phnom Penh, Cambodia

Degen P., Van Acker F., Van Zalinge N. and Thuok N. 2000. Taken for Granted: Conflicts over Cambodia's Freshwater Fish Resources. Paper prepared for the 8th IASCP Conference, Bloomington, Indiana

DoF. 2003. Community Fishery Development in Cambodia. Department of Fisheries

DoF. 2000. Fishery Situation Report for September 2000. Department of Fisheries

DoF. 2005. Annual Report on Fishery Situation 2004 and plan for 2005. Department of Fisheries

Howe C.P., Claridge G.F., Hughes R. and Zuwendra. 1991. Report of Manual of Guidelines for Scoping EIA in Tropical Wetlands. PHPA/AWI Sumatra wetland project No. 5 (Draft), Indonesia

Feldman P., and Rosenboom J. 2001. Drinking Water Quality Assessment in Cambodia. World Health Organization for the United Nations. Phnom Penh, Cambodia

IFSR. 2004. Independent Forest Sector Review. Royal Danish Embassy / Development Cooperation Section and Forest Administration. Phnom Penh, Cambodia

Kurien J., Baran E. and So Nam. 2006. Factors that drive Cambodia's inland fish catch: what role can Community Fisheries play? Policy brief. WorldFish Center and Inland Fisheries Research and Development Institute. Phnom Penh, Cambodia

Hortle K.G., Lieng S. and Valbo-Jorgensen J. 2004. An Introduction to Cambodia's Inland Fisheries. Mekong River Commission Series N0 4. Mekong River Commission. Phnom Penh, Cambodia

Mam, K. 2004. Institutional Framework for Wetlands Management in Cambodia

Mastaller M. 1999. Environmental Management of the Coastal Zone of Cambodia: Assessment of Sustainable Livelihood Alternatives to Mangrove Exploitation. Kampsax International for Danida/Ministry of Environment Coastal and Environmental Management Phase I

MoE. 1999. National Wetland Action Plan. Ministry of Environment and Wetlands International. Phnom Penh, Cambodia

MoE/CZM. 2005. State of Coastal Environment and Socio-Economic Report. Ministry of Environment. Phnom Penh, Cambodia

MRC. 2003. State of the Basin Report: 2003. Mekong River Commission, Phnom Penh. ISSN: 1728:3248

MWBASUP. 2005. The Case Study undertaken in February, 2005. The Mekong Wetlands Biodiversity and Sustainable Use Programme

Neou B., Mam K., Mao K., Kim S. and Srun L.S. 2005. Towards a Holistic Approach to Wetlands Governance: The Legal and Institutional Framework and Economic Valuation of Wetlands Resources in Cambodia. In Oh, E., Ratner, B., Bush, S., Kolandai, K., and Too, T. (eds.) Wetlands Governance in the Mekong Region: Country Report on the Legal and Institutional Framework and Economic Valuation of Aquatic Resources. WorldFish Center. Penang, Malaysia

PRIAC. 2004. Policy Reform Impact Assessment (PRIAC), Cambodia. Impacts of the fisheries policy reforms in Kampong Cham, Pursat and Takeo province. 1st round assessment report. CFDO/DoF, IMM Ltd & DFID

RGC. 2000. Wetland classification system for Cambodia. A report of the Inventory and Management of Cambodia Wetland Project (MRC-Danida). Phnom Penh, Cambodia

Chan S. and Thuok N. 2002. Recent Fisheries Reform in Cambodia

Thuok N. and Sina L. 1997. Review of the Fisheries and aquaculture sector in Cambodia. Paper prepared for the natural resource based development strategy for the Tonle Sap area project. Department of Fisheries. Phnom Penh, Cambodia

Touch S. T. 2001. Fishing Lots Mirror Cambodia's History. The Cambodia Daily, May 5-6, 2001

Van Zalinge N., Degen P., Pongsri C., Nuov S., Jesen J.G., Nguyen V.H., Choulamany X. 2003. The Mekong River System, Proceeding of the large River Symposium. Phnom Penh 11-14 February 2003

Agriculture

Agriculture

Agriculture is central to the domestic economy of Cambodia and integral to the fabric of Cambodian rural life. Although the contribution to the GDP of crops and livestock has declined to 20% in 2004, this is more a reflection of the growth in industry as the absolute value of agricultural output has increased (NIS: 2005). Farm rice production remains significantly important to the food security of the largely subsistent population of farmers and their families and rice consumption is expected to remain high until GDP/capita increases considerably (Nesbitt: 2005). The total cultivated area of Cambodia in 2004 was 2.47 million hectares, 90% of which is committed to rice farming with the remainder to multi cropping systems (NIS: 2005).

Agriculture in Cambodia remains at a reasonably undeveloped state and farms are generally characterized by low input and low output systems. Low input, the generally poor soil quality and the highly seasonal availability of water resources all contribute to comparatively low yields. However, there is considerable scope for increasing the scale, intensity and efficiency of agricultural production (MRC: 2003). The State of The Basin Report (2003), warns that without careful management, increasing agricultural productivity could come at the cost of greater pressures on both land and water resources.

Data Sources

The main source of data for agriculture is the survey data collections of the Ministry of Agriculture, Forestry and Fisheries (MAFF). Data for cultivated area, harvested area and yields occur at national level and according to research studies by NGOs, agricultural production estimates produced by MAFF underestimate crop and

livestock production by around 5-10% (NIS: 2005).

Rice

Rice is the most important crop in Cambodia providing an estimated 70% of nutritional energy needs (SOER: 2004). The most recent data shows the total cultivated area of rice in 2003-04 was 2.3 million hectares, compared to 2.2 million hectares in 2001 (MAFF: 2004). 2.2 million hectares were harvested in 2003 compared to 1.9 million hectares in 2001. Yield per hectare increased slightly from 2.07 tons in 2001 to 2.1 tons in 2003. However, overall production fell from 4.1 million tons in 2001 to 3.8 million tons in 2002 possibly due to flooding. Production then increased to 4.7 million tons in 2003. In 2002, rice production was at its lowest level since the drought in 1998.

Prey Veng and Takeo share 13% and 10% of the total rice cultivated areas respectively. This majority share is mainly due to dry season rice cultivation of which these provinces contributed approximately 21% of the total for 2003-04. The second largest cultivated area of dry season rice is Kandal which has 51,939 ha, equal to 18% of the total. Kandal has the richest soil suitable for rice cultivation with a yield of 3.3 tons/ha. The lowest yield occurs in Oddar Meanchey with 1.7 tons/ha (MAFF: 2004).

In 1995, Cambodia produced a surplus of rice after years of deficiency and continued to remain in surplus from 1995 through to 2000. Nesbitt, (2005), estimates that Cambodia has the potential to produce a 150,000-200,000 tonne surplus of milled rice in a good year using current farming practices. Although Cambodia is currently experiencing an annual rice production surplus,

Rice Growing Area and Production

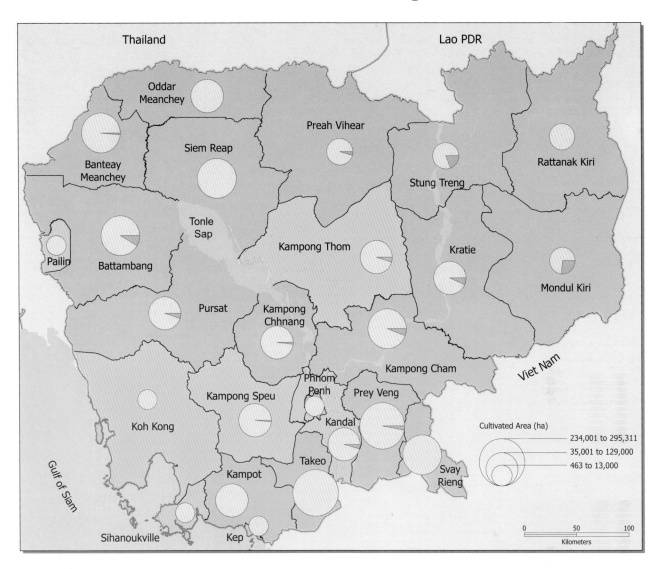

Thailand

Lao PDR

Oddar Meanchey

Preah Vihear

Siem Reap

Banteay Meanchey

Rattanak Kiri

Stung Treng

Tonle Sap

Pailin

Battambang

Kampong Thom

Kratie

Mondul Kiri

Pursat

Kampong Chhnang

Kampong Cham

Viet Nam

Phnom Penh

Prey Veng

Koh Kong

Kampong Speu

Kandal

Cultivated Area (ha)

234,001 to 295,311

35,001 to 129,000

463 to 13,000

Gulf of Siam

Takeo

Kampot

Svay Rieng

Sihanoukville

Kep

0   50   100
Kilometers

Rice Ecosystems

Legend

	Harvested Area
	Non Harvested Area
	Rice Deficit Province
	Rice Surplus Province

Rice Ecosystems

	Rainfed upland rice
	Recession Rice
	Deep Water/Floating Rice
	Rainfed lowland rice
	Water Body
	Provincial Boundary
	International Boundary

Data Sources:
Major Food Crops: Agricultural Statistics,
MAFF 2003-2004
Rice Ecosystems: IRRI Project (CIRP)
International and Provincial Boundary:
Department of Geography 2005
Water Body: JICA Dataset 2002

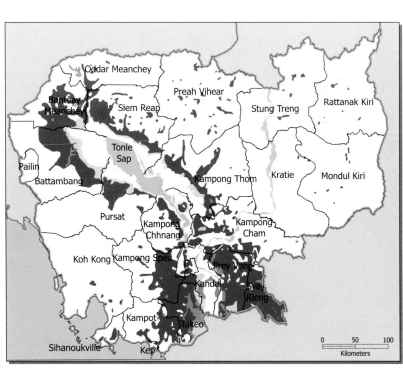

Oddar Meanchey

Banteay Meanchey

Preah Vihear

Siem Reap

Stung Treng

Rattanak Kiri

Tonle Sap

Pailin

Battambang

Kampong Thom

Kratie

Mondul Kiri

Pursat

Kampong Chhnang

Kampong Cham

Koh Kong

Kampong Speu

Prey Veng

Kandal

Svay Rieng

Kampot

Takeo

Sihanoukville

Kep

0   50   100
Kilometers

a majority of the farm households find it difficult to meet their daily requirements and have a surplus for sale and income generation. Additionally, some provinces experience chronic shortages despite the national sufficiency (MRC: 2003). Production levels may be considered fragile as they are highly susceptible to floods and drought.

Contributing factors to an increase in crop yields include the increased availability and application of agrochemicals, better management practices such as IPM, the introduction of improved rice varieties known as High Yielding Varieties (HYVs) as well as the increased availability of agriculture land. As the population continues to grow, agricultural productivity must increase. A recent paper by Nesbitt (2005) analyses population growth rate and agricultural production levels and concludes that at the current rate of population growth, Cambodia will need to increase paddy rice production by 1.57 million tonnes if it is to feed its projected population in 2020.

Rice Ecoregions

The major rice growing areas can be classified into four agro ecosystems which are influenced by rainfall, soil suitability and topography. These are broadly defined as:

Rainfed Lowland Rice Ecosystems

This rice agro ecosystem represents approximately 86% of Cambodia's cultivated rice cropping area and is concentrated around the Mekong River and the Tonle Sap (O'Brien: 1999). It is characterized by flat bunded rice fields which depend almost entirely on rainfall or surface run off. These varieties are adapted to flooded (waterlogged) soil conditions.

Rainfed Upland Rice Ecosystems

This rice ecosystem accounts for approximately 2% of Cambodia's cultivated rice cropping area. These are typically unbunded fields occurring in the upland areas. Upland rice is an integral part of the shifting cultivation areas of the Northeast.

Deep Water/floating Rice Ecosystems

These rice ecosystems occur in low lying areas that accumulate flood water from a depth of 50cm to a maximum of 3m for at least one month during the year (O'Brien: 1999). Deepwater rice production areas account for only 4% of the total annual rice crop and occur in the flood prone areas of the Mekong and Tonle Sap.

Recession Rice Ecosystems

Dry season rice production accounts for 8% of the total rice cropping area (O'Brien 1999). Dry season production is typically located in areas close to the major rivers and their floodplains. Dry season rice production is generally associated with higher yields.

Rice Growing Area, Production and Balance

Province	Harvested Area ha	Yield Tons/ha	Surplus and deficit Tons
Banteay Meanchey	184,562	1.8	72,345
Battambang	205,300	2.2	108,418
Kampong Cham	195,608	2.5	8,005
Kampong Chhnang	108,419	1.7	32,044
Kampong Speu	94,129	1.9	-1,231
Kampong Thom	122,074	1.4	-1,546
Kampot	123,962	2.3	74,136
Kandal	91,845	3.3	-5,617
Koh Kong	7,929	1.6	-19,287
Kratie	33,109	2.9	6,593
Mondul Kiri	9,918	1.9	4,832
Phnom Penh	7,930	2.7	-169,940
Preah Vihear	21,217	1.9	1,554
Prey Veng	286,950	2.2	207,946
Pursat	71,672	1.9	15,267
Rattanak Kiri	22,247	2.1	9,373
Siem Reap	183,544	1.4	22,682
Sihanoukville	10,640	2.7	-13,084
Stung Treng	16,626	2.0	4,441
Svay Rieng	172,397	1.8	98,878
Takeo	232,883	2.6	216,172
Oddar Meanchey	35,708	1.7	19,420
Kep	2,904	2.5	-1,118
Pailin	463	2.8	-3,787

Source: Agricultural Statistics 2003-2004, Food Balance 2003-2004, MAFF

Average Farm Gate Price of Paddy

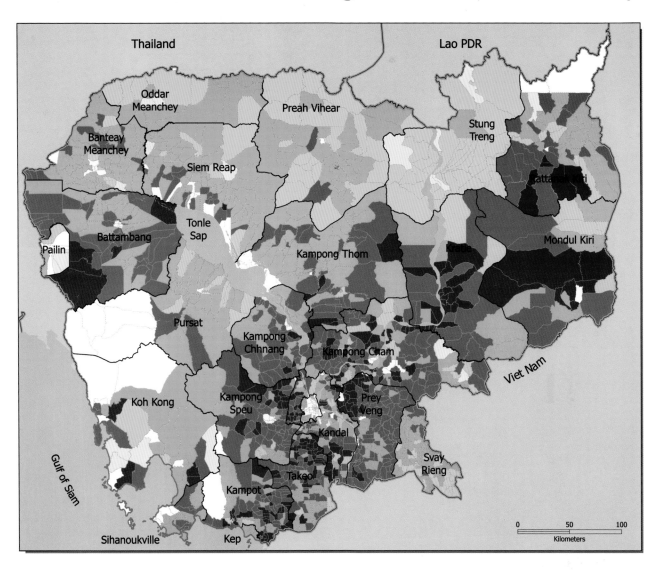

Irrigation

Legend

Price of Paddy December 2004

- 64 - 300 Riel
- 301 - 400 Riel
- 401 - 500 Riel
- 501 - 600 Riel
- 601 - 900 Riel

% of families
with irrigation

- 0.1 - 15
- 15.1 - 25
- 25.1 - 50
- 50.1 - 75
- 75.1 - 100
- No irrigation or no data
- Water Body
- —— Provincial Boundary
- —— International Boundary

Data Sources:
Average Farm Gate Price and Irrigation:
Commune Database 2004
International and Provincial Boundary:
Department of Geography 2005
Water Body: JICA Dataset 2002

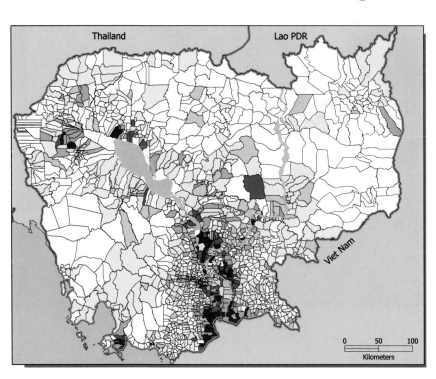

Price of Paddy

The price of paddy fluctuates significantly according to yield, season, variety, quality and location. Cambodian rice prices are also influenced by world market prices, however only a small proportion of local production enters this market. Most rice sold for export is by small scale informal traders who sell to Thailand and Viet Nam. The major official rice exporter in Cambodia is the Angkor Rice Mill Company.

Obviously, in years of low yield, prices are high and in high yield years the reverse is true. Prices are also highest just before the main harvest period in December. Most of the rice grown during the year is sold at this time and thus it is appropriate and useful to analyse price data for this month. The fact that many farmers are significantly in debt by rice harvest and have to immediately sell a large proportion of their crop to repay loans, decreases prices at this time of year. Also contributing to price fluctuations is an increased supply of rice post harvest whilst demand remains stable.

In general, aromatic rice varieties such as Phkar Mali command the highest prices, and as rice self sufficiency and surplus grows, an increased demand for these varieties can be expected. As illustrated in the Average Farm gate Price of Paddy map, at the commune level, the price of rice fluctuates quite markedly. A contributing factor to this is that in communes where the livelihood of the people does not depend on rice, the price of paddy is generally higher than the main rice producing communes. Thus most of the provinces located around the Tonle Sap Lake, the upper and lower Mekong River and the central plain of Cambodia generally have lower paddy prices of 341-390 riel/kg.

With inadequate milling, farmers generally receive a lower price for paddy. With improved processing of their product, farmers will derive a greater return from their farm output. Additionally, improvements in local mills would increase the quality of grain returned to farmers. Other factors contributing to the low price of paddy include poor infrastructure which leads to increased transportation costs, increased supply with little change in demand and further indebtedness with high interest rates from money lenders. Considering the extent of rice production in Cambodia, total income from rice production is very small. For example, when the farm gate price of paddy was set at US$0.08 per kilogram for paddy, the total rice production in Cambodia was valued at US$27 per person (Nesbitt: 2005).

Maize

Maize is the most important non-rice crop. Production levels of Maize declined significantly between 1980 and 1990. This was mainly due to political instability in the major production area of the Northwest. Between 1991 and 2000 production strongly increased by an average of 11 % (SOER: 2004). Often Maize is cultivated along the more fertile soils of river banks. Planting takes place early in the wet season with harvest in August or September just prior to floods. Cultivated areas of Maize are mostly concentrated in Battambang which produces some of the highest yields averaging 5.4 tons/ha. Battambang and Pailin combined produce 253,499 tons of Maize, accounting for 80% of national production.

Maize is cash rather than a subsistent crop and thus has the potential to improve the rural economy. For example, the concentration of Maize in Battambang is largely as a response to supplying feed to the Thai livestock market (WB: 2006). With an improved marketing system, there is great potential for further expansion in the production and income generation of Maize.

Maize Production

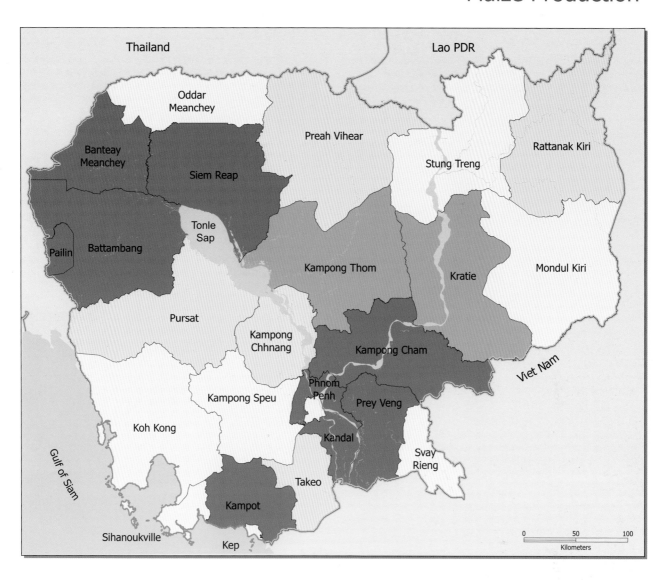

Thailand

Lao PDR

Oddar Meanchey

Preah Vihear

Rattanak Kiri

Banteay Meanchey

Siem Reap

Stung Treng

Tonle Sap

Pailin

Battambang

Kampong Thom

Kratie

Mondul Kiri

Pursat

Kampong Chhnang

Kampong Cham

Viet Nam

Phnom Penh

Prey Veng

Kampong Speu

Koh Kong

Kandal

Svay Rieng

Gulf of Siam

Takeo

Kampot

Sihanoukville

Kep

Legend

Maize Production

	< 1,000 T
	1,000 - 2,000 T
	2,001 - 3,000 T
	3,001 - 236,295 T
	Water Body
——	Provincial Boundary
——	International Boundary

Data Sources:
Major Food Crops: Agricultural Statistics,
MAFF 2003-2004
International and Provincial Boundary:
Department of Geography 2005
Water Body: JICA Dataset 2002

Maize Growing Area and Production

Province	Harvested Area (Ha)	Yield (T/Ha)	Production (Tons)
Banteay Meanchey	7,745	2.0	15,133
Battambang	43,126	5.5	236,295
Kampong Cham	5,748	1.4	7,848
Kampong Chhnang	1,340	1.5	1,983
Kampong Speu	869	1.0	884
Kampong Thom	857	2.4	2,084
Kampot	1,930	1.6	3,101
Kandal	8,421	1.6	13,797
Koh Kong	527	1.1	603
Kratie	1,279	1.8	2,305
Mondul Kiri	249	1.8	446
Phnom Penh	387	1.5	570
Preah Vihear	748	1.5	1,148
Prey Veng	1,768	1.9	3,406
Pursat	482	2.1	1,032
Rattanak Kiri	526	2.3	1,200
Siem Reap	1,629	1.9	3,122
Sihanoukville	76	1.6	123
Stung Treng	782	0.8	625
Svay Rieng	34	1.2	41
Takeo	644	1.7	1,090
Oddar Meanchey	190	1.9	361
Kep	295	0.7	200
Pailin	4,301	4.0	17,204

Crop Diversification

Opportunities for poverty alleviation in Cambodian agriculture are emerging in diversification from traditional wet season lowland rice production to rice-based double-cropping and upland cropping systems. There are relatively large areas of land available for the expansion of upland cropping, especially with improved security and road construction in rural areas. The potential for double-cropping will depend on an understanding of land capability for a range of non-rice crops in the lowlands and uplands of Cambodia and using the principles of integrated farming systems.

Unfortunately, little information on land suitability for field crops is available to facilitate the process of crop diversification. The Cambodian Agricultural Research and Development Institute (CARDI) have carried out a pilot project to assess land suitability for production of field crops. The project determines soil types, farmer practices, identifies major constraints to land capability and produces land capability maps for various field crops (Bell et al: 2005). The Ministry of Agriculture, Forestry and Fisheries (MAFF) and the Ministry of Land Management, Urban Planning and Construction (MLUPC), will conduct a national level land resources assessment to facilitate the process of land use planning and development (Hunter, pers. Comm., 2005).

Diversification holds many risks, especially to resource poor farmers who operate on cash flow. Adopting new farming practices is a costly process with investments necessary to purchase new seed and other inputs. Additionally, farmers are reluctant to jeopardize their food security (Nesbitt: 2005).

Upland Crops

Currently, non-rice crops only account for approximately 10% of the cultivated area in Cambodia. However, this is likely to increase with the demographic population shift to upland areas, improved communications and better marketing channels.

At present, yield of major field crops in Cambodia is relatively low in comparison to other high input yields throughout the region. After maize, pulses are the next most important group of upland crops, with soybean and mungbean together accounting for 3.8% of the total cultivated area in the country. Mungbean's traditional dominance has been replaced by soybean, due to the demand for the latter as a constituent of animal feeds and increased demand from Viet Nam.

Cassava is the most important root crop in Cambodia with an annual production of some 25,000 tons. The area planted to cassava has been expanding steadily since 1990, and this trend is likely to continue while demand as a component of animal feed remains strong and as less fertile, marginal land is brought into production as cassava is adaptable to these conditions.

Upland Crop Production

Province	SESAME		MUNG		SOYA		PEANUTS		CASSAVA	
	Ha	Tons	Ha	Tons	Ha	Tons	Ha	Tons	Ha	Tons
Banteay Meanchey	118	57	7,097	3,568	2,700	1,350	96	48	333	4,783
Battambang	2,397	2,023	6,357	5,405	12,375	23,056	2,910	4,459	1,193	19,712
Kampong Cham	16,224	9,735	8,652	4,365	28,837	26,242	4,484	5,171	13,093	239,968
Kampong Chnang	65	47	1,381	992	0	0	333	333	460	2,410
Kampong Speu	25	10	1,062	1,592	0	0	494	780	3,378	14,812
Kampong Thom	1,108	861	1,419	1,696	2,636	4,221	403	895	1,135	8,111
Kampot	28	27	2,582	2,614	0	0	604	686	733	3,166
Kandal	912	499	3,475	2,989	227	186	1,152	1,816	247	1,532
Koh Kong	0	0	8	8	0	0	0	0	159	1,185
Kratie	2,876	2,174	247	179	181	222	265	319	178	1,024
Mondul Kiri	33	23	281	263	124	180	112	156	257	3,260
Phnom Penh	25	24	13	17	0	0	6	16	60	333
Preah Vihear	1,773	1,831	652	830	936	1,306	1,286	1,593	118	746
Prey Veng	3,709	3,117	2,135	1,761	0	0	715	760	95	592
Pursat	106	64	331	282	2	2	222	185	310	2,132
Rattanak Kiri	252	198	463	370	1,341	2,425	448	679	314	1,742
Siem Reap	526	241	5,440	3,045	0	0	17	17	924	13,020
Sihanoukville	0	0	0	0	0	0	0	0	114	1,359
Stung Treng	177	107	644	415	0	0	281	170	342	1,569
Svay Rieng	0	0	3	2	0	0	12	6	555	3,876
Takeo	0	0	478	447	0	0	156	129	689	4,094
Oddar Meanchey	79	32	303	490	12	6	82	49	214	495
Kep	0	0	0	0	0	0	77	44	114	653
Pailin	1,773	887	375	485	2,660	3,990	122	172	15	75

Upland Crops

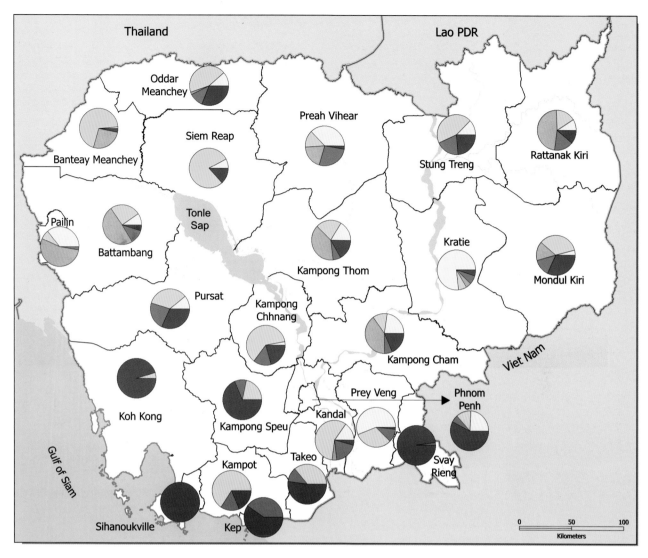

Legend

Harvested Area of upland crops

- Sesame
- Mung
- Soya
- Peanuts
- Cassava

Economic Land Concessions

- Economic Concession
- Evergreen forest
- Semi-Evergreen Forest
- Deciduous forest
- Other forest
- Non forest

Note: Approximately 300,000 ha of economic concessions indicated on map. Total area of approved economic concessions is 791,170 ha. Refer to appendix and page 10 for more information.

Data Sources:
Upland Crops: Agricultural Statistics, MAFF 2003-2004
Economic Concessions: www.maff.gov.kh 2006
Forest Cover 2002: FA
International and Provincial Boundary: Department of Geography 2005
Water Body: JICA Dataset 2002

Indication of Economic Land Concessions

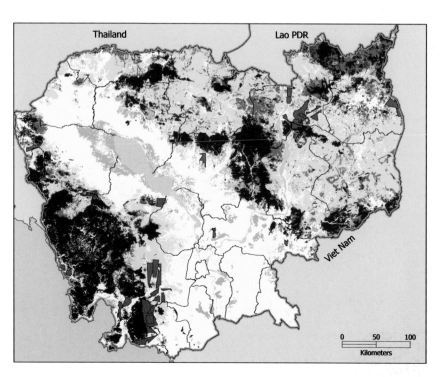

Fruit Trees

In terms of cultivated area, cashew, banana, coconut and mango are the most important fruit crops grown in Cambodia with Kampong Cham, Kandal, Kampong Thom and Kampot the main fruit growing provinces. Kampong Cham's fertile red soils make it particularly favourable for fruit production, most importantly banana and rubber. CARDI and Kbal Kho Research Institutes, under MAFF, have responsibility for fruit tree development. Both are active in this field, and CARDI has recently established a national banana germplasm collection. Research on mango is focusing mainly on varietal improvement. Although the most common tree crop in Cambodia, cashew yields are low. It is unclear whether this is due to the varieties grown or to poor management.

Banana is the most favourable permanent crop and it is grown in all provinces. In addition, Kampong Cham is well known as a banana export province with a total of 10,144 ha of cultivated area dedicated to bananas (MAFF: 2003-04). Kampot ranks as the second largest area to grow bananas with an area of 3,419 ha.

Kampong Cham also has the largest area of cashew nut plantation with 17,136 ha under cultivation. Kampong Thom is the second largest cashew nut producer with 6,371 ha of cultivation. Coconuts are grown in smaller areas and mostly concentrated in Kandal (5,962 ha) and Kampot (3,662 ha). Kampot is also the largest producer of mangos with 2,381 ha under cultivation. This is closely followed by Takeo with 2,379 ha.

Durian, longan, sapodilla and star apple have very small areas of cultivated land. This is especially true of the fruit trees which are mainly grown on homesteads or in the village garden.

IRRIGATION

Irrigation remains the major constraint to intensifying production of paddy and other crops in Cambodia (WB: 2006). The unequal distribution of rainfall and the tendency for the rural poor to be located in marginal areas prone to floods and drought further impedes food security. Moreover, without improved access to reliable water resources, subsistence farmers are less willing to borrow to invest in

high-yield activities such as second crops. Thus, water resources management and control are a basic requirement for increasing agricultural productivity, reducing risk of crop failure and reducing rural poverty.

The extent of irrigation in Cambodia is still low with approximately 7% of the total area of food crops being irrigated (SOER: 2004). The majority of these schemes rely on receding flood waters to irrigate rice with recession rice slowly overtaking lower yielding floating rice systems (MRC: 2003). Additionally, motorized pumps are becoming more common and replacing the traditional manual pumps.

The last extensive study of irrigation systems in Cambodia was conducted in 1993-94 and identified 841 irrigation systems of which 21% were fully operational, 65% were partially operational and 14% were defunct (SOER: 2004). This survey excluded irrigation areas covering less than 10ha.

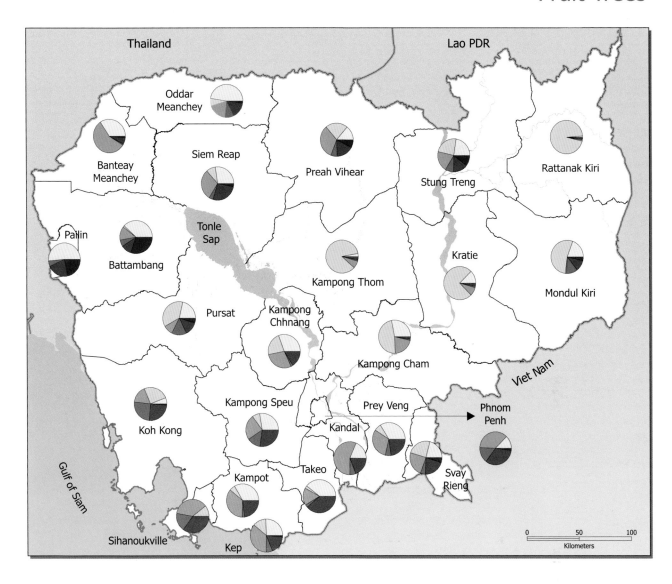

Legend

Harvested Areas

- Banana
- Cashew
- Coconut
- Jackfruit
- Mango
- Orange
- Water Body
- —— Provincial Boundary
- —— International Boundary

Data Sources:
Tree Fruit Crops: Agricultural Statistics,
MAFF 2003-2004
International and Provincial Boundary:
Department of Geography 2005
Water Body: JICA Dataset 2002

Harvested Area of Fruit Trees (Ha)

Province	Banana	Cashew	Coconut	Jackfruit	Mango	Orange
Banteay Meanchey	978	8	1,605	35	178	51
Battambang	1,261	46	446	210	344	1,007
Kampong Cham	10,144	17,136	7,502	485	817	311
Kampong Chnang	267	198	251	18	141	8
Kampong Speu	978	276	857	477	979	32
Kampong Thom	230	6,371	537	99	235	74
Kampot	3,419	576	3,662	251	2,381	102
Kandal	1,985	32	5,962	612	2,015	62
Koh Kong	142	608	402	621	603	27
Kratie	402	2,377	263	41	102	6
Mondul Kiri	180	500	10	104	101	34
Phnom Penh	69	5	198	83	181	11
Preah Vihear	64	100	152	28	77	35
Prey Veng	1,109	232	991	194	758	19
Pursat	259	445	113	176	158	59
Rattanak Kiri	74	6,505	79	83	94	56
Siem Reap	1,238	425	1,362	181	1,219	145
Sihanoukville	6	103	361	175	342	1
Stung Treng	242	253	214	90	157	115
Svay Rieng	504	581	570	115	492	120
Takeo	2,397	175	1,011	153	2,379	56
Oddar Meanchey	416	61	164	77	137	18
Kep	247	127	342	60	170	14
Pailin	19	0	0	2	8	8
Total	**26,630**	**37,140**	**27,054**	**4,370**	**14,068**	**2,371**

Livestock

The increase in livestock in recent years can be seen as a reflection of improved crop production and of the general welfare of farmers (Nesbitt: 2005). Key livestock enterprises in Cambodia are cattle including oxen and buffalo, pigs for breeding and fattening and poultry, mainly chickens with some ducks in areas where water is available. Animal disease is the single most important problem facing the livestock sector. Haemorragic septicemia and foot and mouth disease in cattle, swine fever in pigs and Newcastle disease in poultry are the main concerns. More recently, bird flu has created additional pressures.

Cattle are raised as draft animals for land preparation, kept for breeding and are an important means of transport in rural areas. Cattle are purchased when family cash resources permit and are generally kept as an investment that can be easily liquidated in times of emergency, such as illness or death in the family. Consequently, economic live-weight gain is not a common objective - farmers are more interested in animal survival, and ensuring that draft cattle are in good condition at the time of land preparation. Pigs on the other hand, are very much a farm family cash enterprise. Richer farmers may own a sow and breed and sometimes also fatten piglets. Poorer farmers generally purchase one or two weaners and fatten them for sale. Most farm families keep a few chickens for family consumption, and chicken meat is probably the second most important source of animal protein after fish. Chickens are fed some broken rice and household scraps, but are mainly allowed to run free and scavenge for food. Ducks are raised mainly for the sale of eggs (70%) and some for meat (30%) by farmers who have access to adequate water sources.

The map of families with cattle shows a higher concentration in Cambodia's main rice growing area around the central plain. This is due to higher population density, comparatively greater wealth, the need for draft animals for rice-land preparation and the availability of rice stubble and straw for forage in the dry season. However, these areas experience fodder shortage problems during the rice growing season when most cattle are tethered in the homestead and fed with cut and carry grass.

In contrast, Koh Kong, Mondul Kiri, Rattanak Kiri, Preah Vihear, Oddar Meanchey and Stung Treng have fewer households raising cattle. These provinces have substantial land areas potentially available for grazing. On a percentage basis, Svay Rieng, Kep, Kampot, Kampong Speu and Takeo provinces have the largest proportion of households with cattle.

The map showing the number of families with pigs represents a similar picture with higher numbers of families with livestock in the central provinces. This is also probably due to higher population densities and available cash for investment. Interestingly, on a percentage basis, the more peripheral provinces of Kep, Preah Vihear, Stung Treng and Kampot have the largest proportion of households raising pigs.

Crop-Livestock Interactions

In addition to the obvious importance of cattle as draft animals, there are a number of other important interactions between crop and livestock enterprises. Dried animal manure or manure-based compost is of critical importance for sustaining crop production systems, particularly on sandy infertile soils. Because of its limited availability, manure is mainly used in the rice nursery to promote seedling vigor and to ensure adequate nutrient availability over the extended period that photoperiod sensitive rice varieties may remain in the nursery. Manure is also used for vegetable production in home gardens where it can be applied intensively. In some cases, manure is used in rice-based crop rotations where it is applied to post rice crops such as watermelon, with the residual fertility benefits then being realized in the following year's rice crop in the same field.

Although forage is not widely grown on crop land, crop residues such as rice straw and stubble often provide feed for animals. In addition, grass weeds can provide grazing following field crop harvest and paddy bunds can be an important source of cut-and-carry grass during the wet season.

Type	Trends in livestock (000 heads)		
	1995	2000	2004
Buffalo	764.7	693.7	710.1
Cattle	2,670.1	2,992.7	3,039.9
Pigs	1,967	1,838.3	2,428.6
Poultry	9,762.9	15,249.8	12,990.6

Source: Agricultural Statistics 2003-2004, MAFF

Families with Pigs

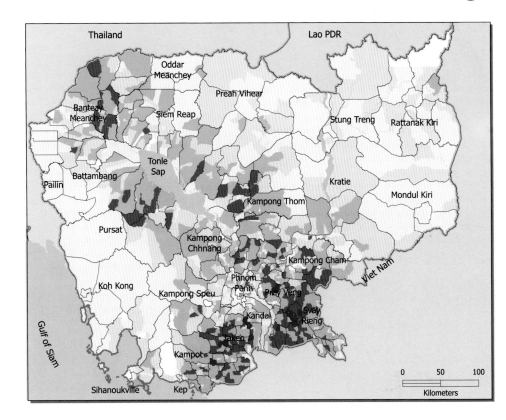

Legend

Families with Pigs

- 3 - 350
- 351 - 750
- 751 - 1,500
- 1,501 - 2,500
- 2,501 - 3,574
- No Data
- Water Body
- —— District Boundary
- —— Provincial Boundary
- —— International Boundary

Families with Cattle and Buffalo

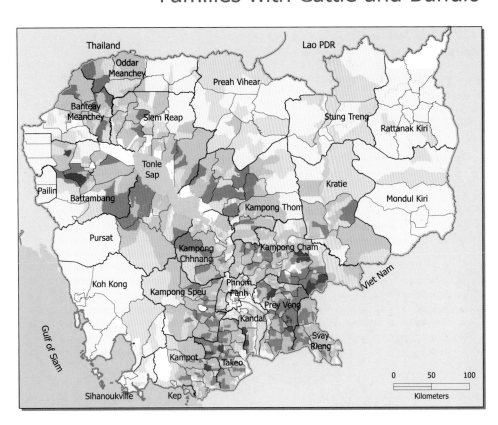

Legend

Families with Cattle and Buffalo

- < 400
- 401 - 800
- 801 - 1,500
- 1,501 - 2,500
- 2,501 - 4,182
- No Data
- Water Body
- —— District Boundary
- —— Provincial Boundary
- —— International Boundary

Data Sources:
Families with Pigs, Cattle and Buffalo:
Commune Database 2004
International, Provincial and
District Boundary: Department of
Geography 2005
Water Body: JICA Dataset 2002

Agriculture

Soils

Morphologically, Cambodia can be considered as a large relatively flat basin, draining gently into the Mekong River delta in Vietnam in the Southeast. The elevation drop is only 40-50m along a 400km axis from Banteay Meanchey in the Northwest to Kandal in the South. Most of the rainfed lowlands have an elevation of < 50m above sea level, even in the Northwest at Battambang.

As can be seen from the rice soil map most of the rice land is centered around the Tonle Sap Lake in the center of the country, and along the Mekong River to its delta in the Southeast. Low hills or uplands are commonly interspersed with the rice-growing lowlands, especially in the provinces of Takeo, Svay Rieng, Kampong Chhnang, Kampong Speu and Kampot. Fringing the central rice growing region are low hills and terraces with lower population density and less intensive agricultural systems. The Southwest, East, and Northern margins are more mountainous and predominantly forest covered, with significant portions designated as nature conservation and protected areas. However, in many of these provinces there are significant lowland and upland areas suited to rice and field crops respectively. Improvements in agricultural production rest on a thorough understanding of the soil resource base coupled with effective land use planning and appropriate policy support.

General Soil Classifications

The soils of Cambodia have developed under a humid to sub humid tropical climate with alternate wet-dry conditions, from the decomposition of acid or basic rocks, colluvial outwash from either or both of these rocks, recent or old alluvial materials and from coastal accretion (Crocker: 1962).

In 1961, a soil survey was initiated by Charles D. Crocker (Crocker: 1962) and an exploratory soils map at a scale of 1:1,000,000 was subsequently produced. The survey gives an inventory of the major great soil groups and elaborates on the geological and physiographic relationships and spatial distribution of these soils. The work established a basis for the country-wide assessment of Cambodia's soil resources and formed the foundation for most of the succeeding soil surveys.

There are several small scale (1:250,000 or smaller) specific-purpose soil surveys in Cambodia, but all are based substantially on Crocker's earlier work. Although the usefulness of Crocker's survey for agronomists is limited by its small scale (1:1,000,000) and unfamiliar nomenclature, Crocker established the link between geological phenomena and the resulting soil development processes and Crocker's work has gained general acceptance in Cambodia up to the present time. (Seng and White: 2005). For a detailed description of Crocker's soil types please refer to the appendix.

Rice Soils

Based on geomorphology, soils of the main rice growing area of Cambodia are divided into three physiographic regions (White et al., 1997):

1. Soils occurring in the old colluvial-alluvial plain. These are formed from previously weathered material that has been transported and deposited at their current location. The areas of old colluvial-alluvial plain are extensive, slightly undulating plains which form the majority of Cambodia's rainfed rice growing area.

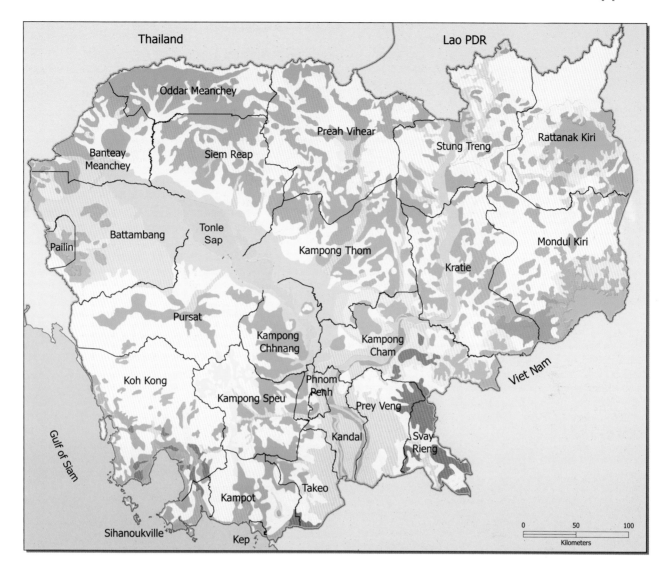

Legend

Soil Type

Acid Lithosols	Planosols
Alluvial Lithosols	Plinthite Podzols
Alumisols	Plinthitic Hydromorphics
Basic Lithosols	Red-yellow Podzols
Brown Alluvial Soils	Regurs
Brown Hydromorphics	

Soil Fertility

Coastal Complex	High Fertility Soil
Cultural Hydromorphics	Medium Fertility Soil
Grey Hydromorphics	Low Fertility Soil
Lacustrine Alluvial Soils	Water Body
Latosols	—— Provincial Boundary
	——— International Boundary

Note: Refer to appendix for soil descriptions
Data Sources:
Soils: CARDI-after crocker, 1962
Soil Fertility: Gene-Ecological Zonation of Cambodia
International and Provincial Boundary:
Department of Geography 2005
Water Body: JICA Dataset 2002

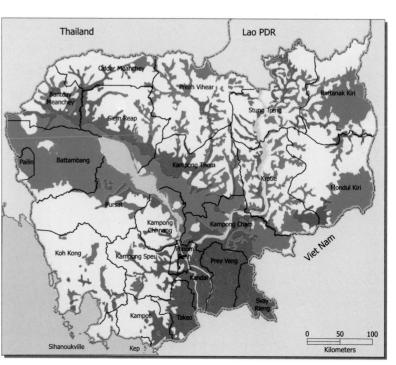

2. Soils occurring in areas of hills and valleys. These soils are developed from decomposition of underlying parent material. They are used for upland rice and non-rice crops

3. Soils of the active floodplains. Soils developed in these areas receive annual deposits of fresh alluvium, and hence are relatively young soils.

The Main Rice Soils

The Cambodian Agronomic Soil Classification (CASC) system together with a manual for identification and management has been widely used for identifying soils in the main rice growing areas (White et al., 1997). The CASC classifies rice soils into 11 soil groups. For a detailed description and management recommendations for the main rice soil groups please refer to the appendix. Most lowland soils of potential use for rice cultivation in Cambodia are low in available nitrogen (N), phosphorus (P), potassium (K), and have low organic matter contents and low cation-exchange capacity (CEC). Hence, nutrient deficiencies represent a major constraint to rice production at present.

Fertilizer use

Fertilizer use in rice has increased significantly from 300 tons in 1989 to 7,900 tons by 1999, but is still very low compared to other countries in the region (FAO: 2001). Despite increased fertilizer demand and use of improved rice varieties, the national average rice yield of 2.1 tons/ha remains low compared to neighbouring countries.

Research has been conducted to determine appropriate rates of chemical fertilizers for the specific soil types identified by the CASC. The recommended rates of fertilizer application, which are based on farmer's socio-economic conditions, vary significantly between soil groups. Nitrogen rates vary from 28-120 kg/ha, phosphorus: 4-15 kg/ha, and potassium: 0-33 kg/ha. Urea, DAP and KCl fertilizers are recommended for most rice soils but other fertilizers, combined to apply the same recommended rate of nutrients, would probably produce similar responses.

The response of rice yield to inorganic fertilizer application varies significantly among the soil groups. On the highly leached sandy soils (Prey Khmer) and acidic clay soils (Koktrap), rice response to combined NPK application remains very poor producing a yield of only 1.8-1.9 t/ha, but on the shallow sandy soils (Prateach Lang) rice yield doubled. On heavier textured soils (Toul Samroung and Bakan), rice yields were generally above 4 tons/ha when combined NPK fertilizer was added. Fertilizer application may result in no increase or increases in rice yield by 13-90%. Fluctuations in the soil-water regime during crop growth causes rice to respond inconsistently to applied inorganic fertilizers (White and Seng 1997).

Other factors that affect rice responses to inorganic fertilizer application include variety, fertilizer application method, weed and pest control and land preparation methods (CARDI: 2002).

Environmental Impact of Fertilizers

At present, fertilizer rates applied in the rainfed lowlands are generally still low suggesting that the negative environmental impact of fertilizer use for rice production is probably minimal. However, nutrient deficiencies are prevalent in most rice soils and despite producing a national surplus in rice, the national average rice yield is relatively low with many provinces experiencing chronic shortages.

More needs to be done to achieve greater yield potential, especially in the rainfed lowlands. In the rainfed lowlands with access to supplementary irrigation, dry season cropping including rice and non-rice crops is becoming more common. The impact of these systems on the environment and socio-economic conditions deserves close examination so that appropriate farming technologies are developed and implemented without causing harm associated with agrochemical use.

Identifying areas in catchment basins that contribute most to nutrient enrichment of water bodies together with periodic monitoring of water quality should be implemented.

Upland Soils

A large proportion of upland soils are prevalent in Cambodia. A major hindrance to the management of upland soils is the scarcity of knowledge about the distribution, properties and behaviors of such soils. There is a need for a practical classification scheme, a land resource assessment and development of sustainable farming systems for upland soils.

Farrolsol over Basltic rock soil profile

Gleysols lowland soil profile

Soils of the Main Rice Growing Areas

Agriculture

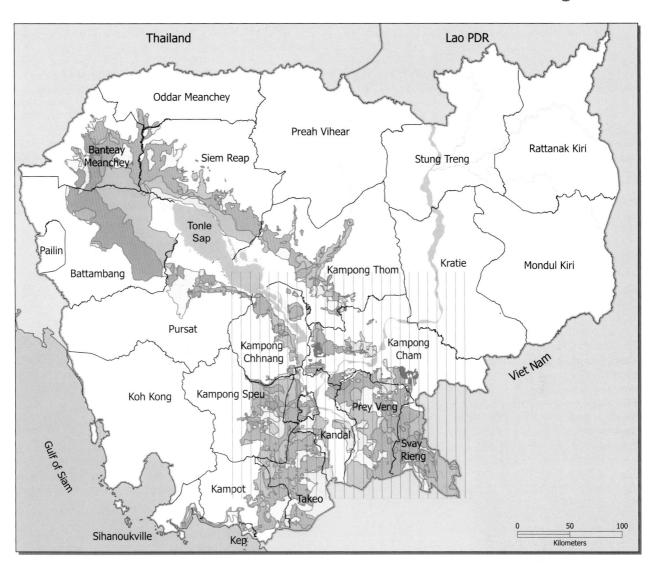

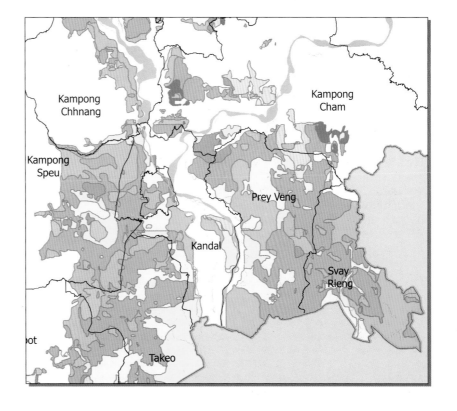

Legend

- Bakan
- Kbal Po
- Krakor
- Kompong Siem
- Koktrap
- Kein Svay
- Labansiek
- Orung
- Prey Khmer
- Prateah Lang
- Toul Samroung
- Water Body
- —— Provincial Boundary
- —— International Boundary

Note: refer to Appendix
for soil descriptions

Data Sources:
Rice Soil: CARDI 2000
International and Provincial Boundary:
Department of Geography 2005
Water Body: JICA Dataset 2002

References

Bell R.W. and Seng V. 2004. Rainfed lowland rice-growing soils of Cambodia, Laos, and Northeast Thailand. In: Seng V., Craswell E., Fukai, S. and Fischer K. eds. Water in Agriculture. Canberra, ACIAR Proceedings 116, 161-173

Bell R.W. Seng V., Schoknecht N., Vance W. and Hin S. 2005. Assessing Land Suitability for Crop Diversification in Cambodia. Paper presented in the Land Resources Assessment Forum for Cambodia, 14-17 September 2004. CARDI, Phnom Penh, Cambodia. (In press)

CARDI. 2002. Annual Research Report for 2001. Cambodian Agricultural Research and Development Institute. Phnom Penh, Cambodia

CEDAC. 2004. Pesticide Use and Consequence in Cambodia. Centre d'Etude et de Développement Agricole Cambodgien

Crocker C. D. 1962. The General Soil Map of the Kingdom of Cambodia and the Exploratory Survey of the Soils of Cambodia. Royal Cambodian Government Soil Commission/USAID Joint Publication. Phnom Penh. Cambodia

FAO. 2001. Selected indicators of food and agriculture in the Asia-Pacific Region 1990-2000. Food and Agricultural Organization of the United Nations, Regional Office for Asia and the Pacific. Bangkok, Thailand

MAFF. 2004. Agricultural statistics 2003-2004. Ministry of Agriculture Forestry and Fisheries. Phnom Penh Cambodia

MAFF. 2005. Report of Annual Meeting, 7-9 April 2005. The Ministry of Agriculture, Forestry and Fisheries, Phnom Penh, Cambodia (In Khmer)

Men S., Nuth S., Ros C., Mak S., Nesbitt H.J., Martin, R. and Cox, P. 2001. Opportunity for increasing agricultural production in Cambodia. Proceedings of an International Conference on the Impact of Agricultural Research for Development in Southeast Asia, 24-26 October 2000. Cambodian Agricultural Research and Development Institute, Phnom Penh, Cambodia, pp 273-286

MRC. 2003. Agriculture. In: State of the Basin Report: 2003. Mekong River Commission, Phnom Penh. ISSN: 1728:324

Nesbitt H. 2005. Lower Mekong Basin:Future Trends in Agricultural Production. MRC Discussion Paper. Mekong River Commission. Vientiane, Laos PDR

Nesbitt H.J. 2005. Water Used for Agriculture in the Lower Mekong Basin. MRC Discussion Paper

Mekong River Commission. Vientiane, Lao PDR

NIS. 2005. Statistical Year Book. National Institute of Statistics, Ministry of Planning. Phnom Penh, Cambodia

Pandey S. 1997. Rainfe Lowland Rice Research: Challenges and Priorities for the 21st Century. In: Fukai S., Cooper M. and Salisbury J. eds. Breeding Strategies for Rainfed Lowland Rice in Drought-Prone Environments. Canberra, ACIAR Proceedings No. 77, 1-12

Seng V. and White P.F. 2005. History of Land Resource Assessment in Cambodia - Lessons Learned. Paper presented in the Land Resources Assessment Forum for Cambodia, 14-17 September 2004. Cambodia Agriculture Research and Development Institute. Phnom Penh, Cambodia. (In press)

Seng, V. Ros C., Bell, R.W., White P.F. and Hin S. 2001. Nutrient Requirements for Lowland Rice in Cambodia. In: Fukai S. and Basnayake J. eds. Increased Lowland Rice Production in the Mekong Region. Canberra. ACIAR Proceedings No. 101, 170-178

SOER. 2004. State of the Environment Report. Ministry of Environment. Phnom Penh, Cambodia

O'Brien N. 1999. Environmental Concepts and Issues: A Focus on Cambodia. Ministry of Environment. Phnom Penh, Cambodia

White P.F. and Seng V. 1997. Response of Rainfed Lowland Rice to P Fertilizer Application in Cambodia. In: Fukai S., Cooper M., and Salisbury J. eds. Breeding Strategies for Rainfed Lowland Rice in Drought-Prone Environments. Canberra, ACIAR Proceedings No. 77, 202-208

White P.F., Oberthur T. and Sovuthy P. 1997. The Soils Used For Rice Production in Cambodia: A Manual for Their Identification and Management. International Rice Research Institute (IRRI), Manila, Philippines

World Bank. 2006. Cambodia Halving Poverty by 2015? Poverty Assessment Report

Education
and Health

Education

The education system represents an important bridge between economic and social development. International evidence demonstrates that improved literacy and education amongst farmers can be a key element of improved agricultural productivity, rural employment diversification and income growth. Education also encourages and promotes the sustainable use of natural resources and leads to a greater understanding of environmental circumstances. Higher literacy rates among women are also linked to a decline in fertility rates and an improvement in their own health as well as the health of their families. With a large proportion of the Cambodian population reliant upon agriculture, improving education standards such as enrollment, attendance and facilities, is an important factor in reducing poverty and improving natural resource management.

The policy priority for basic education is to achieve Education for All (EFA) by 2015. To accomplish quality EFA, the MoEYS recognizes that two main strategies are required. Firstly, there is a need to reduce the cost burden on the poorest families to increase participation of their children in grades 1-9. Secondly, there is a need to improve the internal efficiency of the education system in order for students to effectively move through the primary and lower secondary grades.

The main source of data for education is the EMIS centre in the Department of Planning which produces an annual publication of Education Statistics and Indicators. School principals take responsibility for completing an annual school census form which is then collected and checked for accuracy at district and provincial levels. The main limitations to data representation from this source

is the wide spread occurrence of 'late starters'. While the official age for primary level is 6-11 years old, many children begin school at an older age. To accommodate this, enrollment in the Education Statistics and Indicators is calculated at both net and gross rates.

Education Access and Enrollment

Although the education system gives 'open' access to education, the actual access to each level is still low. Based on education statistics for the MoEYS 2004/05 school year, net admission rates for primary education is 80.6%. The population aged 6-11 years with access to education is at a remarkable 92%, including 91% of the female population. This figure drastically declines when students reach lower secondary with a net enrollment ratio of 26.1%, and further declines in upper secondary with 9.3% net enrollment ratio. These statistics clearly show that while primary access is satisfactory, access to secondary level, particularly in rural and remote areas, is lacking. The efforts at improving access to education since 2001 have been more successful at primary level.

Most children who start school bear the consequences of the internal inefficiency of a system that is characterized by high repetition and drop out rates. Repetition rates are particularly high in grades one and two at 41% and 25% respectively. Another area of major concern is the low primary school attendance rate. According to the 1998 census only 20% of six year olds, and around 40% and 50% of all seven and eight year old children were attending school. Although substantial improvements have been made in the education system since the 1990s, half a million Cambodian children of primary school age remain out of school, most of them living in remote and rural areas.

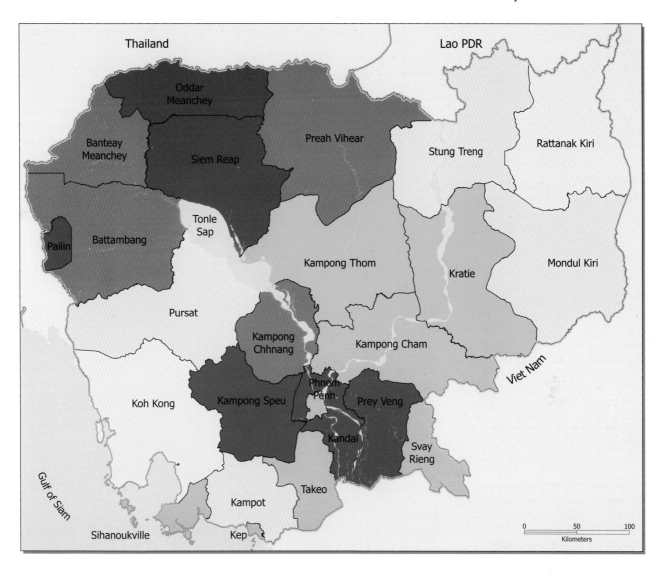

Legend

Gross Enrollment Rate

80.4 - 100 %

100.1 - 110 %

110.1 - 120 %

120.1 - 130 %

130.1 - 138.1 %

Water Body

——— Provincial Boundary

——— International Boundary

Note:
Gross Enrollment Rate -
Total primary enrollment / Population
of primary school age (6-11 years)
mutiplied by 100. Total enrollment is
above 100 because many students
enrolled in primary school are over
11 years old.

Data Sources:
Enrollment: MoEYS 2004-2005
International and Provincial Boundary:
Department of Geography 2005
Water Body: JICA Dataset 2002

Access rates to primary education for boys and girls are almost the same, although drop out rates for girls tend to be higher. Gender enrollment disparity for primary level declined significantly in the last five years, largely due to intensive promotion of female education rights by the RGC, local and international NGOs. Educating women and girls is the key to improved health, nutrition and education of children and families, which in turn can bring high social and economic returns to society. Removing barriers for girls to equal access education certainly benefits both women and men as it guarantees their equal and full participation in the development process.

Cambodian boys and girls start school on an equal footing. They have roughly similar school enrolment rates up to age 10, then girl's enrollment rates start falling behind. Additionally grades 4 and 5 see high drop out rates for girls. Girls represent about one-third of total enrollment in secondary schools. Females are also significantly under represented in technical and higher education.

These outcomes are a combination of a number of social, cultural and economic factors. Firstly, although girls enroll at roughly the same age as boys, earlier drop out rates occur with the onset of puberty and as family responsibilities begin to predominate. Secondly, it is reported that parents are often less willing to invest in educating females, which is a critical factor when parental contributions are a large share of education spending. In addition to this, few rural villages have secondary schools, so attending secondary school typically means traveling long distances or staying away from home. This is culturally unacceptable for girls.

Non Formal Education

Non-formal education constitutes learning opportunities for the vast majority of children, youth and adults in developing countries who are not reached by the formal education system. Most of the illiterate population lives in poverty, in remote and rural areas. The most disadvantaged are women, girls and minority groups.

Another vulnerable group is the 350,000 annual dropouts from formal schooling. All of these are in immediate need and have the right to basic education and literacy provision to improve the quality of their lives. Thus, non formal education has a critical role to play in realizing the RGC objectives of EFA by 2015. Additionally, Cambodia's Poverty Reduction Strategy Paper requires fundamental changes in the knowledge, skills and attitudes of all citizens to engage in behaviours

that will reduce poverty, end exclusion and promote democracy. Non-formal education provides learning opportunities to adults and out-of-school youth to enable full participation in these changes.

The goal of non formal education in Cambodia is to play a central role in the education system to increase literacy rates, teach life skills, and provide the skills necessary to enter the modern work force and respond to the nation's development needs. New policies and targets for non formal education focus on re-entry programs for grades 3-9 for those students who have been out of school for less than three years, alongside equivalency programs for students who have been out of school for more than three years. The major focus is on females and students from poor families. The main targets are:

- Increased re-entry programs into mainstream schooling at grades 3-6 and grades 7-9 with a target of 120,000 per annum from 2005.

Lower Secondary Enrollment

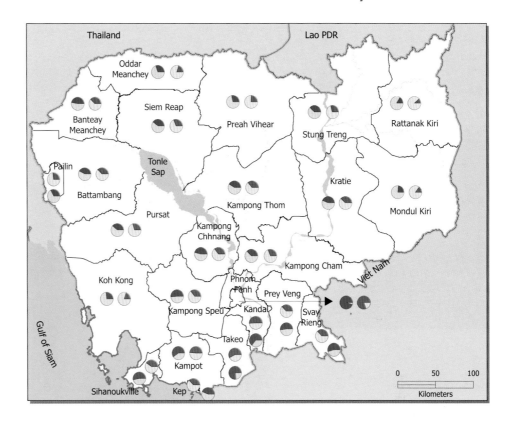

Legend

- ▨ Percentage of Boys enrolled
- ▨ Percentage of Boys not enrolled
- ▨ Percentage of Girls enrolled
- ▨ Percentage of Girls not enrolled
- ▨ Water Body
- — Provincial Boundary
- ━ International Boundary

Note:
Lower Secondary Grades 7-9.
Upper Secondary Grades 10-12.
Refer to Appendix 10 for absolute figures.

Upper Secondary Enrollment

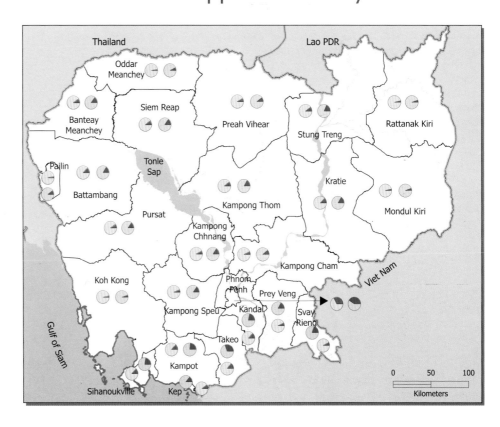

Legend

- ▨ Percentage of Boys enrolled
- ▨ Percentage of Boys not enrolled
- ▨ Percentage of Girls enrolled
- ▨ Percentage of Girls not enrolled
- ▨ Water Body
- — Provincial Boundary
- ━ International Boundary

Data Sources:
Enrollment: MoEYS 2004-2005
International and Provincial Boundary:
Department of Geography 2005
Water Body: JICA Dataset 2002

- Expand equivalency programs for students out of school for more than 3 years with a target of 150,000 per annum from 2005.
- Expanded public / NGO / community partnerships in adult literacy programs in border and remote areas with a target of 120,000 per annum from 2005.

Currently, access and coverage of adult literacy classes is limited. In addition, the selection criteria for the programs vary including on demand, family head of household, out of school youth and links with micro credit and other rural income generating activities. The locations of programs also vary. In some instances primary schools and pre-schools are used as well as community centers, especially in rural areas where many primary schools operate a single shift. There appears to be significant scope for use of schools in early mornings, afternoons and evenings for more expansion of provision. In order to ensure easy access, and remove any potential access barriers, timetabling of the non-formal education program are critical, especially taking into account the participant's domestic and work patterns.

The low level of basic skills in the population has serious implications for Cambodia's comparative advantage in global markets. For example, Cambodia's textile trade has rapidly grown to be worth over one billion dollars a year. With emerging competition from neighbors such as China and Viet Nam who are accorded the same tariff free trading, Cambodia may experience comparative disadvantage if the workforce is largely illiterate. Non-formal education is an important tool to improve literacy and critical thinking skills in order to better prepare the population for the modern workforce and respond to the nations development needs.

Literacy
Estimated literacy levels depend on survey methodology and the definition of the term literacy. As a result there is some variation between countries and even within a country. In Cambodia, the definition of a literate person is someone who has the ability to read and write to a certain extent only. According to this, the literacy rate of those 15 years and over is 67%. In the light of previous literacy campaigns, the literacy rate rose to 68.7% with 81.8% for males and 58% for females. However, the literacy rate in rural and remote areas is far lower than in the towns

A recent literacy survey conducted by UNESCO and UNDP provides clearer definitions of the situation. The survey estimates that 36% of the population or around 2.4 million adults are illiterate (25% male and 45% female) and 27%, or 1.7 million adults, are only semi-illiterate (28% male and 26% female). On this basis, only 36% of the population is literate in terms of being able to use their literacy skills for everyday life and income generation. To improve the situation, the RGC has reshaped the National Literacy Committee with the view to further intensify nationwide literacy activities.

The literacy rates in Cambodia are below many of its ASEAN neighbors, which in many cases have literacy rates of around 95%. The literacy rates of both adults and youth in Cambodia are low and rate second from the bottom among the six ASEAN countries. Given the considerable non enrollment and drop out rates in the primary cycle, as well as the low learning achievements in all grades, a large pool of illiterates can be found among the school age population. Also, about 80% of

the poor live in households headed by individuals with little or no schooling at all. Around four million adults are currently in need of literacy training in Cambodia. With reference to ethnicity, more than 90% of the population is Khmer. Most of the ethnic minorities live in the Northern and Eastern provinces and they generally speak languages with no written tradition. Education indicators in those provinces are remarkably below the national average.

The information available concerning enrollment of adults in non formal education programmes is limited. However, there are several programmes purposely designed to include income-generation, improved school attendance, improved family health and nutrition and a greater awareness of family planning techniques. These programmes, although implemented by the RGC, are mostly run by NGOs. It is estimated that in the government supported programs, around 55% of students acquire functional literacy, while in the NGO programs the figure is about 45%, although the success criteria may vary. The success rate amongst women is only 48% compared to 61% for men. The reasons for this are unclear, but may difficulties for regular attendance by women because of domestic duties.

Educational Facilities
A major factor influencing the high drop out rate in Cambodia is the insufficient education supply, especially in regards to school facilities. At present Cambodia has 6, 063 primary schools, 36% of which are incomplete, meaning they don't provide all classes from grades 1 through to 6. However, there has been a substantial increase in primary schools in remote areas with an additional 155 schools built between 2000 and 2004. Approximately half of all primary schools run double shifts, morning and afternoon sessions to serve the needs of different students. In Phnom Penh where the education facilities are particularly stretched, some schools run triple shifts to meet the demand.

In recent years the lower secondary facilities for grades 7-9 have been expanded but still remain insufficient for the learning needs of students, especially in remote and rural areas. Of the total 1,621 communes only 936 have lower secondary facilities. Additional lower secondary school construction is needed to serve the rapid growth of primary enrollment which will flow to the lower secondary level in coming years.

Distance between primary school and the nearest lower secondary school is not a major access constraint for the majority of grade 6 children. The distance to primary and the nearest secondary school is generally within 3 to 6 kilometers. In summary, only 10% of current primary school students experience long distances between primary/lower secondary education services. Clearly, adopting a commune level cluster model for targeting additional lower secondary provision would significantly reduce these distances.

Access to most upper secondary schooling is more problematic. In the districts without a lower secondary school, students have to travel to another district for both grades 7-9 and grades 10-12. Even in cases where districts have a lower secondary school, many of them require students to travel more than 10-12 kilometers to attend upper secondary education. In other words, improving upper secondary school access will require a careful analysis of the projected demand for

Illiteracy by Gender

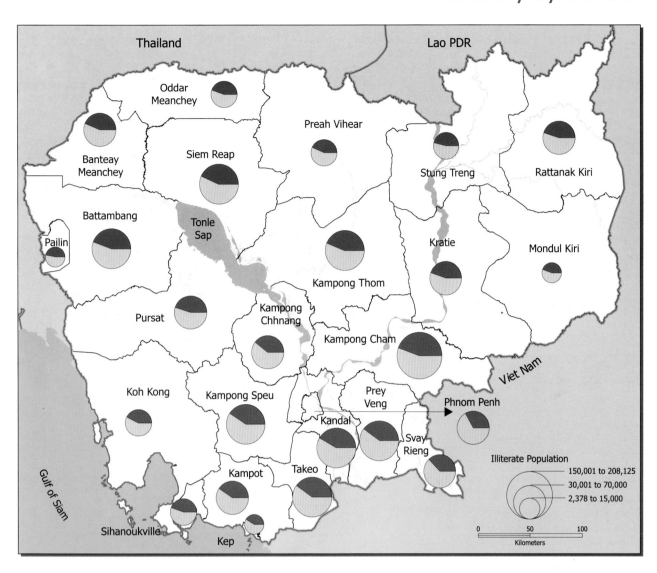

Education and Health

Legend

Illiterate Males

Illiterate Females

Water Body

— Provincial Boundary

— International Boundary

Illiteracy by Gender

Province	Illiterate Males	Illiterate Female	Total Illiterate Population
Banteay Meanchey	26,945	34,610	61,555
Battambang	34,038	42,701	76,739
Kampong Cham	92,695	115,430	208,125
Kampong Chhnang	15,603	23,878	39,481
Kampong Speu	33,830	48,976	82,806
Kampong Thom	44,122	56,260	100,382
Kampot	27,654	40,959	68,613
Kandal	39,926	56,009	95,935
Koh Kong	9,358	12,559	21,917
Kratie	17,180	21,411	38,591
Mondul Kiri	5,999	7,430	13,429
Phnom Penh	13,442	27,022	40,464
Preah Vihear	11,986	15,817	27,803
Prey Veng	45,555	69,574	115,129
Pursat	17,042	20,668	37,710
Rattanak Kiri	19,415	23,595	43,010
Siem Reap	49,181	64,410	113,591
Sihanoukville	7,328	9,169	16,497
Stung Treng	9,081	10,568	19,649
Svay Rieng	17,869	30,263	48,132
Takeo	30,052	45,184	75,236
Oddar Meanchey	11,951	14,747	26,698
Kep	987	1,391	2,378
Pailin	2,990	3,388	6,378

Data Sources:
Illiteracy: Commune Database 2004
International and Provincial Boundary:
Department of Geography 2005
Water Body: JICA Dataset 2002

upper secondary school that can reduce drop out rates at these levels and increase literacy rates in Cambodia.

The average number of students per teacher is 41, although in some areas there can be as many as 53 students per teacher. There is a shortage of teachers mainly because incentives to teach are low. Teacher salaries are poor and don't provide a living wage. Some teachers must supplement their income with other jobs which cuts into class times. Although the national constitution provides free education for primary and lower secondary education at public schools, teachers often need to charge students fees to attend their classes in order to earn a living wage. For many rural families who live by subsistence agriculture, this causes education costs to be one of the highest expenses they face annually and constitutes a significant barrier for many students.

The shortage of teachers is particularly felt in remote areas. At present all new teacher graduates are required to complete two year postings in remote areas. However, with no provision of housing, support or adequate income, most teachers find this extremely difficult.

Since the early 1990s, Cambodia has made considerable progress in expanding education services. As funding for education has improved, dramatic changes have been made. However, both quality and coverage still remain areas of great concern. There is a shortage of school buildings and learning centers, class sizes are often excessive, the number of actual teaching/learning hours is inadequate, new curricula are not yet fully implemented and there is a shortage of core and supplementary teaching materials. Teachers are often ill motivated due to low salaries and poor working conditions. The socio-economic and professional status of teachers is poor. There are few non-monetary incentives such as scholarships, training opportunities, career development or public recognition.

Mean Distance to Education Facilities

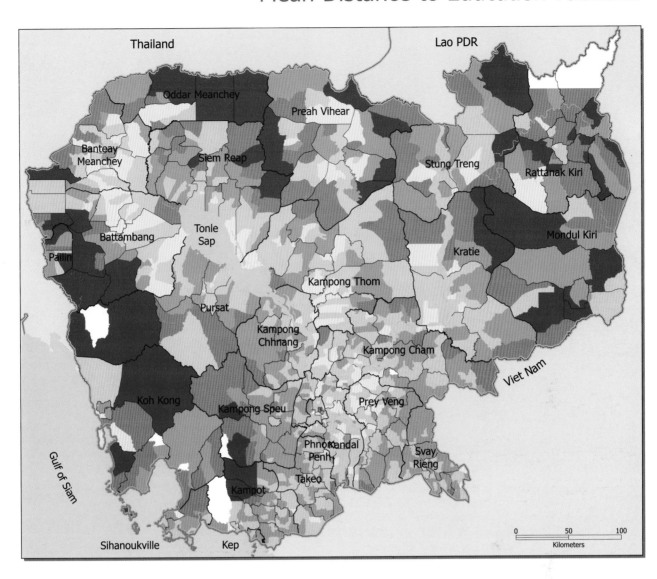

Legend

Mean Distance to Combined
Education Facilities

- <0.5 Km
- 0.51 - 1 Km
- 1.1 - 2 Km
- 2.1 - 5 Km
- More than 5 Km
- No Data
- Water Body
- —— Provincial Boundary
- —— International Boundary

Data Sources:
Mean Distance: Analysis data(combined data) between
Village location and School location: Census 1998
Village location, International and Provincial Boundary:
Department of Geography 2005
Water Body: JICA Dataset 2002

Education Facilities

Province	Pupils per School	Teachers per School	Pupils Teacher Ratio	Pupil Class Ratio
Banteay Meanchey	343.0	7.0	48.7	44.4
Battambang	403.9	8.8	45.7	42.7
Kampong Cham	454.9	9.4	48.2	45.1
Kampong Chhnang	402.8	8.2	49.3	45.4
Kampong Speu	522.5	9.6	54.3	49.3
Kampong Thom	303.7	6.8	44.9	43.5
Kampot	394.9	9.6	41.1	43.8
Kandal	502.4	12.5	40.2	44.7
Koh Kong	290.3	5.0	58.6	43.5
Kratie	262.0	7.6	34.3	39.0
Mondul Kiri	130.1	3.4	37.7	33.3
Phnom Penh	1263.0	40.3	31.3	45.4
Preah Vihear	222.9	5.1	43.4	37.6
Prey Veng	411.9	8.8	46.7	42.1
Pursat	332.0	7.9	41.8	41.0
Rattanak Kiri	152.4	3.1	48.8	36.9
Siem Reap	447.5	7.1	63.1	48.5
Sihanoukville	568.3	13.9	40.8	45.5
Stung Treng	159.9	4.6	35.1	31.0
Svay Rieng	431.5	10.1	42.6	45.0
Takeo	454.7	10.3	44.2	46.3
Oddar Meanchey	252.7	4.4	57.1	39.5
Kep	308.8	9.4	32.9	40.6
Pailin	362.2	7.7	47.2	43.0

Source: MoEYS 2004-2005

The Health Sector

Considerable progress has been made in the health sector in Cambodia in recent years including the eradication of Poliomyelitis, containment of HIV/AIDS and a decrease in the prevalence of Malaria. Despite this marked progress, the health status of the people of Cambodia is among the lowest in the region. Maternal mortality remains high and many children go hungry and die of preventable diseases. To date, the publicly funded health services, especially to the rural poor, are inadequate and overall rates of utilization are low. For most, out of pocket spending on healthcare is a key issue related to indebtedness.

Health is one of the sectors receiving priority attention from both the RGC and external partners. The MoH, considered as one of the strongest ministries, aims to promote peoples health enabling them to participate in the development of the socio-economic sector and decrease poverty in Cambodia. In order to achieve this, the MoH established the Health Sector Strategic Plan 2003-2007.

According to NIS (2005), the main data sources for health and nutrition are the annual and sub annual reports of the Ministry of Public Health and Communicable Diseases, the Cambodian Demographic Health Survey (CDHS) 2000 and the Cambodian Socio-Economic Survey (CSES) 2004.

Coverage and Quality of Health Services
Despite the fact that over 85% of the population live in rural areas, most hospitals and health personnel are concentrated in urban areas, resulting in an unequal distribution of healthcare for Cambodians (Dewdney: 2004). Approximately a quarter of the total population do

not have access to health care at all. Additionally, many of those with access are unlikely to be able to afford it (United Nations: 1998). Moreover, the publicly funded resource-poor facilities present in the rural areas are unlikely to be able to respond to the health needs of the population, especially those households situated in remote areas.

Low salaries for public health staff and limited medical equipment contribute to poor staff motivation, involvement with unofficial pay and poor attitudes towards patients (United Nations: 1998). There are also concerns with health service management regarding limited capacity and corruption (WHO: 2000). In addition to geographical and financial barriers to health care, the common public perception of low quality public health services further prevents people from receiving proper health care. Patients are usually taken to the nearest health centers, referral hospital or private clinic only when their condition deteriorates. This leads to high hospital case fatality rates (Oum: 2005). Overall, it is estimated that only about a third of patients seek treatment at public health facilities. With high out-of-pocket expenditure for health, health care is a major contributing factor to poverty and landlessness (United Nations: 1998).

The 1996 Health Coverage Plan has improved health care access by increasing the number of referral hospitals providing comprehensive care and health centers providing Minimum Package Activities (Table 1). There are currently 67 Operational Districts in Cambodia, each with a referral hospital and a number of health centers. This plan, with support from both the RGC and donors, aims to maximize access to health care, especially for the

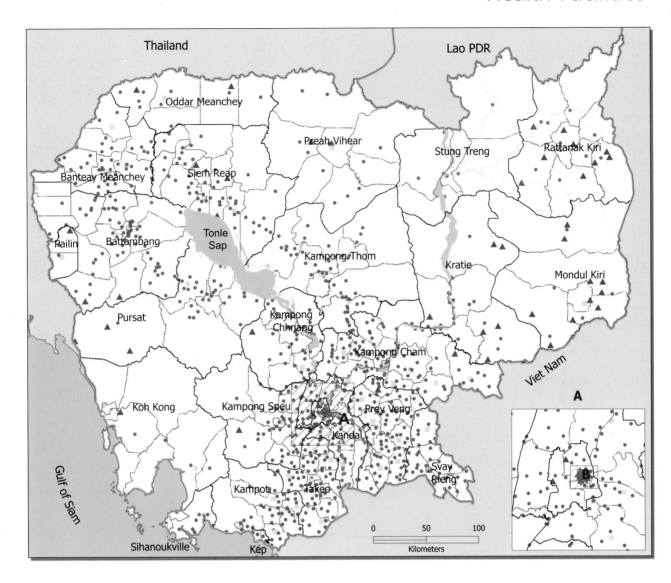

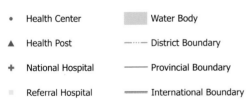

Legend

National and Local Health Facilities

- • Health Center
- ▲ Health Post
- ✚ National Hospital
- ▪ Referral Hospital
-    Water Body (shaded)
- ·-·-· District Boundary
- ——— Provincial Boundary
- ━━━ International Boundary

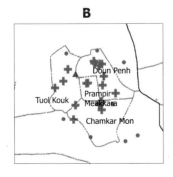

B

Data Sources:
Health Facilities: MoH, National Health Statistics 2003
International, Provincial and District Boundary:
Department of Geography 2005
Water Body: JICA Dataset 2002

National and Local Health Facilities

Province	Health Center	Health Post	National Hospital	Referral Hospital
Banteay Meanchey	49	0	0	4
Battambang	79	1	0	5
Kampong Cham	100	1	0	9
Kampong Chhnang	34	1	0	2
Kampong Speu	47	2	0	3
Kampong Thom	50	0	0	3
Kampot	46	0	0	4
Kandal	88	0	0	5
Koh Kong	9	3	0	3
Kratie	23	6	0	2
Mondul Kiri	6	10	0	1
Phnom Penh	20	3	18	0
Preah Vihear	11	2	0	1
Prey Veng	90	1	0	7
Pursat	31	4	0	2
Rattanak Kiri	10	9	0	1
Siem Reap	54	3	0	3
Sihanoukville	9	0	0	1
Stung Treng	8	0	0	1
Svay Rieng	35	0	0	3
Takeo	70	0	0	5
Oddar Meanchey	11	2	0	1
Kep	4	0	0	1
Pailin	3	1	0	1

rural poor. Additionally, contracting health services to the non-profit private sector aims to improve quality and utilization of health services (Mam: 2005).

At the same time, the government has also tried to build linkages with the community by establishing a health center management committee and feedback committee in order to improve communication and respond more effectively to the needs of the public. Village Health Volunteers have also been selected to ensure the active participation of communities. The Community Based Surveillance System, for instance, is an active surveillance sought to strengthen the community-health facility link while providing timely information about outbreak and disease activities in the remote areas (Oum: 2002).

The Health Workforce
The coverage and quality of health care and health service provision is intimately linked with the types, competency and distribution of the country's health workforce. Currently there is an inequitable distribution of health workers between urban and rural areas with a concentration of doctors, midwives and nurses in Phnom Penh and provincial towns. The average number of doctors per inhabitant is around 1 per 3,124 (MoH: 2005). Low pay with lack of motivation and regular supervision affect the quality of health services. High staff turn over rate and transfer of health staff from the public to the private sector poses even further concern. Meanwhile, it is worth mentioning that the "crash training" during the 1980s following the Pol Pot regime affect, to a considerable extent, the limited availability of skilled and competent staff nationwide (Pers. Comm. Oum: 2005). The rapidly flourishing private health sector, not being adequately regulated, provides services ranging from doubtful to harmful. There is also a preference for traditional healers and traditional birth attendants, especially from people living in the remote areas. This can be attributed to access issues, perception of quality of care, dysfunctional public health facilities and financial restraints.

The MoH aims to develop human resources in a variety of ways. For example, increasing the number of midwives is a key strategy (MoH: 2005). Priority is given to the training and deployment of midwives especially considering the high rates of maternal and neonatal mortality, they can be seen as the frontline workforce responding to an urgent community need. Community empowerment through Village Health Volunteers is also considered an important part of the peripheral health system. Training is provided for volunteers in different areas of health education and family planning promotion. The traditional birth attendants are also included in these activities as a tool to promote safe deliveries and appropriate referral.

Licensing, registration and an accreditation mechanism for health professionals are being developed along with the establishment of professional councils for regulation purposes. Inspection of illegal private practices is being

strengthened at both the central and provincial level. A consumer rights and provider rights package has been developed for piloting in three provinces in 2005. Public health expenditure per capita has been increasing over the years along with the introduction of payment reform in the health sector to improve quality of health services. Other approaches for motivation and human resource management through contracting and performance based incentives have also been improved.

Maternal Mortality
Cambodia's maternal mortality of 450 per 100,000 live births is one of the highest, with a global ranking of 133 (UNICEF: 2004). These figures are probably just the tip of the iceberg of maternal suffering from delivery-related morbidity. Strategically, there are three delays underlying maternal mortality in developing countries including a delay in recognizing danger signs during delivery, a delay in seeking proper care and a delay in receiving proper care at health facilities. Recent studies show that up to 80% of Cambodian women have deliveries outside of health facilities and only 37% of pregnant women deliver with the assistance of a skilled birth attendant (MoH: 2002). As in other developing countries, major direct causes of maternal mortality include hemorrhage, dystocia and sepsis. Another predisposing factor includes the high rate of anemia (more than 50%), among women of reproductive age (NIS: 2000). Maternal Mortality also has an important impact on a large proportion of children as studies show that children whose mothers don't survive delivery have less chance of survival during early childhood compared to their counterparts. In addition to the current high fertility rate, poor contraceptive use and low healthcare coverage, women are unlikely to have access to antenatal care and an adequate delivery service. There has been an alarming decrease in the number of midwifes working outside the capital, and an acute shortage of midwives in remote areas, particularly among the sparsely populated communities (Dewdney: 2004). There are high-unmet obstetric needs while the cesarean section rate is only 0.8% nationally (NIS: 2005). Similarly, the low status of women in Cambodia reflected in the low level of women completing primary education relative to men, results in limited decision-making in the household and poor nutrition status (UNDP: 2004).

The current reproductive health program in Cambodia was started after the general election in the mid 1990s and has yet to meet the needs of the entire population. Currently there are many investments in this field by donors and other international organizations. The national reproductive health program consists of a birth spacing program, safe motherhood initiatives and STD prevention. However, the ability to deliver these essential services is still very much dependent on the existing institutional and human resources which are not at a sufficient level. There are shortages of skilled personnel serving in the rural areas along with weak referral systems. To help alleviate this, training of traditional birth attendants to improve birth preparedness, to recognize danger signs during delivery and the timely identification of referral has been implemented.

Table 1: Health Facility Coverage

Facilities	1998	1999	2000	2001	2002	2003	2004
Hospitals with major surgical operations	23	24	28	30	34	37	41
Functioning health centers	386	514	678	761	812	823	832

Sources: Heng 2005

Mean Distance to Health Facilities

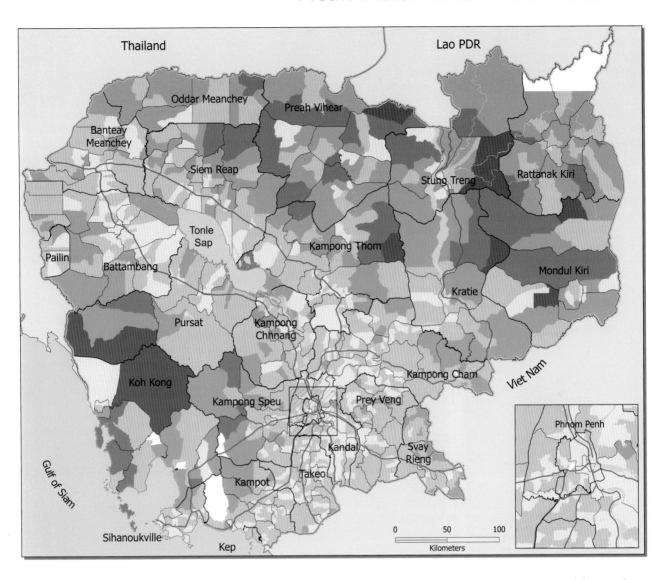

Thailand
Lao PDR

Oddar Meanchey
Preah Vihear

Banteay
Meanchey

Siem Reap

Stung Treng
Rattanak Kiri

Pailin

Tonle
Sap

Battambang

Kampong Thom

Mondul Kiri

Pursat

Kratie

Kampong
Chhnang

Koh Kong

Kampong Cham

Viet Nam

Kampong Speu
Prey Veng

Kandal
Svay
Rieng

Takeo

Kampot

Gulf of Siam

Sihanoukville
Kep

Phnom Penh

0   50   100
Kilometers

Education and Health

Inhabitants per Doctor

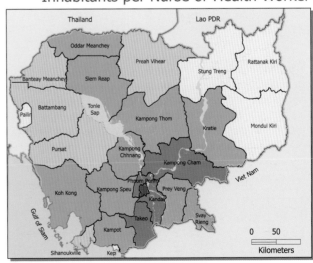

Thailand
Lao PDR

Oddar Meanchey
Preah Vihear

Banteay Meanchey
Siem Reap
Stung Treng
Rattanak Kiri

Pailin
Battambang
Tonle Sap
Kampong Thom
Mondul Kiri

Pursat
Kampong Chhnang
Kratie

Kampong Cham

Koh Kong
Kampong Speu
Phnom Penh
Prey Veng
Kandal
Viet Nam

Takeo
Svay Rieng

Kampot

Gulf of Siam
Sihanoukville
Kep

0   50   100
Kilometers

Inhabitants per Nurse or Health Worker

Thailand
Lao PDR

Oddar Meanchey
Preah Vihear

Banteay Meanchey
Siem Reap
Stung Treng
Rattanak Kiri

Pailin
Battambang
Tonle Sap
Kampong Thom
Mondul Kiri

Pursat
Kampong Chhnang
Kratie

Kampong Cham

Koh Kong
Kampong Speu
Phnom Penh
Prey Veng
Kandal
Viet Nam

Takeo
Svay Rieng

Kampot

Gulf of Siam
Sihanoukville
Kep

0   50
Kilometers

Legend

Mean Distance to
Health Facilities
- < 2Km
- 2.1 - 5Km
- 5.1 - 15Km
- 15.1 - 25Km
- More than 25Km

Inhabitants per Doctor
- < 5,000
- 5,001 - 7,500
- 7,501 - 10,000
- 10,001 - 12,500
- >12,500

Inhabitants per Nurse or
Local Health Worker
- < 400
- 401 - 600
- 601 - 800
- 801 - 1,000
- 1,001 - 1,111

- No Data
- Water Body
- Main Roads
- District Boundary
- Provincial Boundary
- International Boundary

Data Sources:
Mean Distance: Analysis Data Between
Village Location and Health Location
Health Location: Administrative and
Health Facility Mapping 2004, NIS/MoP
International, Provincial Boundary and
Village Location: Department of Geography 2005
Water Body: JICA Dataset 2002

Atlas of Cambodia National Poverty and Environment Maps   115

Neonatal Mortality

The neonatal period is a very vulnerable phase as the risk of a newborn dying is fifteen times higher compared to the subsequent month of infancy and thirty times higher compared to older children. Both the NHS (1998) and the CDHS (2000) showed that 30% of early childhood deaths take place during the neonatal period. This is mostly due to a lack of clean delivery conditions and properly skilled attendants. The current high mortality rate of 45 per 1000 livebirths reflects low antenatal care and lack of access to emergency obstetric care especially in the remote areas (NIS: 2000). The 11% low birth weight prevalence in Cambodia presents additional risk as studies show that 50% of neonatal deaths are associated with low birth weight. Being so strongly linked to the delivery period, newborns in the early few days of life do not receive appropriate care as only one third of pregnant women have the assistance of skilled birth attendants. As a result, newborns are prone to poor feeding, hypothermia and infection during the post-partum period. The high neonatal mortality rate resulting mainly from birth asphyxia, pre-maturity, and neonatal infections including tetanus, reflects the low care coverage among poor households. Poor maternal health and survival was speculated as another important factor for the survival of the newborn and their later childhood.

Currently, there is limited information providing precise mortality data as approximately 80% of deliveries takes place at home (NIS: 2000). Hence, National Health Statistic data which is facility based may not be able to capture true mortality that occurs outside of health facilities. For example, the low neonatal mortality rate in Pailin can be the result of most mortality in the community going unreported. Meanwhile, high mortality rates recorded in provinces such as Kampong Thom and Kampong Cham may be more accurate as there is greater access to public health facilities and local hospitals.

As maternal and newborn health started to receive more attention from policy makers and health partners, moderate progress has been made in improving safe delivery and antenatal care in Cambodia (Mam: 2005). While only 37.7% of pregnant women received antenatal care by skilled staff in 2000, this rate increased to 54.1% in 2002 (MoH: 2002).

Child Mortality

After decades of struggling, the child mortality rate in Cambodia is still high while most other countries in the region have made considerable progress in child health and well-being. One in seven children in Cambodia will die before reaching their fifth birthday. With an under five mortality rate of 140 and an infant mortality rate of 97, Cambodia is seen as burdened with a child survival crisis that needs urgent attention. Infectious diseases including Acute Respiratory Illness and Diarrheal Diseases are major killers in Cambodian children while malnutrition is a main underlying cause of mortality.

Almost 50% of children are plagued by malnutrition with a high rate of

underweight and wasting (NIS: 2000). Micronutrient deficiency such as iron deficiency affects up to 60% of children and women of child bearing age. Likewise, children are a disadvantaged segment of the population who are not only prone to rapidly deteriorating and fatal infectious diseases, but are also very dependent for their survival on health care service provision and the health seeking behaviors of their parents or caretakers. High rates of maternal mortality further affect the well-being and survival of newborns and children. Poor health practice is not unusual among the general population in Cambodia. Child health status is also strongly correlated with the mother's level of education and mother's income as women are more likely to spend their money on a child's welfare compared to other members of the family. High illiteracy rates among mothers lead to delays in disease identification and seeking care. Similarly to neonatal survival, delay in recognizing children's danger signs and delay in seeking appropriate health care are the first two important delays preventing the sick child from receiving proper care in a timely manner. The NHS (1998) and CDHS (2000) show a low percentage of under-five children receiving proper care from health staff. Likewise, only half of the mothers know about the Oral Rehydration Solution (ORS) packets and are even less likely to use it or know how to prepare the ORS when their children have diarrhea (NIS: 2000).

Interventions to reduce child mortality are imbedded in the RGC's initiative to implement a sector wide approach based on the Health Strategic Plan 2003-2007 giving priority to improving the health of women and children (MoH: 2003). Interventions identified as successful in the past along with newly innovative and cost-effective approaches for acute respiratory illnesses, diarrheal disease, neonatal conditions and integrated management of childhood illness are receiving strong political and financial commitments. The integrated multi-sectoral approach to improve food security, access to clean water and sanitation, female literacy rates and poverty reduction strategies should be promoted among the government, donors and in the community. The National Child Survival Strategic Plan is being finalized along with strengthening of Integrated Management of Childhood Illnesses. Other responses include mass media campaigns to promote exclusive breastfeeding and the new prakas on marketing of breast milk.

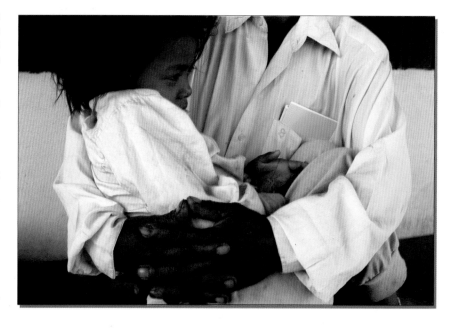

Neonatal Mortality

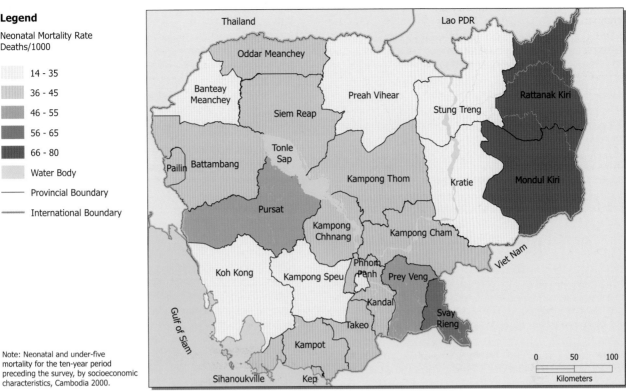

Education and Health

Legend

Neonatal Mortality Rate
Deaths/1000

- 14 - 35
- 36 - 45
- 46 - 55
- 56 - 65
- 66 - 80
- Water Body
- —— Provincial Boundary
- ▬▬ International Boundary

Note: Neonatal and under-five mortality for the ten-year period preceding the survey, by socioeconomic characteristics, Cambodia 2000.

Under-five Mortality

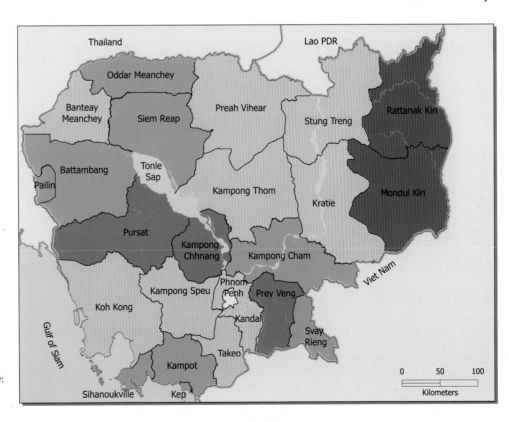

Legend

Under-five Mortality Rate
Deaths/1000

- 50 - 70
- 71 - 120
- 121 - 150
- 151 - 200
- 201 - 229
- Water Body
- —— Provincial Boundary
- ▬▬ International Boundary

Data Sources:
Neonatal and Under-five mortality: CDHS 2000
International and Provincial Boundary: Department of Geography 2005
Water Body: JICA Dataset 2002

Vaccination

Vaccination is one of the most cost effective tools in public health with key roles of protecting newborns and children against common preventable diseases. Supplementary immunization activities increased up to 85% coverage from 2000 to 2004 resulting in a decrease of vaccine preventable diseases (MoH: 2005). However, neonatal tetanus remains a concern due to the lack of clean delivery at birth and low prevalence of women of childbearing age receiving a full dose of tetanus toxoid. The NHS (2002) reported that only 41% of children are fully vaccinated while nearly 20% of the target did not receive any vaccinations at all. Immunizations are usually provided by public health facilities free of charge in combination with routine outreach activities at village level. Low demand, lack of regular supply and access difficulties are still the key barriers for reaching the target particularly in rural areas (WHO: 2004).

The Expanded Immunization Program began in the mid 1980s with support from UNICEF. It initially reached only one third of children and pregnant women but reportedly increased to approximately three quarters of the target by 1995, however, this figure is believed to be an over estimation. One major achievement of the program was the eradication of poliomyelitis in 2000 (Mam: 2005). The WHO recommended a focus on Measles and neonatal Tetanus through supplementary immunization activities (SIA) and the establishment of a nationwide Measles surveillance system in 2000. This resulted in a rapid decrease of measles cases from 13,827 in 1999 to 352 in 2004 (MoH: 2005). Likewise, the SIA provided tetanus toxoid to reproductive age women targeting the high-risk areas. There has only been a slight increase of fully vaccinated 12-23 months children over the period 1998 to 2002 despite considerable effort undertaken nationwide. Recently, Hepatitis B vaccine was included in the National Immunization Programme and is being scaled up from the national hospitals to operational districts at peripheral level (MoH: 2005).

TB and Malaria

The leading causes of morbidity and mortality in Cambodia are infectious and epidemic-prone diseases. Despite the steady decline of malaria and TB cases and death in the past few years, these diseases still present a considerable negative impact on health and economic development in Cambodia.

According to the National Center for Parasitology, Entomology and Malaria Control (2005), burdens of morbidity and mortality from malaria occur in certain geographical areas and during specific seasons. Population movement due to military conflict and natural disasters leads to a considerable number of internally displaced people who are more likely to move to Malaria endemic areas or work in forest-fringed areas exposing them to high risks of contracting Malaria.

The total number of clinically diagnosed and treated Malaria slightly decreased from 132,571 cases and 492 deaths in 2003 to 101,857 cases and 382 deaths in 2004 (NIS: 2000). Malaria mortality rates also decreased from 3.6/100,000 in 2003 to 2.8/100,000 in 2004 while the malaria severe case fatality rate was 8.3% (NIS: 2000). Situational analysis shows a number of important root causes ranging from relentless socio-economic and political instability at the macro level to poor access to health care along with inappropriate health seeking behaviors at the household level. Strategies to combat malaria include marketing of impregnated mosquito nets, health education to promote awareness and protective measures have been undertaken with the collaboration of Cambodia Red Cross volunteers distributing larvicide.

Cambodia is among the top 22 countries considered to have a high TB burden. The current TB infection rate among the general population is 64% while the incidence rate of all TB forms is up to 509/100,000 with a death rate of 95/100,000 (NIS: 2000). The main predisposing factors include low socio-economic status, poor nutrition, overwork and crowding. The rapid spread of HIV in the mid 1990s further reinforces the spread of TB and anti-tuberculosis drug resistance. The HIV prevalence among TB patients was 11.8 in 2003. The National Tuberculosis Program has been working actively with JICA to ensure identification, treatment and follow up care of TB patients. By the end of 2004, TB treatment using DOTS were expanded to all health centers with a curative rate of up to 90% (CENAT). A media campaign has been conducted to increase awareness and encourage care seeking among the general population.

Vaccinations

Legend

% of children who are vaccinated

- 12 - 15
- 16 - 25
- 26 - 35
- 36 - 50
- 51 - 63
- Water Body
- —— Provincial Boundary
- ━━ International Boundary

Note:
Vaccination figures are for children aged 12 - 23 months.
Children considered fully vaccinated are those who have received BCG, measles, three doses of DPTand polio vaccine (excluding polio vaccine given at birth).

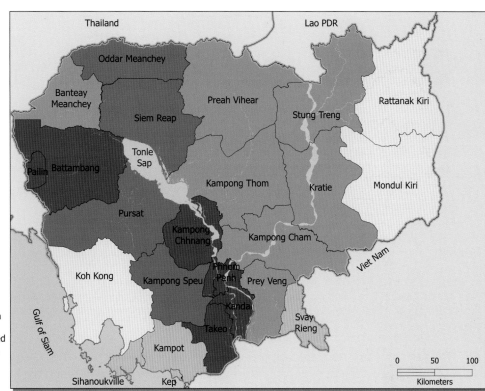

TB and Malaria Prevalence

Legend

Prevalence of TB %

- · 0.06 - 0.12
- · 0.13 - 0.17
- ● 0.18 - 0.21
- ● 0.22 - 0.29
- ● 0.30 - 0.37

Prevalence of Malaria %

- 0.01 - 0.78
- 0.79 - 2.25
- 2.26 - 3.48
- 3.49 - 7.09
- 7.10 - 15.89
- Water Body
- —— Provincial Boundary
- ━━ International Boundary

Data Sources:
Vaccination: CDHS 2000
TB and Malaria: MoH,
National Health Statistics 2003
International and Provincial Boundary:
Department of Geography 2005
Water Body: JICA Dataset 2002

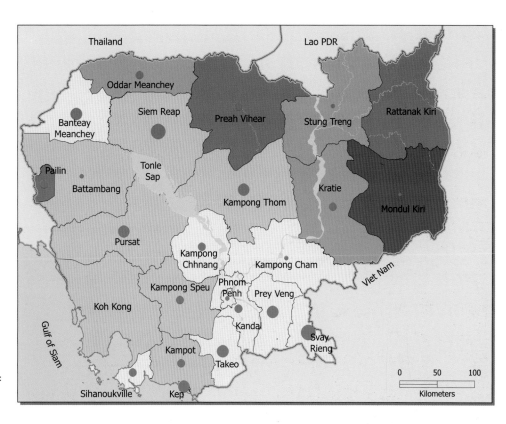

HIV/AIDS

Cambodia has the highest HIV prevalence rate in Southeast Asia although a decline in national prevalence rates and incidence rates among high risk groups has recently been recognized by the Joint United Program on HIV/AIDS (UNAIDS). This is largely owing to a decline in sexually transmitted infections (STI), a significant reduction of risk behavior and an effective prevention program targeting sexual transmission (UNAIDS: 2004).

HIV was first detected in Phnom Penh in 1991 and three years later the first cases of AIDS were diagnosed. The first national HIV Sentinel Surveillance Survey (HSS) was conducted in 1995 by the National AIDS Program (now the National Center for HIV/AIDS, Dermatology and STDs) in 9 out of 24 provinces and cities, especially those bordering Thailand and Vietnam. The target group included direct female sex workers (DFSW), indirect female sex workers (IDFSW), military, police, tuberculosis patients (TB) and women visiting antenatal care clinics (ANC). The sentinel sites have since been expanded and to date, eight rounds of HSS have been conducted covering 22 out of 24 provinces.

The data from the 2003 HSS showed that an estimated 123,100 people live with HIV/AIDS among the adult population aged 15-49 (65,600 men and 57,500 women), equivalent to 1.9% national prevalence. This is a significant decline from the estimated prevalence of 2.1% in 2002. The total number of persons who had AIDS and were urgently in need of care by the end of 2003 was 21,500. The estimated number of people who died from AIDS in 2003 was 20,000 (HSS: 2003). Although the estimated prevalence among brothel-based sex workers (the highest risk group) has declined from 43.9% in 1997 to 20.8% in 2003, incidence of new HIV infections remains high compared to other countries in the region.

National Response to HIV/AIDS

The MoH has made a strong political commitment to the prevention of HIV/AIDS and to the care of people with HIV/AIDS. In 2001 the National Aids Authority developed a national strategic plan to decrease the vulnerability to HIV/AIDS by promoting safe behaviour, focusing on changing aspects of the socio-economic context to support individuals to protect themselves from HIV infection and to cope with the consequences of HIV/AIDS.

Socio-economic Impact

Even at very low prevalence levels HIV/AIDS causes significant increases in illness and premature death among young, productive adults. Informal estimates from NCHADS suggest that HIV/AIDS may be responsible for half of all deaths among young men in their 20s and 30s in Cambodia. This increased morbidity and mortality can have severe socio-economic impacts upon poor rural households and communities where the male household head is usually the primary source of labour. When the majority of the population survives on subsistence farming, these impacts operate through both the costs of illness and lost productivity.

Although prevalence is decreasing in Cambodia, substantial numbers of people are now infected, and will require various forms of health care over the coming decades. Out-of-pocket expenditure by households themselves accounts for more than two-thirds of the $30 annual per capita health care spending in Cambodia. Suggested estimates of the annual cost of treating opportunistic infections is $291 - greater than the annual per capita income of $263, this excludes the cost of antiretroviral therapy. These 'catastrophic health expenditures' are estimated to account for much of the landlessness and new poverty in Cambodia.

As already noted, HIV/AIDS also contributes substantially to lost productivity due to the deaths of prime-age adults in the workforce. The 2001 estimates suggested that lost productivity due to AIDS deaths during 2011 alone would be US$1.7 billion, with US$18 billion being lost between 2001 and 2011. More recent estimates suggest that progress toward reducing poverty will be reduced by 60% per year because of AIDS (ADB/UNAIDS: 2004).

We should not view the impacts of HIV/AIDS only from an economic point of view. There is increasing evidence that young adult illness and premature death can have significant impact on household structure and formation, especially in poor rural farming communities. Where the male head of household is the first to become ill, women, as the traditional primary care-givers, experience considerable additional burdens. In addition, in Cambodia there are some suggestions that men, in these circumstances, will often return to their mother's homes, leaving their wives and families to support themselves. Also, if a husband is infected it is very likely that he will infect his wife and after he dies she will start to experience illness and then die too - and the household will collapse. The number of children orphaned in this way by AIDS could rise from 60,000 in 2001 to 97,000 by 2006, reaching 109,000 by 2011 (NCHADS: 2001). A major element of any multi-sectoral programme needs to be aimed at enabling households to survive, even if individuals die.

Education and Health

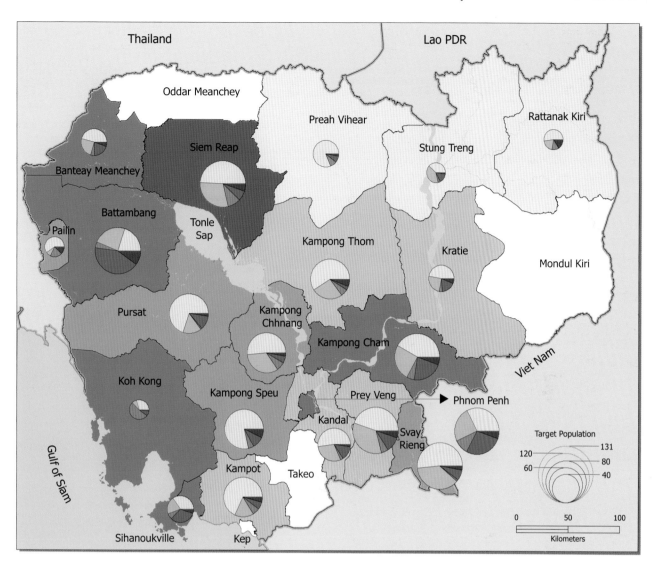

Legend

% of HIV for Target Group

	DFSW: Direct Female Sex Worker
	IDFSW: Indirect Female Sex Worker
	Police
	TB: TB Patients
	ANC: Women Visiting Antinatal Clinics
	No Data

Number of Target Group who Tested Positive for HIV

	26 - 40
	41 - 60
	61 - 80
	81 - 120
	121 - 131
	Water Body
—	Provincial Boundary
══	International Boundary

Data Sources:
HIV/AIDS: Report on HIV Sentinel
Surveillance in Cambodia 2002
International and Provincial Boundary:
Department of Geography 2005
Water Body: JICA Dataset 2002

HIV Prevalence in Target Groups 2002

Province	DFSW Test	DFSW Positive	IDFSW Test	IDFSW Positive	Police Test	Police Positive	TB Patients Test	TB Patients Positive	ANC Test	ANC Positive
Banteay Meanchey	171	64	45	9	170	7	167	26	250	11
Battambang	159	16	130	16	298	7	143	30	600	32
Kampong Cham	133	31	98	14	307	9	98	12	715	18
Kampong Chhnang	68	25	29	7	285	14	197	8	500	12
Kampong Speu	119	39	19	NA	285	6	71	3	498	16
Kampong Thom	84	17	53	5	285	6	140	2	473	11
Kampot	53	18	38	3	297	8	149	4	500	8
Kandal	100	23	40	5	142	1	157	9	495	4
Koh Kong	112	57	71	9	10	9	14	2	211	7
Kratie	90	22	45	6	300	6	64	6	419	11
Phnom Penh	162	30	145	20	169	10	150	24	696	24
Preah Vihear	50	15	17	NA	227	7	37	1	432	5
Prey Veng	151	26	32	4	157	3	319	13	500	9
Pursat	71	45	66	9	302	3	118	12	500	8
Rattanak Kiri	31	4	20	1	140	4	19	NA	399	17
Siem Reap	160	59	150	33	169	11	150	7	500	21
Sihanoukville	148	39	152	25	150	7	90	22	222	8
Stung Treng	65	19	10	3	192	6	44	5	316	7
Svay Rieng	73	26	47	12	300	3	229	12	599	10
Pailin	109	33	24	1	93	9	NA	NA	341	20

Sanitation and Access to Water

While Cambodia has made some progress in providing sanitation services and water to its people it still has the lowest water and sanitation coverage in East Asia (ADB: 2005). Many still rely on groundwater abstraction, rainwater and surface water collection for their water needs and sanitation is almost non existent. This is compounded by poor sanitation practices. In spite of widespread awareness few people use latrines, clean water jars, boil drinking water or properly wash their hands. These conditions greatly contribute to the poor health of Cambodians. Additionally, evidence suggests that time saved by having adequate access to water and sanitation can be used more productively by being involved in 'other activities'. While such activities may not necessarily be income generating, they may include reproductive activities such as child care and thus result in a net gain, if not specifically a monetary one.

There is a variety of data available for water supply and sanitation and discrepancies between the data is generally a result of different definitions of what constitutes safe water and adequate sanitation in the surveys. Many commentators argue that the most up to date data is from the Cambodian Inter-Censal Population Survey 2004 (CIPS), which was used to update census figures. After reviewing the available data, Cambodian sector agencies conclude that 37.5% of the population has access to safe drinking water (33.3% rural and 62.4% urban). 21.9% of the population has access to adequate sanitation (16.4% rural and 55.4% urban), although these figures may be optimistic.

The main consequences of a lack of access to safe drinking water and sanitation facilities, coupled with poor hygiene behaviour, are communicable diseases such as cholera, typhoid fever, parasite infestations and other kinds of diarrheal diseases. This further contributes to the vicious cycle of malnutrition and contagious diseases, especially among the less well-off. Parasite infestation and many other feco-oral transmitted diseases resulting from poor hygiene and sanitation push people further into the cycle of ill health and poverty. Limited access to safe water influences the health burden of skin conditions such as scabies and eye infections. It also increases the incidence of water based transmission diseases such as schistosomiasis and water related insect vectors that cause Malaria, Filariasis and Dengue Fever.

Targets and Strategies for Water Supply and Sanitation

Funding for sanitation and hygiene promotion in Cambodia has been limited, and in the past has not been a priority in budget allocation. In 1999 the Ministry of Rural Development (MRD) developed a "Rural Water Supply and Sanitation Policy Framework and Strategy" (RWSS). In 2003 the "Policy for Water Supply and Sanitation" was officially accepted by the government. In addition to this the "Sector Investment Plan" was last updated in 2005. While the original policy and strategy development predated the MDGs, the national targets for water supply and sanitation are now in line with this.

To help achieve these targets the ADB recently approved an $18 million grant for water supply and sanitation in five provinces over seven years beginning in 2006. In addition to this, UNICEF has made longstanding efforts in community and school sanitation as well as focusing on community water supply. Plan International are formulating a long term program of rural water supply and sanitation, Gret/Kosan completed 18 small piped rural supplies in 2005 and are considering a second phase. There are also various NGOs with small programs including Rainwater Cambodia, Concern, Care and World Vision.

Number of Families with Drinking Water

Province	Water at House	Water within 150m	Other Water	Number of families
Banteay Meanchey	17,116	14,507	69,008	100,631
Battambang	43,125	29,635	92,403	165,163
Kampong Cham	226,870	67,261	48,641	342,772
Kampong Chhnang	45,996	19,644	18,596	84,236
Kampong Speu	54,618	30,192	38,458	123,268
Kampong Thom	64,679	24,948	33,054	122,681
Kampot	26,907	24,050	62,620	113,577
Kandal	82,248	31,483	92,869	206,600
Koh Kong	6,155	4,404	9,684	20,243
Kratie	26,888	9,888	19,774	56,550
Mondul Kiri	3,560	1,717	3,810	9,087
Phnom Penh	5,973	1,224	6,606	13,803
Preah Vihear	10,552	7,354	9,449	27,355
Prey Veng	174,983	19,121	18,443	212,547
Pursat	22,421	15,861	30,557	68,839
Rattanak Kiri	6,208	2,491	13,837	22,536
Siem Reap	67,285	30,984	24,324	122,593
Sihanoukville	8,833	5,713	3,881	18,427
Stung Treng	5,158	3,408	7,292	15,858
Svay Rieng	93,972	14,518	1,872	110,362
Takeo	59,804	38,015	71,095	168,914
Oddar Meanchey	9,406	7,934	11,102	28,442
Kep	1,457	1,907	3,476	6,840
Pailin	2,997	2,101	5,352	10,450

Access to Water

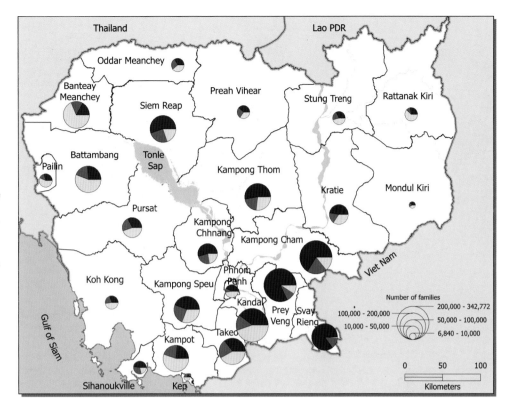

Legend

- ■ Water at House
- ■ Water Within 150m
- ░ Other Water
- ▒ Water Body
- — Provincial Boundary
- — International Boundary

Note:

Water at House: piped water, private pump well or private ring well, usable year round at the house.

Water within 150m: a communal tap, pump well or ring well, usable year round, within 150m of the house.

Other Water: pond, river, rain water or other as the most common source.

Sanitation by Commune

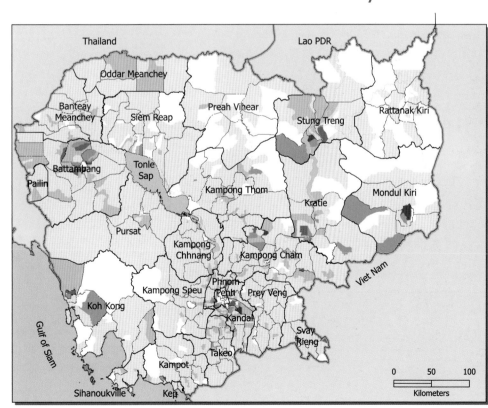

Legend

Percentage of Houses with Toilet

- 1 - 20
- 21 - 40
- 41 - 60
- 61 - 80
- 81 - 100
- No Data
- Water Body
- District Boundary
- Provincial Boundary
- International Boundary

Method:
Sanitation by Commune - Population by Commune / Number of Toilets by Commune.

Data Sources:
Drinking Water and Sanitation by Commune: Commune Database 2004
International, Provincial and District Boundary: Department of Geography 2005
Water Body: JICA Dataset 2002

Education and Health

References

ADB, 2005. $18 Million Grant to Help Provide Clean Water and Sanitation to Poor around Tonle Sap, Cambodia. Accessed at http://www.adb.org/Media/Articles/2005/8642_Cambodia_water/

CENAT Annual Progress Report

CIPS. 2004. Cambodian Inter-censal Population Survey. National Institute of Statistics, Ministry of Planning. Phnom Penh, Cambodia

Dewdney J. 2004. The MoH Health Workforce Development Plan 1996-2005- Third and Final Review. Phnom Penh, Cambodia

NCHADS. 2004. HIV Sentinel Surveillance 2003: Results, Trends and Estimates. NCHADS. Accessed at: www.nchads.org

NIS. 2000. Cambodian Health and Demographic Survey Manual. National Institute of Statistics, Ministry of Planning. Phnom Penh , Cambodia

NIS. 2005. Cambodian Statistical Yearbook 2005. National Institute of Statistics, Ministry of Planning. Phnom Penh, Cambodia

Mam, B. 2005. Summary Report on 2004 Health Sector Achievements. 26th Health Congress, Phnom Penh 01 March 2005.

MoH. 2003. National Health Sector Strategic Plan for year 2003-2007. Ministry of Health. Phnom Penh, Cambodia

MoH. 2003. National Health Statistics Report 2003. Ministry of Health, Department of Planning. Phnom Penh, Cambodia

Oum, P. 2005. Situation analysis of Child Survival Crisis in Cambodia - Master thesis. Johns Hopkins Bloomberg School of Public Health, Unpublished

Oum, S. 2002. Development, Implementation and Evaluation of a Community-Based Surveillance System in Rural Cambodia - Doctoral thesis, London school of Tropical Medicine & Hygiene, Unpublished

Oum, S. 2005. Personal communication with Dr. Sophal Oum, Rector of University of Health Sciences. Ministry of Health, Cambodia

UN. 1998. United Nations Common Country Assessment-Cambodia. Accessed at: http://www.un.org.kh/rcsystem/files/cca.pdf

UNAIDS, ABD. 2004. Study Series: Asia-Pacific's Opportunity - Investing to Avert an HIV/AIDS Crisis.

UNICEF. 2004 The state of the world's children, 2004: girls, education and development. New York

WHO. 2000. Country Cooperation Strategy: Cambodia. Accessed at: http://www.who.int/countries/en/cooperation_strategy_khm_en.pdf

WHO. 2004. AIDS Epidemic Update. WHO/UNAIDS. Accessed at: www.unaids.org

WSP-EAP, 2002. Learning What Works For Sanitation. Revisiting Sanitation Successes in Cambodia. Accessed at http://www.wsp.org/publications/eap_lww.pdf

Appendix

CMAC presenting an updated map on the location of minefields to the local community in Preah Put, Battambang Province.

The Kampong Speu Urban Land Use Planning Project

With the rapid expansion of urban areas due to rural urban migration and an increase in population there is a pressing need for urban planning in Cambodia. As the urban population grows it is necessary to plan an adequate infrastructure to improve living conditions and quality of life. The Kampong Speu Urban Land Use Planning Project aims to improve the Ministry of Land Management, Urban Planning and Construction staff's skills related to land use planning. Furthermore it aims to support the provincial and district authorities of MLMUPC in Kampong Speu regarding their urban land use planning tasks. The German Development Service (DED), provided advisers, project budget, training courses and technical equipment.

Kampong Speu Province is situated in the Plains region Southwest of the capital Phnom Penh. The majority of the population lives in the rural areas with agriculture as the main source of income. The provincial capital, Kampong Speu, is the largest town between Phnom Penh and Sihanoukville on National road 4.

The project started with two working groups in the Department of Land Management and the Department of Urban Planning in late 2002. First, the Urban Planning team focused on the town centre, the Land Management team on the surrounding rural area. Later the teams were merged together.

In the beginning the project worked with topographical maps from the Department of Geography. During a first workshop in the provincial Department of Land Management and Urban Planning Kampong Speu, the team asked the Land Management District officers to sketch the existing land use on transparency sheets, to mark the market places, industrial facilities, tourist sites and protected and concession areas.

In the next step the team verified the information by several field visits to Kampong Speu province with different topics like industry, tourist sites and protected areas. Generally the information of the district officers proved to be true although the sketched boundaries were not so exact. The method was useful to get a fast overview and to learn about the important locations and issues. A first interim report (June 2003) described the general land use situation in Kampong Speu province.

Afterwards the team started to discuss development goals and to draft a land use concept for the urban area and the surrounding landscape. The team changed from sketch mapping to computer mapping during this phase. Because there was only an outdated aerial photo from 1992 available, a balloon photo of Kampong Speu town centre was taken in March 2004. Based on this aerial photo the drawing of an actual map of the town centre was possible. The structure of the first draft report from July 2004 followed the steps of the planning process: Situation Analysis - Development Goals - Strategy.

Two workshops for participation and information of the local stakeholders took place in November 2003 and March 2005. The recommendations and comments of the workshop participants were integrated into the first draft report in July 2004 and the second draft report in July 2005.

Six staff members of the Department of Land Management, six staff members of the Departments of Urban Planning and Research and Regulation and three provincial and district staff participated in the project. InWent contributed to participation workshops, UN Habitat supported the project with ESRI GIS Software within the "1000 cities project".

Aerial Balloon photo showing Kampong Speu centre

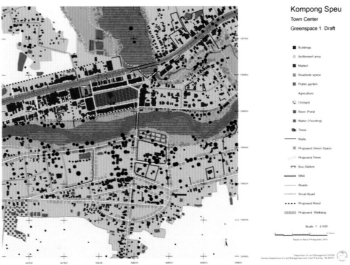

Kampong Speu town centre urban green space planning concept
Note: Map and Legend provided as an example only.

Kampong Speu Urban Planning Process

The following maps intend to give an overview of the urban planning process only

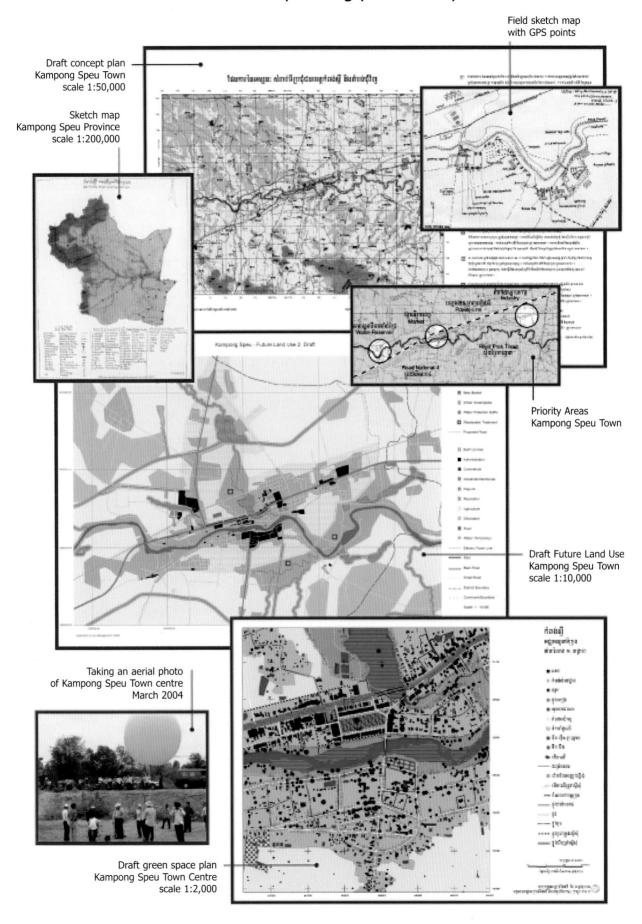

Field sketch map with GPS points

Draft concept plan Kampong Speu Town scale 1:50,000

Sketch map Kampong Speu Province scale 1:200,000

Priority Areas Kampong Speu Town

Draft Future Land Use Kampong Speu Town scale 1:10,000

Taking an aerial photo of Kampong Speu Town centre March 2004

Draft green space plan Kampong Speu Town Centre scale 1:2,000

Rural Land Use Planning and Natural Resource Management

In cooperation with the Ministry of Land Management Urban Planning and Construction (MLMUPC) Seila's Commune and Community-based Natural Resource and Environment Management Project (CCB-NREM) aims to improve sustainable and equitable use of land and natural resources, through participatory community and local level planning and investment. This recognises that sustainable management of land and natural resources is critical to improving people's living standard, both now and in the future. In particular, it supports commune-level governance by:

- providing information on, and helping to define, the spatial framework for land-use planning within the commune development plan
- bringing in tools, methods, and technical support for analysing the natural and other resources available in the landscape of each commune
- providing funds for priority investments in sustainable livelihood activities based on the communes' natural resources and environmental situation

An important tool in this process is the development of commune and/or village level maps showing natural resources (land cover)/ land use and boundaries (community fishery, community forestry, concessions, protected areas and administrative) as a basis for analyses of the present situation, solving conflicts and identify options for future. Participatory Land Use Planning (PLUP) is used in the lowest level of planning in selected areas to include ownership and user rights during the process.

Mechanism for official approval mechanism of the land use maps (in land use plans and (commune) development plans) and the linkages with a broader form of planning need to be strengthened.

The figure below shows the stages of mapping, from general maps based on existing data, through commune level maps improved with participation from commune council and village leaders, to detailed village land use maps and plans. Through this standardized process National data will be improved. CCB-NREM is now active in 10 Provinces and 303 communes and will increase their target area on an annually basis.

Stages of Commune Land Use Mapping

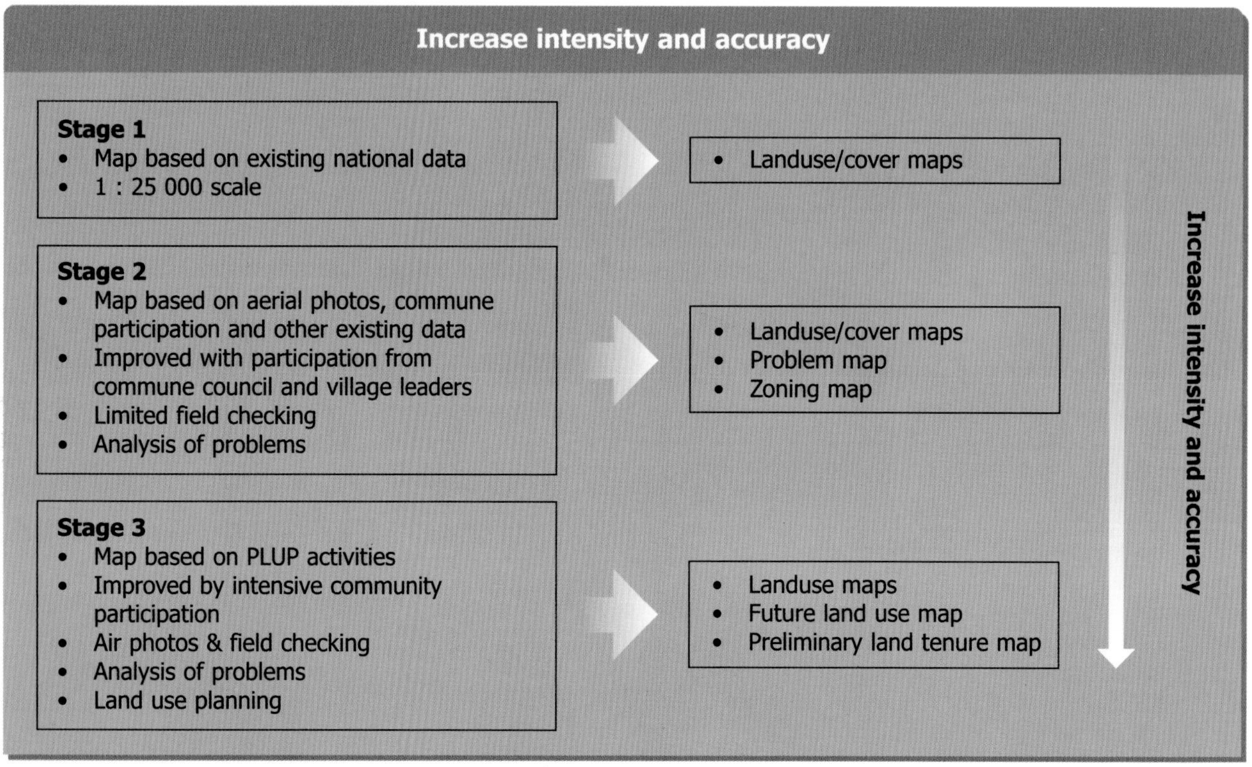

Increase intensity and accuracy

Stage 1
- Map based on existing national data
- 1 : 25 000 scale

→
- Landuse/cover maps

Stage 2
- Map based on aerial photos, commune participation and other existing data
- Improved with participation from commune council and village leaders
- Limited field checking
- Analysis of problems

→
- Landuse/cover maps
- Problem map
- Zoning map

Stage 3
- Map based on PLUP activities
- Improved by intensive community participation
- Air photos & field checking
- Analysis of problems
- Land use planning

→
- Landuse maps
- Future land use map
- Preliminary land tenure map

Increase intensity and accuracy

Demographic Data

Province/City	Population 1998			Sex Ratio	Total HHs	Population annual growth rate in %	Density (Pers/Sq. Km.)	
	Both Sexes	Male	Female				2006	2021
Cambodia-Total	**11,437,656**	**5,511,408**	**5,926,248**	**93.0**	**2,188,663**	**1.81**	**82**	**112**
1. Plain Region	5.898,305	2,820,859	3,077,446	91.7	1,140,167	1.14	297	390
Phnom Penh	999,804	481,911	517,893	93.1	173,678	1.26	4,969	7,769
Kandal	1,075,125	515,996	559,129	92.3	206,189	1.91	374	484
Kampong Cham	1,608,914	775,796	833,118	93.1	312,841	0.35	203	258
Svay Rieng	478,252	225,105	253,147	88.9	98,244	1.04	196	242
Prey Veng	946,042	445,140	500,902	88.9	194,185	1.04	231	274
Takeo	790,168	376,911	413,257	91.2	155,030	1.68	270	338
2. Tonle Sap lake Region	3,505,448	1,698,931	1,806,517	94.0	661,872	2.52	67	94
Banteay Meanchey	577,772	283,358	294,414	96.2	111,856	2.74	122	180
Battambang	793,129	388,599	404,530	96.1	148,356	2.74	90	123
Kampong Chhnang	417,693	197,691	220,002	89.9	82,638	4.13	98	138
Kampong Thom	569,060	272,844	296,216	92.1	106,908	1.08	52	70
Siem Reap	696,164	336,685	359,479	93.7	127,215	1.52	88	29
Oddar Meanchey	68,279	34,472	33,807	102.0	12,531	2.74	17	28
Palin	22,906	12,392	10,514	117.9	4,133	2.74	45	78
Pursat	360,445	172,890	187,555	92.2	68,235	3.62	37	53
3. Coastal Region	844,861	411,739	433,122	95.1	163,341	2.56	65	22
Kampot	524,805	253,085	275,320	91.9	104,993	2.56	82	104
Koh Kong	132,106	67,700	64,406	105.1	24,964	1.47	19	33
Kep	28,660	14,014	14,646	95.7	5,369	2.56	128	226
Sihanoukville	155,690	76,940	78,750	97.7	28,015	1.47	266	437
4. Plateau and Mountain Region	1,189,042	579,879	609,163	95.2	223,283	2.5	23	38
Kampong Speu	598,882	287,392	311,490	92.3	115,728	2.00	110	155
Kratie	263,175	130,254	132,921	98.0	49,326	2.00	31	71
Mondul Kiri	32,407	16,380	16,027	102.2	5,657	2.00	3	5
Preah Vihear	119,261	59,333	59,928	99.0	21,491	2.00	12	19
Rattanak Kiri	94,243	46,396	47,847	97.0	16,758	2.00	12	19
Stung Treng	81,074	40,124	40,950	98.0	14,323	2.99	10	16

Source: NIS Statistical Yearbook 2005.
Note: Population calculations are from the last census in 1998.

Appendix

Age Structure

Cambodia/ Urban Rural/ Province/ Region	Under 5 (0 - 4)	Children (0 - 14)	Economically Productive Age Group (15 - 64)	The Elderly Population (65+)	The voting Age Group (18+)
Cambodia					
Total	11.0	39.0	57.0	4.0	54.1
Urban	9.7	34.0	62.6	3.4	58.5
Rural	11.3	39.4	56.6	4.0	53.0
Plain	10.2	36.5	59.1	4.4	56.4
Kampong Cham	10.6	37.9	57.0	5.1	55.0
Kandal	10.2	37.1	58.2	4.8	55.8
Phnom Penh	7.8	27.8	68.9	3.3	65.0
Prey Veng	10.9	39.1	56.8	4.1	54.0
Svay Rieng	9.9	37.8	58.1	4.1	54.6
Takeo	11.5	39.5	55.7	4.8	53.7
Tonle Sap	11.7	40.4	56.2	3.4	51.9
Banteay Meanchey & Oddar Meanchey	11.5	40.2	57.2	2.6	52.0
Battambang & Pailin	10.9	39.7	57.2	3.1	52.5
Kampong Chhnang	12.1	41.1	54.7	4.2	52.3
Kampong Thom	11.8	39.5	55.5	5.0	53.0
Pursat	11.2	40.9	55.4	3.7	50.7
Siem Reap	13.2	41.2	56.0	2.8	50.6
Coastal	12.3	40.7	56.1	3.2	51.7
Kampot & Kep	12.4	40.9	55.4	3.7	51.6
Koh Kong & Sihanoukville	12.1	40.3	57.6	2.1	51.8
Plateau and Mountain	12.3	41.6	55.0	3.4	51.4
Kampong Speu Kratie & Mondul Kiri	11.5	40.4	55.9	3.7	51.9
Preah Vihear & Rattanak Kiri & Stung Treng	13.1	42.6	54.3	3.1	51.0

Source: CIPS 2004 and 1998 Census, General Report and Provincial Report, NIS, Ministry of Planning.
* Urban-rural figures at province levels are not available due to smallness of sample size.

Indigenous Seed Source Sites

No site	Province	District	Commune	UTM Point	Area, Ha	Species	Name in Khmer	Mother tree
1	Preah Vihear	Tbeng Meanchey	Pal Hal	04 94 650 15 16 781	12.5	Dalbergia bariensis	នាងនួន	78
2	Kampong Thom	Sandann	Tumring	05 51 500 14 38 000	117	Sindora cochinchinensis	ករកោះ	97
						Tarrietia javanica	ដូនថែម	39
						Shorea hypochra	កំព្ញាន, ផ្លែកក្រហម	22
						Shorea guiso	ជ័រចុង	19
						Dipterocarpus costatus	ឈើទាលបង្កួយ	396
						Anisoptera glabra	ផ្ដៀក	323
3	Kampong Thom	Santuk	Kroryear	05 31 601 14 09 923	104	Pinus merkusii	ស្រល់	72
						Fagraea fragrans	តាត្រាវ	72
4	Banteay Meanchey	Mongkul Borey	Phnom Tauch	02 85 596 14 84 344	50	Azadirachta indica	ស្ដៅ	90
5	Ratanakiri	Ochum	Cha Ung	07 06 931 15 20 149	21	Dalbergia bariensis	នាងនួន	21
						Pterocarpus macrocarpus	ផ្ចង់	20
						Xylia xylocarpa	សុក្រុំ	22
6	Ratanakiri	Lumphat	Patang	07 21 626 15 15 900	18	Afzelia xylocarpa	បេង	27
						Dalbergia bariensis	នាងនួន	41
						Pterocarpus macrocarpus	ផ្ចង់	14
7	Ratanakiri	Kaunmum	Teun	07 04 001 15 04 648	20	Afzelia xylocarpa	បេង	26
						Dalbergia bariensis	នាងនួន	17
						Sindora cochinchinensis	ករកោះ	7
8	Ratanakiri	Kaunmum	Teun	07 05 131 15 05 403	30	Hopea ferrea	គគីរថ្ម	88
9	Siem Reap	Chikeng	Kvav	04 51 140 14 84668	20	Pterocarpus macrocarpus	ផ្ចង់	83
10	Siem Reap	Varin	Sre Nauy	04 00 757 15 20 273	50	Dalbergia cochinchinensis	ក្រញូង	121
11	Siem Reap	Siem Reap	Angkor complex	03 76 940 14 85 489	20	Dipterocarpus alatus	ឈើទាលទឹក	43
12	Siem Reap	Svay Leu	Svay Leu	04 30 120 15 00 583	100	Pterocarpus macrocarpus	ផ្ចង់	160
						Xylia xylocarpa	សុក្រុំ	141
						Sindora cochinchinensis	ករកោះ	87
						Haldinia cordifolia	ខ្វាវ	62
13	Mondulkiri	Oraing	Senmonorom	07 27 650 13 58 515	4	Toona sureni	អាំអា	26
14	Koh Kong	Sre Ambel	Doung Peng	03 69 130 12 42 439	10	Scaphium macropodum	សំរ៉ង	78
15	Koh Kong	Sre Ambel	Doung Peng	03 64149 12 56 544	18.5	Sindora cochinchinensis	ករកោះ	37
						Dalbergia cochinchinensis	ក្រញូង	26
						Dalbergia bariensis	នាងនួន	37
						Pterocarpus macrocarpus	ផ្ចង់	33
16	Pusat	Kro-Vanh	Pro Gneal	03 74 329 13 70 194	96	Sindora cochinchinensis	ក្រញូង	45
						Dalbergia bariensis	នាងនួន	69
17	Udor Meanchey	Samrong	Bansayrak	0331972 1581408		Shorea roburghiana	ពពែល	
18	Sihanoukville		Kbal Chhay	0348366 1179581	3 plots	Species trials toward establishment of seed sources.		

Source: Cambodia Tree Seed Project, MAFF

Economic Land Concessions

No.	Name of Company	Province	District	Commune	Area Ha	Purpose	Comments
	Approved Economic Concessions						
1	Leang Hour Hong Import and Export, Agro Industry Development and Processing	Battambang		Takrey	8,000	Sugar cane and Cassava	5,000 ha in Dom Sam Wildlife sanctuary
2	Agro Star Investment	Kampong Cham	Choeng Prey		2,400	Cashew and animal husbandry	
3	Mieng Ly Heng Investment	Kampong Cham	Memot		3,000	Rubber	
4	TTY Industrial Crops Development Import-Export	Kampong Cham	Memot		1,070	Cassava	Exact location unknown. No coordinates
5	VANNMA Import-Export Co. Ltd	Kampong Cham	Memot		1,200	Sugar cane and Cassava	
6	Phea Phimex Co. Ltd	Kampong Chhnang	Baribor, Tekphos, Sammakki, Meanchey		138,963	Tree plantation and paper factory	Exact location unknown. No coordinates
7	Phea Phimex Co. Ltd	Pursat	Kra Kor, Kra Vanh, Sampov Meas		176,065	Tree plantation and paper factory	Exact location unknown. No coordinates
8	C.J Cambodia Co. Ltd 1	Kampong Speu	Phnom Srouch		5,000	Cassava	
9	C.J Cambodia Co. Ltd 2	Kampong Speu	Phnom Srouch		3,000	Cassava	
10	The Cambodia Haining Co. Ltd	Kampong Speu	Aural, Phnom Srouch		23,000	Agro-ind crops and procession factory	
11	Cambo Victor Investment and Development Co. Ltd	Kampong Speu	Aural, Phnom Srouch		28,500	Corn, bean soya bean, rice, cassava and peanut	
12	China National Cooperation for Oversea Economic Cooperation Laod Star Development Co. Ltd	Kampong Speu	Aural, Phnom Srouch		8,000	Agro-ind crops	
13	Golden Land Development Co. Ltd	Kampong Speu	Phnom Srouch	Treng Tra Yoe	4,900	Agro-ind crops ans procession factory	
14	Henan (Cambodia) Economic & Trade Development Zone	Kampong Speu	Phnom Srouch		4,100	Agro-ind crops and animal husbandry	
15	Uk Khun Industrial Plants and Other Development	Kampong Speu	Phnom Srouch		12,506	Cashew, agro-ind crops and animal husbandry	
16	Kimsville Corp.	Kampong Speu	Phnom Srouch		3,200	Agro-ind crops and animal husbandry	
17	Talam Plantation Holding SND. BHD	Kampong Speu	Phnom Srouch		36,700	Oil palm, Rubber and procession factory	Forest conversion, 3,000 ha in Kirrirom NP. Exact location unknown
18	An Mardy Group	Kampong Thom	Balang		9,863	Agro-ind crops and animal husbandry	
19	Cambodia Eversky Agricultural Development Co. Ltd	Kampong Thom	Santuk		10,000	Cotton	
20	Camland Co. Ltd	Kampot	Kampong Bay		16,000	Oil palm	
21	First Bio-Tech Agricultural Co. Ltd	Kampot	Chhouk		10,000	Agro-ind crops and animal husbandry	

No.	Name of Company	Province	District	Commune	Area Ha	Purpose	Comments
22	World Tristar Entertainment Co. Ltd	Kampot	Chhouk		9,800	Corn and procession Factory	
23	China Cambodia State Farm 999 International Co. Ltd	Koh Kong	Sre Ambel		7,500	Agro-ind crops and animal husbandry	
24	The Green Rich Co. Ltd	Koh Kong			60,200	Oil plams, fruit trees and acacia	In PA. Exact location unknown. No coordinates
25	Ratana Visal Development Co. Ltd	Pursat	Krakor		3,000	Cashew and oil palm	
26	30/4 Gianlani Co. Ltd	Rattanak kirri	Oyado		9,380	Agro-ind crops and animal husbandry and proc factory	
27	Global Tech Sdn., Bhd, Rama Khmer International and Men Sarun Friendship	Rattanak kirri	Oyado		20,000	Oil palms, coffee and additional crops	
28	Mong Rethy Investment Oil Palm Cambodia Co. Ltd	Sihanoukville	Prey Nup		11,000	Oil palm	
29	Mong Rethy Investment Cassava Cambodia Co. Ltd	Sihanoukville	Prey Nup		1,800	Cassava and procession factory	
30	Cassava Starch Production Co. Ltd	Stung Treng	Stung Treng		7,400	Agr. and agro-ind crops	
31	GG World Group (Cambodia) Development Co. Ltd	Stung Treng	Stung Treng		5,000	agro-ind crops, animal husbandry and proc factory	
32	Grand Land Agricutltural Development	Stung Treng	Se San		9,854	agro-ind crops	
33	Green Sea Industry Co Ltd	Stung Treng	Siem Pang, Stung Treng		100,852	Trincomali plantation	Exact location unknown. No coordinates
34	Phou Mady Investment Group	Stung Treng	Se San		10,000	Acacia, Trincomali and other crops	
35	Sal Sophea Peanich Co. Ltd	Stung Treng	Se San		9,917	Acacia, Trincomali and other crops	
36	Siv Guek Investment Co. Ltd.	Stung Treng	Se San		10,000	Acacia, Trincomali and other crops	
37	Sopheak Nika Investment Agro-industrial Plants Co.Ltd	Stung Treng	Se San		10,000	Acacia, Trincomali and other crops	
Total Area Size (Approved)					**791, 170 Ha**		

Pending Economic Concessions							
No.	Name of Company	Province	District	Commune	Area Ha	Purpose	Comments
1	Bopha Angkori Mech Trong Kong	Kampong Cham			5,000		Location Unknown
2	Wuzhishan	Mondul kirri			10,000		Location Unknown
3	Yalian International Trust and Investment Co. Ltd & Ocean Space Investment Co. LTd	Mondul kirri			19,900		Location Unknown
4	Tay Seng Import Export	Rattanak kirri			2,000		Location Unknown
5	Grang Land Agricultural Development Co. Ltd	Stung Treng	Se san		9,854		Location Unknown
Total Area Size (Pending)					**46,754 Ha**		

Source: www.maff.gov.kh

Appendix

The General Characteristics of Cambodian Soil Groups after Crocker

Azonal Soils	Area (Km²)	
		Pedologically new, young or formative soils in which the geologic and physiographic factors are the predominant characteristics of the soil. The pedologic profile development processes are not significant.
Acid Lithosols	43,995	Soils which are composed of shallow mantles of weathering material over unweathered rock. They are the result of erosion removal of soil materials as rapidly as the soil materials are developed from rock decomposition. This occurs in the mountain areas and in areas of resistant rock formation where the source rock is acidic sandstone, shale, granite etc. Also in sloping talus colluvium of acid rocks in the mountainous areas.
Basic Lithosols	3,318	Stony soils derived from basalt, limestone, or apatite. The lithosols found on basic geologic formations are economically significant from a mineral resource development standpoint. Also, they have good forest production potential. They are easily recognized by comparing the map of this survey with geologic maps of Cambodia.
Alluvials	15,002	The fresh-water alluvial deposits of Cambodia, bordering the rivers, especially the broad alluvial flats of the Mekong, are geologically recent deposits of effluvia in which pedologic processes of soil formation have not preceded enough to make significant pedological horizon differentiation. Differences which occur in the profile are primarily the result of differences in textural stratification, type, rate and nature of deposition. Subject to nearly annual flooding during the rainy season, the alluvial soils regularly receive additional depositional soil material from the upper watersheds.
Brown Alluvial Soils	1,315	Coarser-textured soils along the Mekong River banks and islands. They are economically quite significant and have different production potential from the finer-textured slack-water alluvials which are usually farther back from the river channels.
Lacustrine Alluvials	10,446	Soils encircling the great lake, Tonle Sap, comprising an area of slightly acid to neutral, very fertile, recently deposited alluvial materials. These soils are normally flooded annually in the rainy season. They are derived from a variety of source materials; as the clay and silt-laden Mekong River flood waters flow back into the lake in the rainy season, and local, mixed basic and acidic source alluvial materials are washed in from the north, west and south of the lake. The soils appear under field observation to have some montmorillinitic clays blended in the profile.
Coastal Complex	1,840	A complex group of the salt-water tidal mangrove swamps of coastal clays and coastal ridges of sands. They are both classified as regosols. This unit is very limited in area, and the soils of the unit differ sharply in their characteristics and production potential.

Zonal Soils	Area (Km²)	
		Pedalfers-Pedologically mature or normal soils formed under humid climatic conditions or conditions conducive to sesquioxide accumulations.
A. Ateritic Soils		Soils of forested warm-temperature and tropical regions.
Red-Yellow Podzols	25,444	Acid soils with leached A horizons and illuvial B horizons of variegated red, yellow and/or grey clay accumulations.
Latosols	6,309	Deeply weathered, uniformly leached, acid soils of fairly uniform characteristics throughout the profile in depth.

Intrazonal Soils	Area (Km²)	
		Pedologically immature or partially developed soils in a formative stage in which a single factor or a group of factors has dominated the morphological development and the resulting characteristics of the soils profile.
A. Hydromorphic Soils		Soils of marshes, swamps, seep areas and flats. These soils are influenced by either a high permanent, a fluctuating (rainy season high, dry season low) or a near surface ground water table.
Planosols	1,665	Soils having one or more horizons abruptly separated from, and sharply contrasting to and adjacent horizon because of cementation, compaction or very high clay content, usually with a fluctuating water table.
Plinthite podzols	17,782	Soils with pronounced accumulations of ferruginous bauxitic concretions at depths varying markedly with erosion and texture of original profile materials, which are formed under the marked fluctuation of the ground water table resulting from pronounced dry season-rainy season moisture variations. These are primarily senile tropical soils and in many areas give indication of being an advanced age stage of the red-yellow podzols.
Cultural hydromorphics	14,055	Soils which have a thin, artificially compacted, impermeable horizon resulting from development into rice fields. While these soils are classified on the basis of recent cultural usage, the shallow impermeable compacted layer has an over riding effect on the physical and production characteristics of these soils. These soils may be found with textural and chemical profile characteristics similar to other soil groups in Cambodia but these have been altered by the effect of the paddy layer.
Grey hydromorphics	17,013	Soils with fluctuating water table at or near the surface most of the layer. These soils have shallow grey surface horizon over heavy-textured, mottled grey, red and yellow clayey substrata. In some great soil group classifications, this class of soils might be designated as low humic glei soils. (The low humic glei soils are an intrazonal group of imperfectly to poorly drained soils with very thin surface horizons, moderately high in organic matter, over mottled grey and brown glei-like mineral horizons with a low degree of textural differentiation.) In this survey, the name "grey hydromorphics" is preferred because the content of organic matter on and in the profile is relatively very low, and the degree or extent of gleization is not distinct from stratification or from parent material characteristics in filed observations.
Plinthitic hydromorphics	1,162	A particular area of grey hydromorphics soils, in the Snuol-Sre Khtum area of Kratie and Mondul Kiri provinces, which, from field observations, appears to have differences from the other soil units of this survey in the features of their development. Field observation indicates that this is the product of an ancient plinthite which has developed on a nearly flat plain which has more recently had impeded drainage and fine soil particles accumulated. These factors have produced a shallow, dark grey silty clay to clay overlying consolidated plinthite.
Brown hydromorphics	6,813	Soils formed under conditions of either high or fluctuating water table developed on colluvial-alluvial parent materials of basic or mixed origin. These colluvial-alluvial areas have a deep, heavy-textured profile. Most areas of this class are relatively highly productive. The color of these soils is medium grey-brown to brown in the upper horizon, with mottled clays in the lower horizons. But for the economic significance, this unit would be combined with the grey hydromorphic soils on the basis of pedologic classification.
Alumisols	3,164	Grey hydromorphic soils which have as a delineating characteristic soluble aluminum and low pH values in the profile to such an extent as to limit plant growth. Delineation is based on a particular set of characteristics, rather than on grouping of characteristics. Significant economic consideration of the effects of the delineating characteristics makes this designation necessary. In areas where soils of this unit occur, locally known as "sol alune", production is limited by occurrence of soluble aluminum compounds and strong acidity, which inhibit plant growth and crop production.
Regurs	6,292	Very dark grey-brown to black, shallow, alkaline clays overlying partially weathered basic parent material. In some areas, the parent material is composed of soft, white, unconsolidated, calcareous granules and light grey clay. They occur especially in the Battambang area, where the regurs have developed over marl derived from outwash of limestone hills in the area. These regurs are the familiar "black cotton soils" as found in India and in scattered places elsewhere in the tropics. Due to the limited total areas of these soils, they are included in the unit of regurs developed from basalt. The basaltic regurs of Kampong Cham, Kratie, Mondul Kiri and Rattanak Kiri provinces are considerably different from the calcimorphic regurs. Basaltic regurs occur in some areas developed on colluvial outwash materials from basalt, and in other areas basaltic round boulders from underlying rock material are found in and on the profile. Pedologically, both kinds of regurs are young shallow soils. The dark granular clay surface extends to a variable depth, averaging thirty centimeters.

Source: Crocker, C. 1962. Exploratory Survey of the Soils of Cambodia. RGC Soil Commission and USAID joint Publication. Phnom Penh Cambodia
Note: Refer to map page 99.

Rice Soil Descriptions and Management Recommendations

Soil Group	Occurrence (%)	Description	Soil Management
Prey Khmer	10-12%	Has a predominantly deep sandy nature with no soil structure or hardpan development. Occur predominantly on old alluvial terraces above the level of natural flooding of rivers.	• Difficult to manage for rice production with low fertility. • pH is acidic. • Limitation of rooting depth is not a problem but low water holding capabilities means the soil is excessively drained.
Prateah Lang	25-30%	A prominent feature of this soil is the sandy textured surface soil overlying loamy or clayey subsoil. Developed from previously weathered alluvium deposited by rivers and/or colluvium derived mostly from sandstone and clay shale.	• Difficult to manage for rice production with low fertility. • pH is acidic. • Shallow rooting depth. • Restricted internal drainage makes soil suitable for flooded rice production. • Tillage is relatively easy.
Labansiek	Less than 1%	These soils have a distinctive red colour and a uniform deep profile. The profile is clayey throughout and the soil is very slippery and sticky when wet. Are pluvial lands and do not occur in the flooded valleys.	• Has moderate potential and responds well to improved management with moderate fertility. • pH is slightly acidic. • Tillage is possible in a wide range of moisture conditions without affecting structure.
Orung	1-2%	Characterized by a sharp boundary between a loamy or clayey textured surface soil and the sandy textured subsoil. This soil sets hard when dry and the surface may crack. Mostly associated with present or ancient river systems.	• Difficult to manage for rice production with low fertility. • Fertilizer management is difficult with nutrients leached into the subsoil or drained by runoff. • Tillage is difficult. • Restricted drainage means that it is difficult to grow water logging sensitive crops.
Krakor	15%	The soil surface is grey or brown when wet and generally light grey to light brown when dry. The subsoil has a firm consistency usually with a loamy or clayey texture. Occurs on floodplains which are inundated for three months or longer.	• Has a good potential to produce high rice yields with good fertility. • Responds well to improved management. • High suitability to irrigation. • Root growth is generally not limited.
Bakan	10-15%	The topsoil has a loamy or clayey texture. The surface sets extremely hard when dry. The subsoil has a loamy or clayey texture. Occurs on colluvial plains and old alluvial terraces.	• Well suited to rice production with low to moderate fertility. • Soil ranges from slightly acidic to acidic. • Tillage is very difficult and the soil must be saturated before plowing. • Restricted drainage prevents cultivation of water logging sensitive crops in the wet season.
Kbal Po	15%	The soil is young and poorly differentiated with the primary difference between the top soil and subsoil being restricted to colour. It is formed of recent alluvial material of the floodplains of the Mekong-Bassac river system and on the Lacustrine floodplain surrounding the major lakes.	• Relatively easy to manage with a high potential for rice production. • Good fertility, with fertility decreasing with distance from the main river channel. • pH is slightly acidic to neutral in the nonthionic phase but the subsoil is acidic and restricts root growth. • the first rains drain rapidly into these soils but later internal drainage is restricted because of the clayey topsoil. • Soils are very sticky when wet causing problems for plowing.
Kein Svay	Less than 2%	Distinguished by a deep relatively uniform profile with a brown surface soil. Texture ranges from loamy to clayey. It occurs on river levees and parts of the backslopes and is typical of meander floodplains.	• Relatively easy to manage with a high potential for agricultural productivity. • Generally requires irrigation if used for rice production. • pH is slightly acidic to neutral. • Root growth is generally not restricted. • Internal drainage is good to moderate on the loamy soils but poor on the clayey soils.
Toul Samroung	7-10%	Characterized by brown or grey clayey or loamy topsoil. Develops moderate to large cracks on drying. The subsoil has slightly higher clay content. Primarily found on slightly undulating plains formed from colluvium and alluvium of mixed origin.	• Well suited to rice production with moderate to high potential and yields respond well to improved management. • Well suited to irrigation. • pH ranges from slightly acidic to neutral. • Tillage is moderately difficult and soil must be saturated before plowing with animals. • Restricted drainage makes it difficult to grow water logging sensitive crops unless good drainage is supplied.
Koktrap	5%	The surface soil is usually clayey, but sometimes loamy. The subsoil has a clayey or loamy texture with abundant red and yellow mottles. Occupies land on the old alluvial terraces and depressions.	• Relatively easy to manage with moderate to high potential for rice production. • Fertility varies greatly between the fertile and infertile phases, however with correct fertilizer application it becomes one of the better soils of the rained areas. • pH is strongly buffed with the pH increasing slowly on flooding. • Rooting depth is limited by a hard plow pan and the clayey subsoil. • Requires only a moderate amount of moisture before its soft enough to plow.
Kampong Siem	2%	Distinctive dark colour, clayey soil texture and deep wide cracking. Often less than 1m of soil overlying the parent rock. Occurs in low areas of a varied undulating landscape of small hills and rises or at the foot slopes of larger hills.	• Well suited to rice production. • Fertile. • Ph ranges from slightly acidic to slightly alkaline. • Rooting depth is generally not limited, although the soil may be shallow. • Internal drainage is initially very rapid. • Extremely sticky when moist and difficult to plow with a four wheel tractor.

Source: White, P.F. etal, 1997. The Soils Used for Rice Production in Cambodia. A Manual for Their Identification and Management. International Rice Research Institute. Manila, Philippines.
Note: Refer to map page 101.

Gross Enrollment Ratio in Primary, Lower and Upper Secondary School based on CSES 2003-2004

Province/City	Primary School			Lower Secondary School			Upper Secondary School		
	Female	Female	Female	Female	Female	Female	Female	Female	Female
All Cambodia	**124.3**	**129.5**	**127.0**	**46.0**	**58.4**	**52.2**	**17.5**	**23.7**	**20.8**
Phnom Penh	122.4	129.2	126.0	103.2	109.0	106.0	50.9	64.4	57.3
Kampong Cham	116.9	131.0	124.1	38.9	45.4	42.3	11.2	14.7	13.0
Kandal	140.6	129.6	134.6	54.4	67.2	60.5	14.5	26.7	20.6
Prey Veng	136.2	138.7	137.5	29.5	50.2	39.6	10.1	10.6	10.4
Svay Rieng	132.8	143.0	137.8	35.1	68.6	51.1	6.7	23.2	15.6
Takeo	133.4	121.8	127.4	53.6	107.1	77.5	16.9	38.0	28.0
Banteay Meanchey	126.5	132.0	129.3	29.0	42.1	35.8	13.2	12.7	12.9
Battambang	121.4	137.0	129.4	59.6	52.4	55.8	20.6	20.8	20.7
Kampong Thom	108.3	128.6	118.3	46.7	49.8	48.4	12.6	19.4	16.4
Siem Reap	117.3	125.5	121.3	25.7	43.5	34.7	9.9	13.5	11.9
Other Tonle Sap	121.2	128.9	125.0	39.6	46.0	42.7	13.2	18.0	15.4
Coastal	123.9	124.6	124.3	49.0	47.1	48.1	21.3	27.9	24.7
Kampong Speu	131.4	137.1	134.2	32.7	59.0	45.0	10.5	22.1	16.8
Mountain	106.4	107.9	107.2	27.8	42.4	35.5	11.3	13.9	12.7

Source: NIS Statistical Yearbook 2005.

Net Enrollment Ratio in Primary, Lower and Upper Secondary School based on CSES 2003-2004

Province/City	Primary School			Lower Secondary School			Upper Secondary School		
	Female	Female	Female	Female	Female	Female	Female	Female	Female
All Cambodia	**75.1**	**76.8**	**76.0**	**17.1**	**15.6**	**16.4**	**8.5**	**8.6**	**8.5**
Phnom Penh	85.6	90.1	87.9	49.4	47.9	48.7	29.6	30.7	30.1
Kampong Cham	71.2	75.3	73.3	11.8	12.4	12.1	6.7	5.3	6.0
Kandal	81.1	82.4	81.8	19.5	18.3	18.9	7.2	9.0	8.1
Prey Veng	77.1	77.6	77.3	12.4	6.9	9.7	3.7	1.8	2.6
Svay Rieng	77.9	81.5	79.7	13.2	17.1	15.0	3.2	7.8	5.7
Takeo	81.1	81.3	81.2	20.3	27.1	23.3	5.6	8.7	7.2
Banteay Meanchey	77.6	76.1	76.8	10.8	11.6	11.2	5.1	6.1	5.6
Battambang	79.5	80.6	80.1	26.3	17.3	21.5	12.4	9.7	10.9
Kampong Thom	69.8	70.5	70.1	13.8	11.7	12.7	2.7	5.5	4.3
Siem Reap	71.3	70.2	70.8	11.0	9.4	10.2	6.2	5.4	5.7
Other Tonle Sap	72.5	77.2	74.8	10.2	9.2	9.7	3.7	4.0	3.8
Coastal	75.6	75.6	75.6	16.6	11.0	13.9	8.0	12.0	10.1
Kampong Speu	70.5	71.6	71.0	9.3	7.4	8.4	3.9	5.3	4.6
Mountain	61.3	59.9	60.6	7.1	10.9	9.1	3.4	3.8	3.6

Source: NIS Statistical Yearbook 2005.

Metadata Table

Map	Aggregate	Source	Limitations
Territory Overview			
Regional Location	Region	World Dataset	
Administrative Boundaries	Provincial, District and Commune	Department of Geography 2005	Many administrative boundaries are disputed and continually being updated.
Geographical Relief	National	JICA Dataset 2002	Selected data.
Rainfall and Temperature patterns	National	FAO	Extrapolated grid data from satellite interpretations.
Dry Periods	National	Gene-Ecological Zonation of Cambodia (Tree Seed Project FA/ Danida /DED) 2003	Based on 104 meteorological stations and a few regional stations. Limited accuracy in areas with low station coverage and restricted data collection periods.
Landuse	National	JICA Dataset 2002	Automated Landsat, spot data and aerial photo interpretations with limited field checks.
Poverty Level by Commune	Commune	WFP 2002	Calculated based on Census data from 1998.
Landmine and UXO Contamination	National	Level 1 Survey 2001 CMAA	Provides limited information on precise location of mines and accidents. Survey teams require more time for accurate data collection.

Map	Aggregate	Source	Limitations
Population and Settlement			
Population Density	Commune	Commune Database 2004	Data collection by village chief and commune council. Quality check by MoP by comparing trends.
Population Age Structure	District	Commune Database 2004	Data collection by village chief and commune council. Quality check by MoP by comparing trends.
Urban-Rural Population	Provincial	Commune Database 2004	Data collection by village chief and commune council. Quality check by MoP by comparing trends.
Population Projection 2020	Provincial	NIS Statistical Yearbook 2005	Based on 1998 census data.
Housing Type	Provincial	Commune Database 2004	Data collection by village chief and commune council. Quality check by MoP by comparing trends.
Household Size	Commune	Commune Database 2004	
Households with Amenities	Provincial	CIPS 2004	
Transport Infrastructure and Market Locations	National	Commune Database 2004	Transport infrastructure under permanent improvements and some seasonally weather based deteriorations Market locations uncertain due to administrative readjustments.
Transport Facilities by District	District	Commune Database 2004	Ongoing changes.

Map	Aggregate	Source	Limitations
Natural Resources			
Terrestrial Vegetation and Landuse Patterns	National	BPAMP (MoE)	Based on several different satellite interpretations and aerial photography.
Land Cover Non Forested Areas	National	JICA Dataset 2002	Automated Landsat and Spot Data interpretation with rough or uncertain LUCC class distinctions.
Forest Concessions	National	IFSR 2004	Official data of MAFF - FA, no information about the status of concessions.
Forest Cover 1976, 1997 and 2002	National	Mekong Secretariat, MRC, FA	Based on different non comparable forest types and classes as well as satellite interpretation methods. Scientifically not precisely comparable data.
Forest Disturbance	National	IFSR 2004	Based on model with the assumption that forest disturbance increases with roads and villages. Does not take population density into account.
Village Locations	National	CMAA 2001 (Level one Survey)	Not including new villages founded in the upland areas of Cambodia in recent years.
Community Forestry	National	FA 2005	Uncertain limits and boundaries of CFI areas at commune level.

Gene-Ecological Zones	National	CTSP, FA	For tree species purpose only. Caution with the determination of the specific nature of the seed source near the border of two distinctive ecozones.
Seed Source Sites	National	CTSP, FA	Limited Species.
Protected Areas and Protected Forests 2002	National	PA: MoE, PF: FA, MAFF	Mostly non officially approved or located boundaries. Official demarcation ongoing within the process of state land mapping.
Geology	National	Department of Geology, MIME	Under continuous improvements. Uncertain data based on pre 1970 interpretations.
Mineral Resources	National	Department of Geology, MIME	
Projected National Transmission Grid and Hydropower	National	MIME 2005	Mostly projected and planning data
Fuel Used for Cooking	National	CIPS 2004 and 1998 Census	

Water Resources

Topographical Map of the Mekong Basin	Regional	MRC - DEM	Based on 1996 and 1998 to 2000 1:100.000 data set
Population Density of Wetland Areas	Commune	Commune Database 2004, Department of Geography and UNESCO	Boundaries of wetlands derived from MRC based on flooding data from DGM.
Wetlands and Catchment Areas	National	Wetlands: ASEAN Regional Center for Biodiversity Conservation. Catchment, Flooded Area: MRC 2002. Discharge: JICA Dataset 2002	Boundaries of wetlands derived from MRC.
The Tonle Sap Biosphere Reserve	National	Department of Natural Resource Assessment and Environment Data Management	
The Coastal Zone	Provincial	Mangrove: CZM, MoE 2005. Coral Reef and Sea Grass: UNEP	Data collection in the CZ is only recent and ongoing.
Small Scale and Marine Fish Production	Provincial	Agricultural Statistics 2003-2004, MAFF 2004	Inconsistent terminology in regards to fish catch. Respondents often don't consider themselves fishers.
Fish Production and Fishing Lots	Provincial	Fish Catch: Agricultural Statistics 2003-2004. Fishing Lots: MAFF 2001	Data generally based on market quantity rather than household consumption.
Community Fisheries	National	DoF 2005	
Arsenic Hazard	Provincial	Point data from Feldman and Rosenboom 2000, Arsenic risk map UNICEF 2004	Number of wells

Agriculture

Rice Growing Areas and Production	Provincial	Agricultural Statistics 2003-2004, MAFF	Several doubts about serious recording at district level.
Rice Ecosystems	National	IRRI Project (CIRP)	Rough classification based on agronomic data, little ecological data or sociological data incorporated.
Average Farm Gate Price of Paddy	Commune	Commune Database 2004	Data only collected in December.
Maize Production	Provincial	Agricultural Statistics 2003-2004, MAFF	Limited accuracy in tonnage.
Upland Crops	Provincial	Agricultural Statistics 2003-2004, MAFF	Does not include agricultural concessions.
Fruit Trees	Provincial	Agricultural Statistics 2003-2004, MAFF	Does not include agricultural concessions or homestead trees.
Families with Pigs	Commune	Commune Database 2004	No data about total number of herd.
Families with Cattle and Buffalo	Commune	Commune Database 2004	No data about total number of herd.
Soil Types	National	CARDI-after crocker, 1962	Outdated classification system and very rough data.
Soil Fertility	National	Gene-Ecological Zonation of Cambodia	Classification based on outdated Crocker system.
Soils of the Main Rice Growing Areas	National	CARDI 2000	According FAO legend 1998 with local Khmer soil type names

Education and Health

Primary Enrollment	Provincial	MoEYS 2004-2005	Enrollment only. No attendance or continuous education over 4-6 years.
Lower Secondary Enrollment	Provincial	MoEYS 2004-2005	Enrollment only. No attendance or continuous education.
Upper Secondary Enrollment	Provincial	MoEYS 2004-2005	Enrollment only. No attendance or continuous education.
Illiteracy by Gender	Provincial	Commune Database 2004	Data collection by village chief and commune council.
Mean Distance to Education Facilities	Commune	Analysis data (combined data) between Village location and School location: Census 1998	Village centre to education location only. No point data distinction for primary and lower/upper secondary locations.
Health Facilities	National	MoH, National Health Statistics 2003	Location of building only. No information about service quality.
Mean Distance to Health Facilities	Commune	Analysis data between Village location and Health location	Village centre to health center location only.
Inhabitants per Doctor	Provincial	NIS/ MoP	Nationally recognized doctor only. No information about service quality.
Inhabitants per Nurse or Health Worker	Provincial	NIS/ MoP	Nationally recognized health workers only. No information about service quality.
Neonatal Mortality	Provincial	CDHS 2000	Recorded cases inside the national health system only.
Under-five Mortality	Provincial	CDHS 2000	Recorded cases inside the national health system only.
Vaccinations	Provincial	CDHS 2000	Recorded cases inside the national health system only.
TB and Malaria Prevalence	Provincial	MoH, National Health Statistics 2003	Hospitalized cases only.
HIV/AIDS Prevalence	Provincial	HIV Sentinel Surveillance 2002	Small sample frame.
Sanitation by Commune	Commune	Commune Database 2004	Data collection by village chief and commune council.
Access to Water	Provincial	Commune Database 2004	

Appendix

Authors and Contributors

Introduction
Save Cambodia's Wildlife

The Geography of Cambodia
Mr Ith Sotha, Director, Department of Geography, MLMUPC

Climate
Mr Thy Sum, Climate Change Office, MoE

Poverty Mapping
Mr Khim Ratha,
Vulnerability Analysis and Mapping, WFP

Landmine and UXO Distribution
H.E. Heng Ratana, Deputy Director General, CMAC

Population and Settlement
Mr Yem Suong, NIS, Ministry of Planning

Transport Infrastructure and Market Locations
Mr Chan Sophal, Poverty Specialist, The World Bank

Forest Resources and Community Forestry
Mr Nong Divan, Deputy Chief, Forest Industry and Trade Development Office, FA, MAFF
(Modified by Technical Committee)

Forest Trends
Mr Hour Lim Chhun, National Advisor, Natural Resources and Environment Programme, cdc

Non Timber Forest Products
Project Team: Managing Natural Resources for Poverty Reduction: Policy Research on Resource Benefits and Management Options Programme. CDRI

Protected Areas
Mr Sok Vong, National Programme Coordinator, Mekong Wetlands Biodiversity Conservation and Sustainable Use Programme, MoE

Gene Ecological Zones and Indigenous Seed Source Sites
Mr Sok Srun, Senior Project Officer, Cambodia Tree Seed Project, FA, MAFF

Geology and Mineral Resources
Mr Sieng Sotham, Director, Department of Geology, MIME

Energy
Mr Victor Jona, Director, MIME

The Mekong River and Wetlands
Mr Mam Kosal, Team Leader: Biodiversity and Climate Change, UNDP

The Coastal Zone
Mr Vann Monyneath, National Coordinator, Environmental Management of Coastal Zone Programme, MoE

Fisheries
Ms Kaing Khim, Vice Chief of Community Fisheries Development Office, DoF

Agriculture
Mr Sam Vitou, Director of Institute of Local Development, CEDAC

Soil Types
Mr Seng Vang, Head of Soil and Water Sciences Programme, MAFF

Education
Ms. Tho Ory, MoEYS

The Health Sector
Ms. Phalyka Oum, Co-ordinator for TWGH Secretariat, MoH

HIV/AIDS
Dr Ly Penh Sun, M.D, MSc, Chief of Technical Bureau, NCHADS, MoH

Kampong Speu Urban Land Use Planning Project
Mr. Kuoch Thay, Department of Land management, Urban Planning and Construction

Technical Committee
H.E. San Sy Than, Director General NIS (Chairman)

Mr Mogens Laumand Christensen, Minister Counsellor, Danida Resident representative, Royal Danish Embassy

Mr Ith Sotha, Director, Department of Geography

Ms Solinn Lim, Director, Save Cambodia's Wildlife

Mr Ignas Dümmer, Natural Resource and Environmental Management Advisor

Mr Jan-Peter Mund, Faculty Advisor, Royal University of Agriculture

Mr Chan Sophal, Poverty Specialist, World Bank

Ms Tep Saravy, Vulnerability Analysis and Mapping Officer, WFP

Mr Khim Ratha, Vulnerability Analysis and Mapping Officer, WFP

Mr Piseth Long, Senior Programme Officer, Royal Danish Embassy, Danida

Mr Prom Tola, Consultant

Technical Peer Reviewers
Christopher Barlow, MRC

Amanda Bradley, Community Forestry International

Iain Craig, Agriculture Extension, MAFF

Peter Cutter, BPAMP, MoE

Anne Erpelding, GTZ

Marcus Hardtke

Peter Kaufmann, GTZ

Jan-Willem Rosenboom, Senior Water and Sanitation Consultant, WSP

Ralf Symann, DED Advisor

Atlas Project Team
Save Cambodia's Wildlife
Loreen Kerrigan, Coordinator
Julie Sanderson
Hing Phearnich
Srun Vicheka

Cartographer
Phnom Penh Geoinformatics Education Centre

Designer
Red Lotus Publishing
012 870 560

Photographers
Asian Images
Magnum Photos
Save Cambodia's Wildlife

Acronyms and Abbreviations

CARDI	Cambodian Agricultural Research Institute	EAC	Electricity Authority of Cambodia
CASC	Cambodian Agronomic Soil Classification	FA	Forestry Administration
CDC	Council for Development of Cambodia	GIS	Geographic Information System
CDHS	Cambodia Demographic and Health Survey	ICZM	Integrated Coastal Zone Management
CDRI	Cambodia Development Resource Institute	IEA	International Energy Agency
CECS	Compendium on Environment Statistics in Cambodia	IRRI	International Rice Research Institute
		IUCN	International Union for the Conservation of Nature
CIPS	Cambodia Inter-Censal Population Survey		
CMDG	Cambodian Millennium Development Goal	JICA	Japanese International Co-operation Agency
CMAA	Cambodian Mine Action and Victim Assistance Authority	MAFF	Ministry of Agriculture, Forestry and Fisheries
		MoE	Ministry of Environment
CNMC	Cambodian National Mekong Committee	MoEYS	Ministry of Education, Youth and Sport
CSES	Cambodian Socio-economic survey	MoH	Ministry of Health
Danida	Danish International Development Assistance	NEAP	National Environment Action Plan
DoF	Department of Fisheries	NIS	National Institute of Statistics
DoG	Department of Geograph	NPRS	National Poverty Reduction Strategy
DOTS	Internationally recommended TB control Strategy	PLUP	Participatory Land Use Planning
DFW	Department of Forestry and Wildlife now FA	RGC	Royal Government of Cambodia
DFID	Department for International Development	UXO	Unexploded Ordinance